MAKING SENSE OF THE JOURNEY

This is a book of memoirs about the changes that time brought into the lives of the authors, depression-era babies whose youth and adulthood were bracketed by World War II, the Korean War, Vietnam, and the Cold War. They have also witnessed the emergence of the new global world, a kaleidoscope of new nation-states that flooded the United Nations with a new spirit.

Specifically, the writers are Mennonites whose lives have spanned a social and theological sea change that affected them all. They were born into a Mennonite polity of tightly knit rural communities, and they wrote their memories out of an era in which that reality became fractured. They are now middle class; and their frame of reference in their adult lives has been largely institutional and professional, for most of them have been movers and shapers in Mennonite institutions.

Theologically the writers embrace an evangelicalism rooted in sixteenth-century Anabaptism and a commitment to the Anabaptist vision of Harold Bender. They were among the first to grasp the power of that vision and the possibilities it offered. In a time of social change Anabaptism offered both an explanation of what they believed and helped them nourish that centuries-old sense of being an alternative to magisterial Protestantism.

Actually, the accounts in this book reflect the experiences and stories similar to those of hundreds of Mennonites whose lives were changed in this disruptive era. In the process they transformed the Mennonite church. No more could Mennonites be *Die Stillen im Lande*.

—*Notes from the "Introduction"*

Anabaptist Center for Religion and Society Memoirs

Ray C. Gingerich, Series Editor

This series of autobiographical accounts is typically published by Cascadia Publishing House and copublished with the Anabaptist Center for Religion and Society (ACRS) and Herald Press. ACRS/EMU sponsors the series, determines the particular focus of each set of stories, and in consultation with the publishers, volume editors, and authors, is responsible for the content.

VOLUME 1
Making Sense of the Journey: The Geography of Our Faith
Robert Lee and Nancy V. Lee, Editors

VOLUME 2
Continuing the Journey: The Geography of Our Faith
Nancy V. Lee, Editor

Note: Except for a few corrections plus minor changes to accommodate the shift of publishers—such as the revised title and copyright pages as well as updated Library of Congress information, this 2009 Cascadia edition (ISBN 978-1-931038-71-3) of volume 1, *Making Sense of the Journey*, is identical to the original edition released through ACRS in 2007 (ISBN 978-0-9799625-0-9). ACRS and Cascadia are offering this Cascadia edition to enhance the significant distribution and promotional efforts ACRS is already making on behalf of its publications.

ACRS MEMOIRS · VOLUME 1

Making Sense of the Journey: The Geography of Our Faith

*Mennonite stories integrating faith and life
and the world of thought*

Edited by
Robert Lee and Nancy V. Lee

Foreword by
Loren E. Swartzendruber

Cascadia
Publishing House
Telford, Pennsylvania

copublished with
Anabaptist Center for Religion and Society
Eastern Mennonite University
Harrisonburg, Virginia *and*
Herald Press
Scottdale, Pennsylvania

Cascadia Publishing House orders, information, reprint permissions:
contact@CascadiaPublishingHouse.com
1-215-723-9125
126 Klingerman Road, Telford PA 18969
www.CascadiaPublishingHouse.com

Making Sense of the Journey
Republished 2009 by Cascadia Publishing House
a division of Cascadia Publishing House LLC, Telford, PA 18969
Copublished with Herald Press, Scottdale, PA
Copyright © 2007 by Anabaptist Center for Religion and Society, Eastern Mennonite University,
Harrisonburg, VA. All rights reserved.
Library of Congress Catalog Number: 2009042026
ISBN 13: 978-1-931038-71-3; ISBN 10: 1-931038-71-6
Book and cover design by Suelyn Swiggum
Jan Luyken's (aka Luiken) historical engraving Jesus and Peter on the cover design is taken from David Martin (1639-1721), *Historie des Ouden en Nieuwen Testaments: bverrykt met meer dan vierhondred printverbeeldingen in koper gesneeden* [History of the Old and New Testaments: trans. with over 400 hundred engraved copper plates by Jan Luiken], published 1700 by Pieter Mortier, Amsterdam. Used courtesy of Menno Simons Historical Library, Eastern Mennonite University.
Except when otherwise noted, portrait photography by Ray C. Gingerich

The paper used in this publication is recycled and meets the
minimum requirements of American National Standard for Information
Sciences—Permanence of Paper for Printed Library Materials, ANSI Z39.48-1984.

Excerpts copyright © 2006 and used by permission of Cascadia Publishing House, Telford, PA: C. Norman Kraus, "From Mennonite Fundamentalist to Critical Anabaptist" is a revised version of "From Mennonite Fundamentalism to Critical Anabaptism: My Story," in C. Norman Kraus, *Using Scripture in a Global Age: Framing Biblical Issues*. Portions of Ray Gingerich, "The Quest for an Authentic Faith that Engages the World," appeared as "Reading the Bible in Search of Jesus and the Way" in *Telling Our Stories*, ed. Ray Gingerich and Earl Zimmerman.

Library of Congress Cataloguing-in-Publication Data
Making sense of the journey : the geography of our faith : Mennonite stories integrating faith and life and the world of thought / edited by Robert Lee and Nancy V. Lee ; foreword by Loren E. Swartzendruber. -- Cascadia ed.
  p. cm. -- (ACRS memoirs ; v. 1)
Originally published: Harrisonburg, Va. : Anabaptist Center for Religion and Society, Eastern Mennonite University, 2007.
  Includes bibliographical references and index.
  Summary: "The Mennonite writers of this book were Depression-era babies who amid experiencing World War II, the Korean, Vietnam, and the Cold wars, helped Eastern Mennonite College and North American Mennonites develop more global perspectives and commitments"--Provided by publisher.
  ISBN-13: 978-1-931038-71-3 trade pbk. : alk. paper)
  ISBN-10: 1-931038-71-6 (trade pbk. : alk. paper)
  1. Christian life--Mennonite authors. I. Lee, Robert, 1928- II. Lee, Nancy V., 1931- III. Title. IV. Series.

BV4501.3.M25212 2009
378'.071977550922--dc22
[B]

2009042026

16 15 14 13 12 11 10 09   10 9 8 7 6 5 4 3 2 1

*To the generation of Mennonites
born in the great depression era
who embraced the Anabaptist vision
and helped transform the Mennonite Church
in a disruptive modern world
shaped by World War II
and the Cold War*

CONTENTS

FOREWORD by Loren E. Swartzendruber ... ix
PREFACE ... xi
INTRODUCTION by Albert N. Keim: *Who We are* ... 1

PART I: MAKING SENSE...

Albert N. Keim
*In Search of a Worldview:
What Did I Know and When Did I Know It?* ... 7

C. Norman Kraus
From Mennonite Fundamentalist to Critical Anabaptist ... 25

Calvin W. Redekop
A Link in the Chain, an Unprodigal Son, a Wandering Pilgrim ... 41

Ray Gingerich
The Quest for an Authentic Faith that Engages the World ... 63

PART II: ...IN THE CHURCH AND COMMUNITY

Myron S. Augsburger
My Journey: Reflections ... 91

Edward B. Stoltzfus
*Jesus, Where Are You Taking Us?
Tradition, Vision, and Contemporary Culture* ... 115

John R. Martin
A Life of Twists and Turns ... 131

Titus W. Bender
A Journey toward Embracing God's Wider Family ... 147

PART III: ...IN THE UNIVERSITY AND SOCIETY

Samuel L. Horst
Reminiscences of an Eighty-Six Year-Old ... 173

Harold D. Lehman
    From Park View to Wider Horizons   191
Gerald R. Brunk
    From Rocking Horse to Rocking Chair   205
James R. Bomberger
    An Ordinary Boy with Extraordinary Experiences   217

PART IV: ...AND GLOBALLY
Paul Peachey
    A Hippocratic Mid-Life Course Change   235
Esther K. Augsburger
    From India to Virginia   257
Calvin E. Shenk
    My Pilgrimage: Missional Education   277
Nancy V. (Burkholder) Lee
    An Unexpected Life   289

APPENDIX by Calvin W. Redekop   313
    An Unfinished Story: The History of the Anabaptist Center for Religion and Society
NOTES ON CONTRIBUTORS   321
INDEX   329

FOREWORD

The monthly breakfast series sponsored by the Anabaptist Center for Religion and Society offer a priceless opportunity to hear the stories of those who have given their lives in service to the church. Each of us is profoundly shaped by our personal histories, and we grow in our understanding of others by hearing their stories.

During my seminary years, I was employed as an admissions counselor and associate campus pastor at Eastern Mennonite, and I frequently ate lunch in the faculty-staff lounge in the Administration Building. There I heard my elders philosophize, tell stories, and debate the current issues. There was much humor, and tears were occasionally shed. It was a wonderful education for which I paid very little!

Preparing for what I thought would be a career in pastoral ministry, I occasionally asked my mentors, "Where do you get all of the stories that you regularly share with others through sermons and teaching or in the faculty/staff lounge?" They assured me that with life experience would come plenty of stories and that the time would eventually come when deciding what not to share would be the major challenge. Now I understand.

It is surely a challenge for a retired faculty member, administrator, or college president to share his or her story in just an hour over breakfast. One can assume that each one had to make difficult choices about what not to include. In this volume we are given the opportunity to reflect again on those individual stories, and for that I am grateful.

Eastern Mennonite University and the entire church owe an immense debt of gratitude to each individual willing to openly share significant experiences that formed each one intellectually and spiritually. As for all of us, some life-changing events seemed relatively insignificant when they occurred. Placed in the historical context of a longer life, however, we appreciate the power of those events to change the trajectory of one's journey. We are also reminded of the pervasive experience of unmerited grace transmitted through the community of faith.

To God be the glory for the faithfulness of those who have traversed the land, leaving markings for the next generation's journeyers. May we continue to learn from their wisdom!

Loren Swartzendruber, President
Eastern Mennonite University

PREFACE

The Anabaptist Center for Religion and Society (ACRS) was founded by a group of retirees living near Eastern Mennonite University who wished to share their growing vision for integrating and re-imaging Anabaptist faith and life in contemporary academia and the church. In seeking a common identity and purpose in the formation of ACRS, they soon discovered striking differences that for mutual understanding required the sharing of their life stories. (See Cal Redekop's "Appendix" for a history of the beginnings of ACRS.) This sharing began informally but soon led to regular monthly presentations of the now popular "ACRS Monday Breakfast Series." The sixteen personal memoirs here represent the first volume of these presentations. (The dates of each presentation and any major revision are indicated at the end of each memoir.)

Part I of this book reflects the early discussions "Making Sense..." of their personal journey of faith, as told by a historian, theologian, sociologist, and theological ethicist. In "Part II ... in the Church and Community," theologians, evangelists, pastors, teachers, and a social worker explore the geography of their journeys of faith and service. In "Part III ... in the University and Society," scholars and professors of American and world history, education, and literature integrate their faith and professional disciplines with their life and work. Finally, in "Part IV ... and Globally," leaders and educators in peace, art, mission, and the English language and culture describe how their work and faith became international.

The editors would like to thank the sixteen contributors for their openness in sharing their personal stories and their careful work on their manuscripts.

Special recognition goes to Ray Gingerich, ACRS director, for organizing what became known as the "ACRS Monday Breakfast Series," which made this book project possible. Ray did double duty in compiling the index and serving also as the professional photographer for this book.

Our thanks, too, to our daughter, Suelyn Swiggum, who did the cover and interior design and prepared this book for the printer.

ACRS also thanks Eastern Mennonite University, in particular Provost Beryl Brubaker, who also served on the ACRS Steering Committee, for support and subsidy of this publishing venture, which may appropriately contribute to "celebrating the vision" for the ninetieth anniversary of EMU (1917–2007).

INTRODUCTION

Who We Are

Albert N. Keim

Memoirs are not, strictly speaking, history. Each is a biography, a focus on one life. Their charm lies in the twists and turns of the often unanticipated events that changed and shaped that life. Memoirs are also full of irony as unexpected consequences come out of carefully planned initiatives. Most of all, memoirs help explain how people became what they were, a product of the story itself or the inferences and nuances between the lines. In that sense memoirs are especially interesting to contemporaries, for the stories sharpen a multi-dimensional picture, providing new planes of understanding. In that sense there is a bit of the voyeuristic about memoirs.

This, then, is a book about time, events and character. The stories in this book are stories of time and the changes it brought in the lives of the authors. The fundamental reality of history is time—but which time one experiences is critical. The writers of this book were Depression-era babies whose youth and adulthood were bracketed by World War II, the Korean War, Vietnam and the Cold War. They were also observers of the emergence of a new global world made up of a kaleidoscope of new nation-states that flooded the United Nations with a new spirit. Those global events were grounded in their consciousness.

Specifically, the writers were Mennonites whose lives spanned a social and theological sea change that affected them all. They were born into a Mennonite polity of tightly knit rural communities, and they wrote their memories out of an era in which that reality became fractured.

They are now middle class; and their frame of reference in their adult lives has been largely institutional and professional, for most of them were movers and shapers in Mennonite institutions. In fact, most were connected with Eastern Mennonite University.

The humble self-effacing personalities of the authors are palpable. Writing a memoir was difficult for them, for it involved a focus on the self. This generation grew up in an ethos in which the group (church) trumped the individual. To call attention to oneself was simply unseemly—probably un-Christian.

Of course, a book of memoirs by people with a common commitment becomes an opportunity to aggregate their shared beliefs. Certainly the overriding generality in this book is a commitment to the Mennonite church, a church that not only governed the authors' worldview but also offered employment and service. Indeed, it is difficult to imagine a group of people whose commonalities are so all encompassing.

Theologically the writers embrace an evangelicalism rooted in sixteenth century Anabaptism and a commitment to the *Anabaptist Vision* of Harold Bender. This group of people was the first to grasp the power of the vision and the possibilities it offered. In a time of sociological change Anabaptism offered both an explanation of what they believed and helped them nourish that centuries-old sense of being an alternative to magisterial Protestantism.

It also helped them deal with the new American evangelicalism reflected in the aggressive work of groups like the National Association of Evangelicals, a movement with substantial appeal to many Mennonites. While many identified themselves as evangelical Christians, their evangelicalism was tempered by powerful commitments to discipleship *(Nachfolge Christi)* and an ideal of service in the name of Christ. Moreover, the WWII Civilian Service Program (for conscientious objectors to war) and the service of many of these people in post-WWII relief work converted them into world citizens transcending boundaries and nation-states. Actually, the accounts in this book reflect the experiences and stories similar to those of literally hundreds of Mennonites in this era who went abroad for service and returned changed persons. In the process they transformed the Mennonite church. No more could Mennonites be *Die Stillen im Lande*.

Certainly another shared characteristic is their almost compulsive devotion to service to their church. Almost all of the writers did some voluntary service and then spent their adult lives working for the church for a pittance. In 1970 full professors at EMU earned less than half that of assistant professors at state universities. Only in the late 1960s did EMU institute a retirement system for its employees. Yet its faculty served with a sense of vocation not unlike that of priests in Catholic orders.

For a generation buffeted by such powerful winds of change, the generational question could hardly be avoided. How have their children taken their values and adapted to the new world they inhabit? In earlier times they might have become, if not copies of their parents, at least practitioners of their values. Now in what is a confusing and uncentered culture, the remedies of the past simply appear less useful. It thus becomes a generational responsibility to recite what has been learned and valued most with the hope that some of the things one generation stood for still have some traction with their children.

Mostly we do memoirs to help orient ourselves and our children to our past. Writing forces us to remember and to take stock of our lives. How did we become what we are? What are the disappointments and the surprises? How does what we are square with what we intended? For some the urgent question is this: What difference did our lives make in the scheme of things? This is not a Mennonite question, but it is present nevertheless. Ultimately we cannot escape the question of the meaning of our lives.

Life is a mystery, and the best memoirs reflect that mystery. Good lives are those which bring hope and courage in the midst of that mystery. This book reflects that struggle.

April 2007

PART I

Making Sense…

ALBERT N. KEIM

In Search of a Worldview: What Did I Know and When Did I Know It?

Lebenswelt

The muscles in Grandpa Miller's arms flexed and sweat streamed down his face into his beard and dripped onto his blue work shirt as he pushed the big wooden-wheeled "muck" wheelbarrow through the soft soil. I was on my knees holding on to the front of the wheelbarrow with my stubby three-year-old fingers. Several hundred feet ahead I could see my mother and father with an uncle, two cousins and several hired hands. They were also on their knees, bent over, busily pulling carrots out of the black soil and placing them in rubber band bunches ready for my grandfather, who hauled them to the washhouse on his wheelbarrow. On the return trip to the field I got to ride in the wheelbarrow.

It was midsummer 1939. My grandfather and I with the rest of the carrot harvesters were part of a small community of Old Order Amish, some 70 families in all who lived in a kind of bucolic oasis between the bustling cities of Akron and Canton, Ohio. At night the city lights turned the sky to the north and south into a pale reddish-orange, ominously it seemed to my childish imagination, like the fearful end of the world my father sometimes talked about during our evening devotions. Cities, I knew, were places where worldly, that is, non-Amish, people lived. There was a small town only two miles away, but to us it was an alien and hostile place, for on our weekly trips to the grain mill townsmen would sometimes taunt us with cries of "dumb Amish" or "yellow bellies," the latter a reference to our non-participation in the good war, WWII.

One effect of growing up Amish during WWII was to make me extremely self-conscious of my Amish identity, especially when at the age of seven in 1942, I had to ride a yellow school bus to first grade at a large (600 students) public school in town. About 50 of us were Amish or Mennonite, a very visible minority with our funny haircuts, barn-door trousers, apron dresses and white caps. Our only relief from incessant harassment came each spring when an influx of migrant African-Americans came to school. They were despised even more than we Amish.

My father was an unusually devout and conscientious man whose affable demeanor softened his limited ability to accept much distance between his ideals and human frailty. After his ordination as an Amish minister he became a reformer, dedicated to eradicating moral and spiritual problems endemic in our Amish community, particularly the widespread practice of bundling, or as we called it, "bed-courtship." He was also intent on changing the understanding of salvation; the Amish believed one could not know until death if one was saved. My father was an evangelical; he believed conversion to be a powerful experience whose effect could not be misunderstood. His diagnosis of the conventional Amish position on salvation was that of course they did not know if they were saved since they had never been converted. One effect of my father's preoccupation with this issue was to make me an early rebel against Amish ideas. It also introduced me to some rudimentary theological ideas early in my life. My interest in logical explanations for belief began in that period of my life.

In that tightly knit community I was a child surrounded by grandparents, uncles, aunts and many degrees of cousins. One cannot grow up in an Amish community such as mine without being forever impressed by the benefit of communal mutuality. Human beings are capable of constructing religious-cultural systems with social environments that are amazingly good places to live, especially in the Amish case, for children. The highly structured gentle environment was just what a child needs to thrive and grow. Quite frankly I cannot imagine a more desirable environment in which to spend a childhood. Unfortunately the Amish community is not as good an environment for intellectually ambitious adults. Only by the conscious denial of the free range of one's intellect can one be a functioning member of an Amish community. Therein I suspect lies one of the great paradoxes of human life: well-functioning communities require a substantial restriction of human freedom. That restriction of freedom can be perpetuated by a comprehensive ideological or religious milieu that sharply limits the range of individual autonomy.

Ironically it was my devout and conscientious father who set in motion the events that led me out of the Amish community. My father was so deeply concerned about war and its effects on his church and his children that he did not want me, his eldest, or any of the young men in his congregation to be conscripted by the military. Thus when I was seventeen, he persuaded the people of his congregation to migrate to Ontario, Canada, where there was no conscription system. Unfortunately one of my sisters is severely handicapped, and the Canadians would not let my family immigrate to their country. It was a fateful event in the life of our family. Had we moved to Ontario, we would almost certainly have remained an Amish family. Instead we moved to Virginia, my parents became Beachy Amish, my father became a bishop, and today only my handicapped sister remains a member of my parents' community.

In my case, within six months of failing to go to Canada, I registered for the draft and in 1955 was drafted. I declared myself a conscientious objector and was given a two-year Mennonite Central Committee assignment in Europe. I became a member of an organization called PAX, whose task it was to build villages for Mennonite refugees from Poland. In the course of those years I also worked in Austria, Switzerland and the Netherlands and did a month-long stint on a kibbutz in Israel.

I went to Europe Amish, but by the time I returned, it was clear to me that I could not be an Amishman. I had discovered the world was simply too rich and complex to be narrowed down to the relative simplicity of an Amish life. At the time I could not have put it in those terms, but that was about the essence of the matter.

It was one thing to determine not to be Amish; it was another to fashion an alternative life. At age 23 I had a marketable skill—bricklaying—but I also sensed that I could not be a bricklayer for the rest of my life. Across the Blue Ridge Mountains from my family home was a place I had only vague knowledge of: Eastern Mennonite College. On a whim one day when it was raining and therefore unsuitable for bricklaying,

I visited the college and talked to the Dean about whether they would enroll someone like me who had never quite finished the seventh grade. The kindly Dean, Ira Miller, had seen many farm boys of my type before and urged me to take the GED exam, which he assured me would determine whether or not I could enroll. When I managed somehow to make a nearly perfect score, something he had never seen before, he not only assured me that I had been admitted, he even offered some financial assistance.

So I came to Eastern Mennonite College. It was a near-perfect environment for me, a kind of halfway house, not unlike the Amish community of my childhood. What was different was that the communal boundaries had expanded and were more opaque. The fundamental criteria for a communal ethic—that communal values precede personal values—were very much in force. Whether from youthful combativeness or some sense that such an understanding of the relation of the individual to society was inimical to the pluralist individualism, which I had already begun to embrace, I chafed at the restrictions the college imposed on its students. In retrospect I now understand how valuable that environment was for me, given my uncentered character at the time.

Actually the restrictive quality of the college was mitigated by the fact that soon after I arrived at EMC, I fell in love with a fellow student, Leanna Marie Yoder. After my freshman and her junior year we were married, and during my junior year we became parents. Marriage to Leanna and the birth of Melody changed my life profoundly. My overly cerebral preoccupations shifted as I discovered both what it means to be loved and to love unconditionally. Now a tiny universe of three souls bound together not by thought but by the deepest springs of human feeling and emotion became the centerpiece of my life. For the first time I sensed that many of the most profound insights about life and its meaning can be apprehended but not logically expressed. In fact it came to me that language diminishes understanding. One's deepest insights cannot be adequately expressed by language. In any case, having a family helped make my understanding of reality more complex and multi-faceted.

It was during this period of my life that I began reading the Jewish scholar, Martin Buber, whose then recent *I-Thou* (1958) helped me see the fundamental mutuality which all human beings share. It was a wonderful corrective to my personal inclination to embrace an individualistic self-definition, which was the vogue in the larger American academic culture of the time. It was also in this period, while I was trying desperately to escape the dogmatic biblicism so forcefully invoked at EMC, that I discovered the writings of the Concern group, a set of young Mennonites who had been or were studying theology at European universities. What I learned from them changed my life. They taught me two things: God is a pacifist and the hermeneutical community is the best guide for life.

The idea of the pacifist God derives from the nature of Jesus' life and death, which illustrates that human beings are radically free to believe or not to believe in God. God limits himself—his power—so that humans can be free to choose or reject his presence in the world. This insight, so opposite anything I had been taught before about the nature of God, made it possible for me actually to believe in God for the first time.

The idea of a pacifist God also implies that human beings are not only free but also responsible to act in the world as agents of divine purpose. This idea was worked out in greater detail by theologian Harvey Cox, whose books *Secular City* and *God's Revolution and Man's Responsibility* make the point that the fundamental human problem is not selfishness, but sloth, the refusal by humans to take responsibility for the world and its care. The appeal of this idea for me was that it helped me jettison my somewhat sectarian notion that God's primary interest is the church community.

The Concern group's emphasis on the hermeneutical community appealed to me because it offered an alternative to the hard-edged biblicism taught with such force at EMC. The college made, it seemed to me, an iconic object of the Bible. The Concern group had a better alternative: to see the Bible not as a holy book but as a source of information meant to be used by God's people as they searched for the purpose and meaning of their lives. The best venue for finding one's direction in life thus lay not in intensive Bible reading, but in the context of a small group of believers gathered together in Jesus' name to find direction for their lives, hence, the idea of the hermeneutical community.

That the idea of the hermeneutical community should be of interest to me is a bit surprising in retrospect. Did I really want to become enmeshed in another community that defined my life? Actually at the time I did not, but I was also fleeing from the notion of the iconic Bible. The hermeneutical community gave me a reprieve from that. Thus I embraced, theoretically at least, the idea of a faith-community that could offer a means to establish a basic foundation of truth. I was hungry for truth, but I did not want it to come from an iconic holy book.

The decision to go to graduate school was made for me by my ability to take tests successfully. Even though my grade point average in college was a bare 3.0, my GRE scores were unusually high. When my professors at EMC saw my scores, they immediately pushed me to go to graduate school. Somewhat naively I applied to only one school, the University of Virginia, mostly because it was nearby. Surprisingly I was accepted and even offered a tuition scholarship.

Now for the first time I learned what academic life was really like, for at the university life was all about scholarship, the single-minded pursuit of knowledge. At EMC learning had been considered an important value, but one was never allowed to forget that the real endgame was faith. Everything had to be subsumed under that. At the university the goal was the objective, tolerant and single-minded pursuit of scholarship. The generation of new knowledge was the whole point. I loved it. For the first time in my life I was doing what I loved, not required—in fact not allowed—to see scholarship as somehow residual to the primary pursuit of faith. I loved that secular environment.

Intoxicated with my newly found freedom from religious priorities, I selected an esoteric topic for my MA thesis, whose only end was the search for new knowledge. I made medieval history my primary field and wrote my thesis on an obscure 12th century English Bishop and Abbot. I explored how he managed his diocese and monastery. Much of the resource material was in Latin or medieval English. It was simply delightful, for not only was I doing work no one else had done before, but it was deliciously impractical. The only reason for doing it was to add a tiny smidgen to the sum total of our knowledge of medieval history. For once in my life I was doing something for which there was no practical or transcendent reason.

So enamored was I by the ambiance of an Ivy League university that I began dressing like an Ivy Leaguer. The au courant uniform was a blue button-down shirt, red tie, tan khaki trousers and blue blazer. Through my college years I had continued to wear my Amish-Mennonite plain coat. Now I changed uniforms, overjoyed to be free to don an Ivy League form of dress. Even my way of dressing advertised the new community of scholarship that I had joined. I was very happy.

After my MA I completed my PhD at Ohio State University. By then some of the gloss had worn off the scholarly enterprise, and I realized that while I could be happy getting deeper and deeper into an ever more narrow area of medieval history, I did need a justification for my life and work that transcended scholarship. I was shocked by how practical minded undergraduate students were and realized that learning more about medieval bishops was not going to be of great interest to the people I would be spending the rest of my life trying to teach. Therefore, I shifted to recent American history and focused on public policy, a topic that literally drips with practical and contemporary relevance.

We loved our life at Ohio State. We lived in a neat little house on the edge of the campus. Leanna taught first grade at one of the schools, and Melody was in the third and fourth grades. Melody always came home for lunch, and she and I established a wonderful bond that we still cherish a half-century later. We also attended our first truly satisfactory Mennonite church during those years. Neal Avenue Mennonite church was one of the first GC-MC churches, and its members were almost entirely professionals or graduate students at the university. Here for the first time I found a blend of tolerant pluralism in theology and lifestyle that I had sought but never found before.

Since this was the late sixties, the Vietnam War was at a near crescendo. In worship and Sunday school classes we were engaged in a nearly continuous dialogue regarding how to act in relation to the war and its atrocities. Our arguments were not whether to protest the war, but how and at what points. For Leanna, Melody and me it was a profoundly inspiring period in our lives. We believed we had found an operational hermeneutical community.

One effect of our experience at Neal Avenue was to confirm our identity with the people called Mennonite. And it made it rather easy to say yes to President Myron Augsburger when he invited me to return to EMC in 1971. That decision was a fateful one. I had offers from a college in Michigan and a junior college in Ohio, but we opted for EMC. At the time we thought we would return to EMC for a few years and then move on to a secular school somewhere. That never happened largely because the job opportunities for historians collapsed in the 1970s. I literally could not have found a job elsewhere had I tried. But I did not try, for by 1977 I had agreed to become Dean of EMC; and by the time I discovered I did not enjoy administration, I was fifty, in a mid-life funk and no longer ambitious enough to strike out on any new enterprises. I had also gotten deeply involved in Mennonite research, and EMC was as good a place to do that as anywhere. Thus four books later I am still at EMU, a bit bemused by my forty-year perch on this 100-acre plot of God's earth. I never intended to be here this long.

Weltbild

History as I will use it here refers to everything constructed by human beings, past, present and future. I begin with history because it offers some explanation about the purpose and direction of life. History can be constructed only by creatures who transcend instinctive behavior by their ability to reason and think. Actually thinking is almost certainly the more important function, for it is by thinking that humans are able to attach meaning to the physical and mental constructions and behaviors they create or perform. But reasoning comes first because reasoning is the process by which the human brain organizes the stimuli and sensations the human organism encounters in the world. For most organisms it is instinct that manages or copes with the environment. In humans it is reason that performs that function. But thinking would be virtually impossible if reason were not buttressed by memory, for it is memory that offers the possibility of transcending and changing past behavior and knowledge to create new possibilities. Thinking is essentially the process of taking reason and memory and fashioning a meaning by making choices about the future.

To put this in perspective, one has to ponder the remarkable event that occurred sometime in the evolutionary cycle when the actions of those destined to become human ceased to be merely instinctual. Animals live through the biological laws of nature, unable to transcend nature. Animals lack the ability to penetrate beyond the senses and understand the essence behind sense awareness. They cannot, therefore, have a sense of truth even though they may be able to determine what is useful. Animal existence is one of harmony with nature. Animals are equipped to cope with the conditions they meet.

At some point in the evolution of human beings harmonious adaptation to nature became less passive; in fact, emancipation from the coercive power of nature ensued. Thus a new form of life came into being; life became aware of itself. Self-awareness, a product of reason, imagination and memory, disrupted the harmony of human beings in nature. Human beings became freaks of nature, subject to and aware of physical laws, but unable to change them. Human beings became aware of their powerlessness, of their own death and their inability to avoid death. To be human was to be trapped in a profound dichotomy, suspended in both nature and history.

Reason, a great blessing, is also a profound curse. Human beings are the only animals who can be bored, the only animals that find their existence a problem that requires a solution. This problem can be illustrated by reference to the situation of a human baby. Babies have lost the instinctual traits of nature but are not yet equipped with new tools to replace the lost instincts.

The paradise myth in the Bible expresses the situation perfectly. In original Eden people lived instinctually in nature, in harmony with nature, but they lacked self-awareness. It was an animal paradise. Eviction from paradise was a product of self-awareness. Eden was guarded by two angels with fiery swords; instinctual innocence could not be revisited by human beings.

The human conundrum is that humans are no longer in nature, yet they cannot escape nature. Neither their mental nor instinctual equipment is completely adequate. They can imagine infinity but cannot transcend finitude. For late-twentieth century human beings nature has become a much-diminished force in their lives. Hence the real home of modern humanity is not nature, but history.

History is thus the arena of meaning for human beings, explaining who we are and what our life-purposes should or might be. It is in history that humans construct culture (language, art, religion, politics, science), which becomes the repository of human knowledge and the guide for on-going development.

History is also the context for the construction of social systems.

Human beings are profoundly social in their essential nature, a condition deriving almost certainly from their prolonged dependency at birth. However, I suspect that sociability may also be connected to the complex synergy of human emotion (feeling) and rationality. We may be able to love animals, but that interaction can never approach the complexity or the quality of human relationships.

Perhaps the modern city is the quintessential example of the degree to which humans have fabricated a human environment (history) as an alternative to nature.

History is in the first instance world construction. In its second meaning it has to do with purpose and direction. Where is the human enterprise heading and for what reasons? In my earliest memory lies a vague dread of the end of the world. The adults about me tried to act as though they looked forward to the world's end, but I always sensed that even they found the idea pretty terrible. At the center of that point of view was the assumption that the historical enterprise was simply not going to be viable over the long haul; sooner or later the ship of fools was going to sink. Or rather, in the triumphalist tradition I grew up in, it was really a rescue. My father's favorite song was, "When the trumpet of the Lord shall sound and time shall be no more," something he claimed to long for, but which was certainly a very world-denying form of expectation. Time, the very stuff of history, was not only considered something ephemeral but actually an evil that needed to be replaced by something timeless: eternity.

I must confess that I cannot accept that devaluation of time (history), not because the end-of-the-world stuff seems so dreadful nor because I am an optimist. Actually, I am pretty pessimistic about the human prospect for the future. I am genuinely worried about my grandsons' futures. I find it hard to believe that their generation will be able to escape the nightmares we in the twentieth century have inflicted on each other. But I cannot embrace the end-of-the-world business, because it is so antithetical to that other idea I hold, which is that human life (existence) has meaning only if in fact that meaning can be found in this life. I suspect I am helped by the fact that I also espouse a transcendent presence in the cosmos, of whose role and about whose activity I am genuinely mystified.

I try to live by the belief that we human beings have been designed (adapted) to exist in this world as it is and that when we live our lives meaningfully—that is, intelligently and benevolently—we can actually experience a substantial degree of hope and optimism. Now I know that is something a relatively healthy, wealthy and secure person like myself can claim. It would be far harder to do so if I were a poor person or a victim of unmerited cruelty or tragedy. However, one of the great mysteries of life is the fact that even in the midst of tragedy, people find hope or at least a willingness to persist with their lives.

What Is Truth?

One evening as I watched *60 Minutes* on CBS, Morley Safer interviewed the Reverend Professor Peter J. Gomes, Plummer Professor of Christian Morals and Pusey Minister in The Memorial Church at Harvard University. Gomes is a remarkable man, one of America's most distinguished preachers, a black man who is also homosexual. Among the startling observations he made in the interview was his take on the biblical injunctions regarding sex and marriage. The Israelites, he pointed out, developed the biblical injunctions regarding sexual relationships because they were a small wandering band of people trying to steal land (the Old Testament story recounts the first time the children of Israel stole Palestine; the second time they are doing so is in our own time), which belonged to a more populous people. Having lots of Israelite babies was a priority if they were to succeed in displacing the Philistines. Procreation was thus a major preoccupation for them, and the rules of sexuality in the Bible reflect that historical priority. In our world, Gomes argues, where human reproduction is only a marginal aspect of sexuality, the issues of sexuality acquire profoundly different understandings. While Gomes himself is celibate by moral choice, he also believes single-sex marriage ought to be legalized and blessed by the Christian church.

My point in this digression is not to discuss the issues Gomes raises but to highlight him as a practitioner of a postmodern worldview. Gomes does the postmodern thing exceedingly well, which is to see human truths—the explanations and rules we invoke for our most profound human questions and behaviors—as always relative to time and circumstance. The truths enshrined in the holy books, regardless of the religion, are themselves derived from the exigencies of the human enterprise. The truths became sacred and all-powerful because at various times historical circumstances demanded authoritative truth. As a result, the world is full of authoritative truth-claims, almost always couched in transcendent language: the language of transcendence is itself a product of time and place. I find such an understanding of truth attractive, despite an awareness that it also poses really big issues about how any truth claims can actually become authoritative in such a radically relativistic environment.

As a historian I am impressed that most human beings have sought to believe too much too completely. Agnosticism or skepticism is not an attitude most human beings find attractive. One of the arguments commonly made for authoritative beliefs is that they are necessary for social order: if we were all agnostic, anarchy would become endemic and human life impossible, the argument goes. Perhaps, but the evidence seems to suggest that more dangerous, historically, have been those ideologies and faiths that claimed too much authority, especially when they were embraced by structures of power. Almost always such combinations become life-denying and world-destructive.

However, the issue I find intriguing is not how truth claims arise or become convincing. What I want to know is how one can sort out the desirable ones from those which are bogus? Or to put a more positive spin on it, which ones are more compelling? From a postmodern perspective, the world is rich with such truth orientations, and one should revel in the sumptuous smorgasbord available. I agree that the array of worldviews present in the world is a wonderful boon, but the burden we face is how to construct a diet that nurtures our lives without unsettling our stomachs. In a pluralistic world the criteria for truth choices become central issues.

The issue thus becomes not so much "What is truth?" as "Which truths?" No doubt the most common response is the utilitarian one: "What works best?" usually followed by, in our self-absorbed times, by "for me?" If we lived in a world where needs and choices were equal, such a laissez faire approach to the marketplace of truths could be relatively benign. Unfortunately such is not the case, for truth choices are not made on an even playing field. We make our selections, not in abstraction but existentially in the context of our real lives. Thus even if we were to adopt or fashion a logically coherent worldview, its connection with our real lives would still need to be demonstrated; so our truth choices should be based not on "What works" or "What makes sense." The most fundamental criteria have to be grounded in my *sitz im leben*, my real situation in life, including my history, my roles and responsibilities, and my acumen. Ultimately truth can be truthful that is embodied in human life, or the life that is lived.

As a university teacher I was constantly tempted to embrace or propound truths that had scant connection to the lives of my students. I would justify such forays in pedagogical terms, or explanations that truths perhaps not relevant now would be useful later. The rationale was not entirely bogus; there is a lot of merit in anticipating the future. The problem is that truth suspended or waiting for relevance has a very short half-life, but more poignantly most of what we really believe deep down in our gut emerges out of the humus of human pain and struggle. I am not advocating that experience is the ultimate reservoir of truth; rather my point is that ideally we can get the best grasp on truth by linking experience with knowledge and reflection.

Therefore, one answer to how to select truth is that it needs to be grounded in our particular real-life histories. The great German historian, Ernst Troeltsch, came to a similar conclusion in the 1920's when his students, perplexed by the plurality of worldviews they confronted, inquired of the great man how one should choose. His answer was that the choice might most happily be made on the basis of propinquity; the tradition from which one came. His comment anticipated the argument made by Thomas Kuhn in his *Structure of Scientific Revolutions* (1962). Kuhn believed all explanations of the world and their meaning are mediated through the symbols and language of a particular tradition that has evolved over time. As long as the symbols and meanings comport with experience, they maintain their plausibility; that is, they are convincing to those within the tradition. But as time changes the experience of a people, the symbols are replaced by new ones that are more plausible. Troeltsch had something like that in mind when he warned his students against assuming too easily that they could adopt a Buddhist worldview with convincing plausibility. My point is that one basis for truth choice is to embrace what is nearest at hand, our own tradition.

Weltanschauung

In this section I want to identify several elements of my worldview, not so much to create coherence but because sometimes, as in pointillist paintings, the true texture can be seen only when the separate elements are made apparent.

We live in a world of change, movement and development; and we ourselves are always changing and developing. In his *Modes of Thought* Alfred North Whitehead makes the point that the world we inhabit is part of a dynamic evolutionary process. Reality is always undergoing flux and change. Human beings belong to and are equipped to live in this dynamic world that has produced us. Thus one axiom of a satisfactory worldview must be its openness and awareness of the dynamic quality of the cosmos we inhabit. Almost certainly one of the great human challenges is to find ways to embrace change when things seem, as they often do, to be out of control.

We live in a world that is societal in quality. Everything is related to and affected by and influences everything else. We human beings belong together, move together, work together and find our fulfillment in participation. This is true from the most mundane to the most transcendent experiences. All truth, all beauty, all of life is found in relationship. As Americans we live in a culture whose most valued ideal is the unfettered individual. Our economic ideology, our political philosophy, and our central religious understandings all make the individual the focus of action and truth. If as I am arguing, our fundamental existence lies in mutuality, our culture must be terribly out of sync with the way the world is really designed. I find the so-called "chaos theory" of James Gleick (1987), which emphasizes the integral interconnections of everything in the universe, to comport well with the key mutuality claims made by Jesus. The universe is profoundly societal in its essence.

I believe that the world (cosmos) is kept in order more by persuasion than by coercion. God is a pacifist whose will and purpose can always be rejected, but whose uncoerced invitation to respond offers the possibility of novelty and renewal in history. Coercion is a profoundly reactionary tactic, for it can enforce what is already present; its ability to enhance the new is severely limited and can at best impose order so that persuasion can become possible. Genuine freedom is only possible where decision and choice is uncoerced. It is through uncoerced decision and the responsibility that such free choice brings that consequential change becomes possible in the human domain. One of the great causes all human beings must ascribe to is preserving genuine freedom. The warrant for practicing unfettered choice lies in the very nature of the universe itself.

Because freedom to choose lies at the center of the cosmic order, morality becomes possible. Morality is more than knowledge of good and evil; it is the decisions people make in light of their knowledge that make moral life possible. The volitional character of human action makes the issue of right behavior the centerpiece of human experience. When the existentialists claim that all of life is decision, they are more than half right. The other half is that all of life is right behavior. We inhabit a relentlessly moral universe from which there is no escape. The question of right and wrong is woven into the very warp and woof of our existence.

Lebenswelt Revisited

The three year old stretched his too short legs as he clambered up the ladder to the ten-foot high platform of the grey metal sliding board. "Come on up, Grandpa," he shouted as he flung himself down the slide at breakneck speed. The grandfather, his knees painfully protesting, slowly climbed the ladder and with a rush slid down the sliding board. The play continued until the boy and grandfather were tuckered out. By then the petting zoo was open, and the two spent much time getting acquainted with a yard full of farm animals. They concluded their day at the park with a game of tag on a big jungle gym. The time was midsummer 1996. The place was Long's Park in Lancaster city. The three year old was Jonathan Keim-Shenk and the 60-year-old grandfather was me. That forenoon in Long's Park was a time of pure pleasure for both of us, and for me it brought back memories of that time 57 years earlier when I had played with my grandfather by catching rides on his "muck" wheelbarrow. What a different world Jonathan lives in than the one I had inhabited at his age!

I am impressed that in my youthful world, work and play were mostly intermixed; in Jonathan's world it is nearly always separate. It is that functional separation that seems to me to call for new ways of understanding the world and the meanings we bring to our lives. Jonathan is growing up in a highly segmented world where age, gender, knowledge, experience, even truth are functional categories that define our lives. In the absence of a spatially and socially functional community, the deliberate selection and integration of such categories becomes a major life task. The family typically becomes the epicenter of a series of loosely related activities defined by such categories. Unfortunately the family is a very fragile social entity unless it has some strong roots in a larger communal matrix. Suburbs are at best neighborhoods of friendly strangers whose proximity is nearly always accidental and communally non-functional. The real danger in this segmented world is that people come to define themselves by categories that are too narrow or too functional, such as "I'm a salesman," or "I'm a homosexual," or "I'm a grandfather." Replacing such categories with more comprehensive ones has to be an important goal.

The challenge for Jonathan will be to find or construct a community with which he can interact. For Jonathan's generation a major life task will almost certainly be the search for a viable community. For me it has been something quite different; a search for freedom from a community about which I was ambivalent. In many ways my life task has been less socially focused because I had a functioning community whose presence I could take for granted but was more intellectually demanding. The very robust quality of my community—the EMU campus and the Mennonite church—made the intellectual work more arduous, for my community has had a strong premodern ideational base. I could therefore enjoy the benefits of a strong community while flirting with the invigorating ideas of a postmodern worldview.

Ultimately we all yearn for a sense of significance, for reassurance that our lives are not simply accidental blips on the cosmic screen. We have to live with a sense of mystery, put nicely by that opinionated patriarch

Paul, who said that we see through a glass, darkly. He also said that if we hang in long enough, the mystery might even be cleared up. My guess is that the leap of faith he advocated might have been easier for him than it has been for me. But the fact of the matter is that the uncertainty and patience his promise requires may be about as close as we can get to a reassuring answer. In good postmodern fashion I would rather suffer the uncertainty and be uncommitted. Certainty would be nice, but that demands a suspension of unbelief of which I am simply not capable. I like historian Herbert Butterfield's advice: "Cleave to Christ and for the rest be totally uncommitted."

March 2005

C. NORMAN KRAUS

From Mennonite Fundamentalist to Critical Anabaptist

I was born in rural southeastern Virginia in a decade of radical cultural change dubbed the "Roaring Twenties," the post-World War I decade that preceded the stock market crash of 1929 and the depression that followed. It was a period when men fell in love with their automobiles, when the cowboy rolling his own cigarette became an iconic figure, when women received the vote, cut their hair, took off their corsets and scandalously shortened their skirts. But it was also the time when a strong conservative movement of fundamentalist and Pentecostal reaction to the new cultural climate was developing.

I was five years old when the stock market crashed, and my earliest memories are of depression times when my father, who was a plasterer, had a difficult time finding work or collecting his wages even when he had worked. Then in 1932 Franklin Roosevelt was elected and began to introduce his new democratic socialism. I remember very well, when Roosevelt was reelected president, the fear that his NRA, CCC, and Social Security programs caused in conservative religious communities like the Mennonite Colony in which I was born. We lived in a rural area where the paper was delivered by the mail carrier, and I brought in the mail the morning after the election. I remember Roosevelt's picture on the first page. It struck a note of fear in my own eight-year-old heart.

Our church leaders were much more comfortable with non-political Fundamentalism and anti-worldly Pentecostalism than with the politically liberal policies of the new administration, and they feared that the end-time prophesies of the "anti-Christ" and the satanic number "666"—the "mark of the beast"—were beginning to be fulfilled. Many also believed that these programs were the signs of "communist" influence. Conservative politicians were making lists of anti-Americans, and it was whispered that Mennonite leaders H. S. Bender and Orie O. Miller were on the list. I shall never forget the evening when Bishop George R. Brunk passed that information on to my parents and the other guests visiting in our living room at Eastwood (the last farm within the eastern perimeter of the colony).

I knew little of the new freedom that the cultural changes of the twenties introduced. I was born into a tightly bounded religious community called "the Colony," which had been settled by Pennsylvania Dutch Mennonites on a farmed out plantation located on the peninsula near Denbigh courthouse about half-way between old Newport News and Williamsburg. (The whole area has since been incorporated into Newport News.) We were surrounded by a post-plantation, rural English society that had been jolted awake by the military development of the area during World War I and was just beginning to be important as an ongoing military center.

Although there were no physical fences or walls, as some Newport News citizens thought, the topographical boundaries as well as the moral and spiritual boundaries of the Colony were clear to me. I could have told you exactly which open fields and wooded areas belonged to it, where the Mennonite community ended and the "world" of non-Mennonite culture began, where I was comfortable and at home and where I was a "damned Mennonite." I grew up in two clearly delineated cultures, one represented by the public school and one by the religious community with its controlling center, the church.

It had not always been that way; but while I was growing up, this church community was firmly controlled by the bishop, George R. Brunk, (I), a towering, impressive figure who was determined to protect his flock from the onslaughts of the devil. As the occasion required, he confronted foes as different as Billy Sunday, the raucous revivalist preacher, the corrupt local sheriff's political machine, and the Virginia state school board, fighting for the rights of the Mennonite community.[1] When the community telephone rang six shorts, the community emergency alert, we would sometimes hear his voice announcing, "Lock your screen doors. The Jehovah's Witnesses are in the area." In the community itself he dominated both the social and theological climate, so I cut my theological eyeteeth on a premillennial interpretation of the King James Version of the Bible as the infallible, literal word of God. The major problem with Fundamentalism, George R. used to say, was that it was not fundamental enough! We Mennonites kept the "all things" commanded by Jesus in the great commission (Matt. 28:20 KJV).

An Expanding World

From this restricted and sheltered beginning my life has expanded and grown in the pattern of a chambered nautilus. I do not remember any major revolts, only in-process course corrections. It may be hard for those of you who have grown up in the Shenandoah Valley to believe, but my first major culture shock came when I entered Eastern Mennonite School as a high school junior in 1940 and had a roommate from Pennsylvania who wore a necktie. In all other respects he was a quiet, conscientious Christian boy who would not even buy an ice cream cone on Sunday! I just could not put the two things together.

And my first theological divergence from Denbigh orthodoxy came when I returned to the college division of Eastern Mennonite School in 1943 to enter the ThB program. I began my course of study with New Testament Greek and Systematic Theology. Chester K. Lehman, who taught the latter, gave us a Mennonite adaptation of the "Old" Princeton theology, which embodied and defended Reformed orthodoxy. While he adopted a more Arminian version of that theology, which allowed for human free will, he did not modify its uncompromised non-millennialism, which "spiritualizes" the 1000-year reign of Christ at the end of the age. That roiled premillennialists like Menno J. Brunk, who claimed it was a first step away from biblical literalism and opened the door to Liberalism. Brunk, who had been educated at the Dallas Theological Seminary, the center for premillennial dispensationalist theology, used to say, "If the literal meaning of the text makes sense, it is nonsense to make any other sense of it."

Instead of finishing my ThB degree at EMS as initially planned, I went to Goshen College for my last year and earned a BA degree in Bible, the difference being that a Goshen degree was an accredited liberal arts degree. Although I had to take mostly liberal arts courses in order to complete the requirements for a BA degree in one year, I became aware that Goshen was not the beehive of liberalism that I had been led to believe. As would become much clearer in my experience later as a pastor, the differences between eastern and mid-western Mennonitism were far more related to their difference of origin in the Mennonite and Amish traditions and in their acculturation patterns on the eastern seaboard and the mid-western frontier. This was a major step in expanding my view of the "world."

Going to Goshen in those days was tantamount to betraying the conservative cause, and to my great surprise I was asked to return to Eastern Mennonite School to take over Harry Brunk's high school history and government classes since the college was expanding its liberal arts curriculum. Even though my degree was concentrated heavily in Bible and I had not taken courses in history, government, or teacher education, I welcomed the unanticipated chance to become a teacher. Up to that time I had expected to go either into the ministry or to the foreign mission field, but a call to the ministry depended on being chosen by lot. That would have meant simply finding a job and waiting, and since I had broken ranks by going to Goshen College the wait could have been a long one!

I taught at Eastern Mennonite School from the fall of 1946 to the spring of 1949 and then returned to Goshen to complete a seminary degree at Goshen Biblical Seminary, fully intending to come back to Virginia; but, as my mother-in-law used to say, "It was just not to be so." Sometime during the spring of 1949, Dean H. S. Bender stopped me on the sidewalk at the west end of the administration building and asked me whether I would be willing to accept ordination in the Indiana-Michigan Mennonite Conference. I demurred that I had planned to return to Virginia, but he assured me that an ordination need not mean a permanent assignment in Indiana.

With that understanding I accepted ordination and an assignment at the Maple Grove Mennonite congregation, a small rural church in Topeka, eighteen miles east of Goshen. Little did I know that during that same time an investigation of the Eastern Mennonite School faculty was in progress that would have made my return there as a teacher quite impossible in any case. But that is a story for another time.

The year 1950 was a momentous one for Ruth and me. We had been married in the spring of 1945 while I was still in the Bible School program at Eastern Mennonite School and had moved into a small second story apartment in Park View just off the campus. We fully expected to finish the year at EMS, but an unplanned pregnancy prompted us to transfer to Goshen the next fall. Ruth was from Elida, Ohio, and had attended Goshen College, so moving in that direction for the birth of our first child felt comforting to her. Now in 1950 our third child was on the way, and I was finishing seminary with no prospects of a job that would support us. Churches were not yet supporting their ministers.

It was at this point that Dean Bender again approached me about the possibility of my teaching in the Bible Department at Goshen. He also inquired whether I would be interested in going on to graduate school, perhaps in Germany, a suggestion that greatly interested me.

After graduating from Goshen Biblical Seminary in the spring of 1951, I began teaching there that same fall. At that time the Bible department and the seminary were still integrated. Students in the seminary received a BA degree with a major in Bible after four years of study and a ThB the fifth. Since Bender was taking a sabbatical that year, he assigned me two of his ThB courses to teach—the Acts of the Apostles, and Romans and Corinthians, and in addition as was customary for new teachers, the Greek language courses. That year and the following one were especially stressful since I was also pastoring at Topeka and often went out there two and three times a week. Congregations were not yet supporting ministers, and the nine-month salaries at the College were low enough that I had to get a job over summer to keep my growing family alive.

Graduate Education

In the autumn of 1953 I went to Princeton Theological Seminary on Dean H.S. Bender's recommendation. By then the twins had come along, so there was a family of seven to plan for! The two older girls, who were in elementary school, went to live with their grandmother Kraus in Denbigh (now Newport News), Virginia; and the rest of us moved into a newly refurbished seminary apartment at 21 Dickerson Street, Princeton, New Jersey. It was a fabulous and full year! Besides completing a Master's program, including writing a thesis, which was later published, I often preached in the Mennonite churches of Bucks County, Pennsylvania. Ruth got a part-time job, which she enjoyed; and with the apartment only a block from the library, I studied at home as much as possible.

This was my first experience of genuine graduate work, and I anticipated going to Europe to study church history if we could get the money together. But at Princeton I got a new vision for what I thought was needed at that juncture in the Mennonite Church. For the first time I was introduced to the field of American church history and theology, and I came to realize that this was a missing piece in the academic curriculum in our college and seminary. We were concentrating on Bible and Anabaptist-Mennonite history but paying very little attention to the religious culture we were living in. At that time, for example, the shelves of the Goshen College library did not contain books that Bender and his colleagues considered "liberal," and theological analysis of American trends was virtually non-existent.

Thus I majored in American theological studies and did a thesis under Dr. Lefferts Loetscher entitled *Dispensationalism in America: Its Rise and Development*, which was later published at his suggestion by John Knox Press. In the 1940s and 1950s prophetic interpretation was still a major issue in Mennonite theological circles. Bender, however, was uninterested in and apparently unimpressed by my thesis. To my knowledge he never included a review of my book in *The Mennonite Quarterly Review*. A few years later when I returned from Duke University, I suggested to him that we ought to include a requirement in American Church History in the budding seminary curriculum, but he remained quite unconvinced.

The Princeton faculty offered me a generous fellowship to continue my study for a doctorate, but President Paul Mininger pressed me to return to Goshen. Because J. Lawrence Burkholder was finishing his degree at Princeton, the college was short on faculty and would need to hire another teacher if I stayed away any longer. Moreover, if I decided to extend my study leave, the college could not guarantee me a continuing job. Since we were operating with virtually no cash reserves and I was not yet on the tenure track, we had few alternatives.

The next three years were crowded with activity and tension. John W. Miller, who had been sent to study in Switzerland in preparation for teaching Old Testament at Goshen Biblical Seminary, returned that same year. His continuing connection with the Concern group, in which Irvin Horst, Paul Peachey, Calvin Redekop, David Shank, and John Howard Yoder were also members, and his undisguised espousal of the critical analysis of Scripture soon lost him the good graces of Dean Bender. I agreed with John's communal ecclesiology, which identified the essence of church as "primary relationship," and together with him was involved in fostering small *koinonia* groups, which we considered the primary expression of the church. We sponsored visits by *Bruederhof* (Hutterite) leaders to the campus and engaged in extended private discussions with them. Also, we organized a small communal group of faculty, who practiced economic as well as spiritual responsibility for each other.

At the same time other theological and ethical issues were emerging. The thesis that J. Lawrence Burkholder had written at Princeton, which questioned the ethical relevance of the Hershberger-Bender position on absolute nonresistance, caused quiet but intense tension on campus. My own questioning of the doctrine of scriptural inerrancy, which to that time had not been openly challenged, caused uneasiness. In addition, the popularity of the Billy Graham campaigns and the introduction of this emphasis into Mennonite circles by the Brunk and later Augsburger tent campaigns put great pressure on the seminary to be more evangelistic in its emphasis. We spent more than one seminary faculty meeting discussing the meaning and methods of evangelism, and Dean Bender sought rapprochement with George Brunk by helping to bring his tent meetings to a field just east of the college in 1952 and giving him a place on the college podium.

During these same three years, the seminary faculty was debating the merits of discontinuing the ThB curriculum and developing an accredited graduate seminary program. Bender had decided to move in that direction, but not all of the professors fully agreed. Paul Mininger, who later became the president of the college, was the most hesitant. As a bishop, he was very aware of the implications in the church of such a step. With the use of the lot to choose ministers already in sharp decline—we were only beginning to use the word pastor—a three-year graduate seminary curriculum would be a big step in the direction of a professionalized and salaried ministry. At the college level, of course, it would require the reorganization of the Bible and religion curriculum as an integrated undergraduate program. I am convinced that the experience of these three years on the faculty was well worth the delay in my doctoral program.

In 1958, the year my book on Dispensationalism was published, I was given a major fellowship by Duke University to continue my graduate studies in American Church History and Theology, and this was followed the next two years by the newly established Rockefeller Theological Fellowship. I was particularly interested in going to Duke in order to study with H. Shelton Smith, who had recently published *The Changing Conception of Original Sin* (Scribners, 1955), a historical study on original sin in the American theological tradition. This was the period when the challenge to the old Liberalism by Karl Barth, Emil Brunner, and in America, Reinhold Niebuhr, was at its height of influence. Along with my study of the American religious scene I continued my interest in political theory and philosophy. These were the years of the opening Civil Rights movement, and I was caught up in the excitement of the local Durham developments.

The three years at Duke gave me a badly needed and much appreciated chance to escape my sectarian boundaries and the tensions that were developing at Goshen College in the last years of Bender's tenure. He was deeply involved in the formation of the new graduate seminary program growing out of the existing five-year ThB program, but he refused to relinquish chairmanship of the Bible Department. He apparently intended to have J. Lawrence Burkholder appointed as Bible department chairman, but Lawrence left Goshen to teach at Harvard Divinity School. I was still at Duke University, and in any case, as Albert Keim notes in his biography of Bender, he did not trust me to lead a College Bible Department independent from the seminary.[2]

A Cultural Revolution

My generation was caught in the middle of a major cultural and philosophical revolution that had already impacted the Mennonite church following World War I and continued unabated following World War II. Men like Bender and Orie O. Miller had brokered one stage of the transition and were loath to give up power. The power brokers in eastern conferences like Lancaster and Virginia managed to hold on for several more decades. Those of us who chose not to be managed took our lumps, and the consequences were especially severe for those in the biblical and theological fields. But we realized that the generation of college students whom we were teaching faced a still more uncertain and unmanageable future than we had. For us at Goshen College the crisis point in the changing cultural climate was 1967–68, the year of the McCarthy presidential campaign. From that point and through the next few years students aggressively pushed for radical revision in both the educational and moral disciplines on campus. The college was no longer to be accepted *in loco parentis!*

In the early 1970s we talked about the "generation gap" that had developed, which was compared to the gap between first generation immigrants and their U.S.-born children. At Goshen College while we were trying to introduce students to Anabaptism as a paradigmatic option to Mennonite Fundamentalism, we were clobbered with the anti-Vietnam war protest and the "Woodstock" phenomenon. In this context our Anabaptist model of discipleship got interpreted too often as a variation of the "Jesus Freaks," radical social protest, and communalism. Those students who rejected this more radical interpretation tended to get lost in individualistic ventures or return to the denominational fold.

During those years, student attendance at chapel and especially Sunday morning services dropped off precipitously; and some of us younger faculty, who were inclined toward more social activism and a less institutional view of the church as an organic body, tended to sympathize with them. Already in the 1950s, as noted, we had begun forming *koinonia* groups, which we considered our primary church groups. We began even to have household communions, much to the chagrin and anxiety of our elders. During the 1960s and 70s, students also formed such *koinonia* groups and households, and out of these independent but cooperative groups we formed a new congregation—"assembly"—of small groups.[3] People belonged to this assembly through participating in a small group. A majority of our members were students, and for the first few years we met on campus. Ultimately we purchased a deserted cheerleader uniforms factory on 11th Street and refurbished it for our purposes.

For lack of an otherwise chosen name, the congregation became known as "Assembly"; and the congregation continues today as an authentic Anabaptist alternative to the traditional Goshen churches.

This involvement with the small groups movement represents what I might call the ecclesiastical concern that has dominated my life work. I was committed to a genuine ecumenical fellowship of believers, but it seemed to me that ecumenism needed to begin at the congregational level, not with institutional executives' meeting in international conferences. It needed to begin with "the two or three together" with Jesus in their midst, searching for existential answers to the personal and social questions of the day.

My Cross-cultural Work

When I left the college in 1980 and went to Japan under the Mennonite Board of Missions, I still saw our basic task as attempting to form alternative Christian communities, not simply to convert individuals to Christ. For most Japanese people, conforming to the Japanese culture, i.e., "being Japanese," provided their self-identity. Christianity was a "foreign religion," which might be added on to their unique Japanese identity—respected but not integrated into their sense of identity. My concern was finding how to help these people understand and experience the significance of Jesus for the formation of a new self-defining community—neither Jew nor Greek, Buddhist nor Christian, Catholic nor Protestant, Mennonite nor Lutheran—to experience what it meant to be "in Christ" as a new social reality.

During my nearly thirty years on the Goshen College faculty, I had taken a number of leaves of absence for overseas assignments. Most of these had taken me to various countries in Asia. My family joined me in spending 1966–67 in India, where I taught at Serampore Theological College, the college founded by William Carey, Joshua Marshman, and William Ward in 1818, about twenty miles up the Hooghly River from Calcutta. After India's independence, Serampore became the hub of seminary education in India since it held the independent legal charter, which had been granted to Carey by the king of Denmark in 1827. When the British left India in 1948, Christian seminary education was organized under the legal umbrella of the Serampore charter. For me this was the beginning of a cross-cultural experience that was to prove an irresistible pull in the years to come.

In the intervening years I served on the Overseas Committee of the Mennonite Board of Missions and did a number of teaching and pastoral assignments under the auspices of MCC and various Mennonite mission boards in India, Taiwan, Vietnam, Philippines, South America, and East Africa—Ethiopia, Tanzania, and Kenya. Then in 1975 at the invitation of Takio Tanase, who had been a student of mine at Goshen College and was a leader in the Hokkaido Mennonite Church, we spent a full semester of my sabbatical in Japan on a teaching mission in the Mennonite churches. Besides my connection with Tanase, several of the Japan missionaries had been seminary colleagues and/or students of mine. Thus when we decided to resign from the College at the end of 1979 and pursue a cross-cultural teaching mission, Japan seemed a good location from which to operate.

I should pause to mention that this experience of teaching in many different cultures, often with an interpreter, had a major impact on my view of the Bible and the question of how to communicate its message. Teaching the Gospel of John in English from the Greek text to students from perhaps ten different language backgrounds, for which English was at best a second language but the only language they had in common, was a formidable challenge! And preaching to tribal pastors in the mountains of the Philippines through a chain of multiple translations by interpreters who knew only two of the three languages involved heightened one's appreciation for the priority and precedence of the Holy Spirit as both inspirer and interpreter of Scripture!

The Hokkaido mission was begun at a *"kairotic"* moment in the history of Mennonite missions. Although Japan was in an economic and cultural crisis as a result of the war, it was not a third-world culture. The Christian message did not have the implicit motivation of economic advancement behind it to boost its acceptance. The Japanese people were well educated and relatively well acquainted with modern western culture; and under the virtually dictatorial direction of Douglas MacArthur Japan was transitioning into democracy. Most of the original missionaries came from Goshen College inspired by the "Anabaptist vision" of Harold Bender, which fit this new democratic pattern very well. And with fifty years of Mennonite mission history in Asia behind them, they were determined to plant an indigenous Japanese church in the Anabaptist tradition.

My purpose for going to Japan was not to plant new churches, but to nurture churches that were just now coming of age. I was convinced that an "Anabaptist" theology needed to be mission oriented—what we are today calling "missional"—and speak existentially to the cultural situation. After some thirty years of studying and teaching historical theology, I now wanted to write such a theology—a theology aimed not so much at systematizing an orthodox theological thought pattern as developing an authentic theological analysis and expression of the significance of Jesus for twentieth century culture. Furthermore, I had become aware through my cross-cultural teaching that western culture and its questions about Jesus and God by no means provide the only perspective from which to do God-talk. Indeed, the western theological debate of the last two thousand years had almost become incestuous with inadequate formulations and answers giving birth to yet more controversial questions and answers.

What our Japanese churches needed, it seemed to me, was a critical analysis of western theology based on an indigenous contextual interpretation of Scripture. After all, the scriptural narratives were not configured in the pattern of Greek dualistic categories. Indeed, there are aspects of Japanese tradition that are nearer to the ancient Hebrew culture than to modern Western culture. I felt that the Japanese should be free to understand Jesus as a full expression of the Divine reality without necessarily formulating it in the Platonic form of Trinity and, further, to explain the atonement in terms of their own shame culture, rather than the legal guilt culture of the West. They needed to understand and interpret God in the context of Shinto divine naturalism or Buddhist mystical humanism rather than in terms of Greek dualism and transcendence. One church leader put it succinctly when he told me, "We know what the missionaries taught us, but to speak frankly it does not make good sense to us." And again he commented to me that for him with his Buddhist background "Jesus gets in the way of God." It was with this challenge ringing in my ears that I taught and wrote for seven years in Japan until the summer of 1987.

I still remember the customs officer who greeted us at San Francisco, or was it Seattle, on our return. He took a long look at my passport, and as he handed it back said, "Welcome home." From our home base in Hokkaido we had traveled to many locations in Asia—the Philippines, Taiwan, Hong Kong, Thailand, India, and Australia—for extended teaching missions. We had come to love dearly our Japanese brothers and sisters and our mission colleagues in the work of the church, and Asabu-cho, Sapporo, really had been home. Riding the train through the mountains between Sapporo and Obihiro where I taught classes was a genuine pleasure. The early morning train rides home where I would order a tube of potato crisps and a cup of very black coffee for breakfast were especially pleasant. But that "welcome home" in heartfelt American English warmed my heart! We were heading to Goshen to take up interim residence at 615 College Avenue until the house was sold and we could move on to Harrisonburg, Virginia, for our retirement. We had come almost full circle. I completed that circle ten years later when my adult children and I buried Ruth's ashes in the cemetery of Warwick River Mennonite Church at Newport News, Virginia, where I had grown up.

A new epoch began for me in 1998. Ruth had died quite unexpectedly the year before of acute leukemia. In the autumn of 1998 Rhoda Hess and I were married. Rhoda, the daughter of Reuben and Kathryn Short, grew up in the Archbold, Ohio, area where her father was a minister in the Evangelical Mennonite Church. She had been widowed for several years during which time we became acquainted in a small support group. After a ten-day wedding trip to China, we settled in at 1210 A Harmony Drive and began our new venture together. She has been engaged in mediation work and has continued to take course work at the Center for Justice and Peacebuilding at EMU. I have continued writing, and in addition to several articles, I published two books with Cascadia Press. The latest one, entitled *Using Scripture in a Global Age: Framing Biblical Issues*, appeared in March 2006.

February 2004
Revised April 2007

Notes

1 See David L. Zercher, "Between Two Kingdoms: Virginia Mennonites and the American Flag," *The Mennonite Quarterly Review* (April 1996, 70: 165–190).

2 See my "The Professor and the Dean," *Mennonite Historical Bulletin,* (LXII, 1, January 2002), pp. 6–8.

3 See my Chapter 10, "A Theological Reflection on the beginning of the Assembly Congregation," in *Using Scripture in a Global Age: Framing Biblical Issues.* Telford, PA: Cascadia Publishing House, 2006.

CALVIN W. REDEKOP

A Link in the Chain, an Unprodigal Son, a Wandering Pilgrim

Most students of human behavior have realized that thought and experience cannot be separated. Recent research and reflection have reemphasized the intimate relationship between the mind and the body, the biological/genetic and the environment, in all human actions and thinking. Scott Holland states the case succinctly as follows:

> Reason is not disembodied, as the tradition has largely held, but arises from the nature of our brains, bodies and bodily experience. This is not just the innocuous and obvious claim that we need a body to reason; rather, it is the striking claim that the very structure of reason itself comes from the details of our embodiment... by the specifics of our everyday functioning in the world.[1]

It is not my intention to expound on this point here but merely to indicate why I relate my experience and my thought world so closely in my story.[2] One of the ways to condense this complex relationship/ phenomenon is to employ metaphors. Reflecting on my story, I have come up with three metaphors that may help to provide the underlying motifs of what has been significant in my experience: a link in a chain, an unprodigal son, and a wandering pilgrim.

Regarding the first metaphor, a link in a chain, I have always been aware that I have never been a free floating or independent agent, but a continuous part (link) of a human chain of existence and experience.

From my first conscious moments I have realized that I have received almost everything from those around me and, further, have passed it on with precious little "value added" of my own, to use an economic term. Regarding the second metaphor characterizing my life experience, an unprodigal son, I have figuratively "stayed at home" to work in "my father's house"; I never seriously rebelled or "left home." I loved my family, congregation(s), community and physical environment. I always needed the assurance and affirmation of my family, church, friends and community. Of course there were often tensions and disagreements, but never enough to suggest leaving my "world" psychologically, socially or religiously.

The third metaphor, a wandering pilgrim gaining refreshment and sustenance at wayside fountains and inns, may also be more appropriate for Mennos as a people than first meets the eye.[3] I have been fortunate, through no great foresight of my own, to move about and eat and drink of the cultural ambrosia of a variety of communities, localities, subcultures and even societies. These have made my thought life all the more multilayered and complex, even contradictory and paradoxical. I will not emphasize the theme of these three metaphors specifically, but I believe that they help to organize and elucidate the substantive.

A Brief Review of Relevant Experiences

I was privileged to be born into Russian Mennonite ancestry. My father, born in 1900, the son of a Mennonite Brethren elder, Benjamin Redekop, and his wife, Susanna, immigrated to Canada in 1913 from the Russian Ukraine. In 1916 the family moved to Lustre, Montana, where Benjamin was elected to co-pastor the local Mennonite Brethren congregation. Nurtured in a stern and pious household—after all, an elder was to be a model for the Mennonite Brethren community—my father inherited some of this legacy, which affected my immediate family's "tone." In spite of that "burden," Dad had a very subtle, sly, sometimes cynical sense of humor. The interplay of these two forces, his piety and more worldly-wise savvy, made him an intriguing parent. He was well known for his descriptive one-liners and humorous retorts.[4] As a leader, he held local church and public offices and was drafted to become the mayor of Mountain Lake to help "clean up the town." He reluctantly agreed and was drafted for another two terms.

My mother, Katherine Wall, born in 1901, was the daughter of Reverend Jacob A. Wall, the minister of the Evangelical Mennonite Brethren congregation in Mountain Lake. In 1875, Katherine's grandfather, Aaron A. Wall, had moved his family to Mountain Lake, Minnesota, where he and Isaac Peters founded the Evangelical Mennonite Brethren Church, an outcome of the agitation for reform that had already begun in the Ukraine. This new church was aimed at "renewing" the *Kirchliche* (the official Mennonite Church). Katherine's father also carried the burden of being a model in the reformed new Mennonite church, but by temperament he was as calm and pacific as Benjamin Redekop was energetic and bold. Along with his father, Aaron, Jacob A. Wall was endowed with a healing and ameliorating personality. Aaron, for example, was known widely as a "bone doctor," a trait continued by Jacob, the son.

In 1916 Jacob Wall was called to shepherd the newly planted EMB congregation at Lustre, Montana. The Redekop and Wall families homesteaded on the open prairie about four miles apart. The Reverend/Elders Redekop and Wall worked well together and would probably have melded the two separately organized three-year old congregations of immigrants into one but for the re-emergence of strong MB exclusiveness.

My parents played an unintended scene in one of the acts of this ongoing play. When Katherine and Jacob fell in love and declared their intention to marry in the year 1920, they went to their respective fathers to receive their blessings and to arrange for the marriage.[5]

The co-pastor of the MB church, who also subsequently entered the discussion, said to the betrothed, "I assume you will join the MB church, so we will have to arrange for a baptism by immersion since the EMBs practice only sprinkling."

At 20 and 19 years of age respectively, the youths were rather flustered. They replied, "We will need more time to think about it."

After some discussion in both families, Mom and Dad met with the three elders. Mom directed her words toward the strict MB elder and said, "Elder _____, I was baptized by my father Jacob A. Wall upon the confession of faith when I was 17 years old, and to be baptized again would be a repudiation of my conversion, the validity of my faith and my father's office." (This is a transliteration from the Low German as we remember how Mom told the story).

Grandfather Redekop supported her decision, and thus my father became the only member of the Redekop family to leave the MB church and join a Mennonite group that was not as "pure" as the MBs considered themselves. This may have been the most confrontational my mother ever became, and I still marvel at her courage; for after all, she was one of 'those peaceful [*vredliche*—in low German] Walls."[6]

My parents bought a farm in 1922 and struggled to survive in the severe frontier environment with the rest of the fifty families who had settled there from 1916 on. The "conquest of the prairies" provided the backdrop for the challenges of building a community, a religious society, and a family. The promising crops of the mid-twenties and the beginnings of the terrible droughts of the early 1930s formed an indelible story in every person's memory including mine. A recent book, entitled *The Worst Hard Time: The Untold Story of those who Survived the Great American Dust Bowl* by Timothy Egan (Houghton Mifflin, 2006) in many ways speaks authentically for those of us who experienced the Mennonite settlement in northeastern Montana with almost Gothic realism.

My older sister, I, and two younger sisters and brother provided one of the many small family units that dotted the treeless landscape, usually separated by a mile in very direction. The public schools served as centers for community activities, while the "meetinghouses" (*Bethaus* in German, *Bethoos* in low German, pronounced Bayt-hoos) provided the locus for all religious and many clan/family events such as weddings and funerals. Many were the special prayer meetings called by the congregation to pray for rain, which never came.

These personal vignettes provide one little window into the "world" I inherited and in which I lived, an infinitely rich Dutch-Russian heritage that came to include the amazingly complex communities in Holland, West Prussia, Russia, North America, Mexico, Brazil, Uruguay, Bolivia, and especially Paraguay. The effects of these continuous large migrations that originated in Holland and entailed settlements in Russia, Canada, the United States and Latin America were deeply imbedded in the folklore to which I was exposed as I grew to adulthood.

My family had relatives in many states west of the Mississippi River, in Canada, Mexico, Paraguay, and especially in Russia. The Marxist-Communist era, including the Gulag saga of Russian twentieth-century life, was also a part of my family history. Though the connections became very sparse and dim after the chaotic emigrations, in the recent decades after the cold war ended, we slowly became aware of what had happened to those who had remained in Russia after the 1870s. We now know that three of my uncles and an aunt were sent to concentration camps. The aunt died in the camp of starvation, another uncle simply disappeared, and numerous other cousins and related members suffered terribly in many contexts or disappeared.

I have thus in recent years become more respectful of the immense expansive society and also pathos of the Russian Mennonite "golden years" and then the terrible Stalinist scourge. My wife, Freda, and I have visited some of these major settlements to pay homage. *The Redekop Book,* which Freda so painstakingly compiled and wrote, contains extensive accounts of this story, which is only now becoming more deeply ingrained in my psyche. A further painful reality is that part of the clan that remained is rapidly amalgamating into Russian society, losing their Anabaptist heritage at this very moment.

I am also a product of the pietist movement among the Russian Mennonites, but I became fully aware of this only after writing a history of the Evangelical Mennonite Brethren (EMB), *Leaving Anabaptism* (Pandora Press, 1998), some seven years ago. I discovered that my maternal great-grandfather, Aaron A. Wall, co-founder of the EMB church along with the renowned Isaac Peters, had been converted under the preaching of Eduard Wuest, the leading German pietist revivalist who sojourned among the Russian Mennonite Colonies for some years (in the 1840s) and was largely responsible for the pietist awakening there. My paternal grandfather, Benjamin Redekop, was also a direct heir of the pietist renewal, which latter sparked the renewal movement out of which the Mennonite Brethren emerged.

I grew up in the Peters-Wall division, later the Evangelical Mennonite Brethren Church at Lustre, until I was 13, and Mountain Lake, Minnesota, thereafter, which earlier had clearly stated its goal of recovering the original Anabaptism; but the pietist influence inherited from the Ukraine, and then nurtured in North America was not able to resist the addition of American fundamentalism and revivalism. Thus by the time I was in my teens, I was struggling in a turbulent pietist-revivalist sea. As was the expected practice, my parents expected me, without question, to attend the nearly annual revival meetings staged at the EMB *Bethoos,* and three times I marched down the aisle to repent of my new sins and renew my faith in Jesus, beginning at age seven, under the preaching of a leading EMB preacher George P. Schultz, who had studied at "Moody's." In 1940, our family moved to Mountain Lake, Minnesota. All the denominations in the community cooperated in the annual community revival in which a more renowned revivalist such as Oscar Lowry, Dan Gilbert or Merv Rosell extended the altar calls. Arnold's Park, Iowa, became the annual summer "Retreat" where we heard leading speakers such as John R. Rice, William B. Riley or R.G. LeTourneau present the gospel of faith and prosperity.

I was not deeply aware of the faith and legacy of Menno Simons in my EMB community, although his name was occasionally recited in sermons. Moreover, in the early 1940s I had become so thoroughly influenced by the growing war hysteria and patriotism in Mountain Lake, especially in high school and among my peers, that when my selective service number came up, I registered as 1-A at Fort Snelling. My parents were shocked and saddened by my decision. Providentially (?) I failed the physical exam (for total deafness in one ear) and hence was required to do farm work until the end of World War II in 1945, when I was released from that assignment.[7]

Now I was free to decide what to do with my life. Farming did not seem an option for a number of reasons. Meanwhile, the emotionally coercive, fundamentalist-revivalistic atmosphere permeating the Midwest and the Mt. Lake community began to lose its power over me. A close friend and I had become skeptical of the hyper-evangelism and even began to doubt the motivations of many of the evangelists themselves who came to town. My friend, released from the draft a year earlier than I, decided to go to Goshen College. My parents had long felt that "the children should get a college degree." Though at a sacrifice for them, they reluctantly encouraged me to leave the farming operation, and I entered Goshen College in January 1946. This was the event that most dramatically changed my life's trajectory. This move reintroduced me to my Anabaptist heritage although the "externals" in forms of attire and practices I experienced at Goshen College were almost too much of a shock. Nevertheless at Goshen College I was tutored in Anabaptism by many of the pillars of the Old Mennonite church, though in my naive state I was not aware of their stature, all of whom I now greatly admire:

S.C. Yoder, Melvin Gingerich, Guy F. Hershberger, J.C. Wenger, Harold S. Bender, Howard Charles, Ernest E. Miller, J. Lawrence Burkholder, Atlee Beachy, and others. Ironically in this context, I began to sense that my extensive Russian Mennonite tradition was not equally significant. Conrad Grebel was much more important than Menno Simons, or so it seemed. Nevertheless Goshen College gladly accepted us "Russian Mennonites."

I joined MCC in the fall of 1949 since that choice seemed the only way for me to continue in the vibrant faith/action synthesis of my newly discovered Anabaptist faith and to maintain my relationships with the Russian Mennonites. MCC expressed for me the essentials of the Anabaptist faith and action I had recovered. Fortunately it also reconnected me with many Russian Mennonite leaders and reaffirmed the legitimacy of the Russian Mennonite part of Anabaptism.

At MCC I became acquainted with—and in many cases worked for—an expanded roster of luminaries, like O.O. Miller, C.N. Hostetter, C.F. Klassen, H.A. Fast, C.L. Graber, Harold S. Bender, William Snyder, J. Winfield Fretz, and Heinrich Duerksen, to name a few. In my work with MCC in Europe I had personal contacts with such European Mennonite leaders as Abraham Braun, Dominee Hylkema, Van der Zijp, Benjamin Unruh, Richard Hertzler, Fritz Kuyper, and many more. This MCC network also introduced me to North and South American leaders such as Erland Waltner, J.B. Toews, J.A. Toews, B.B. Janz, J.J. Thiessen, C.A. DeFehr, and Paraguayans Heinrich Duerksen, Martin W. Friesen, and others. These persons represented a wide cross-section of the larger Mennonite global community, and I became deeply inter-twined with this network of European and American Anabaptist-Mennonite leaders and identified with the greater Mennonite ethos and history. They became the models for my life work. I truly have felt that I have known many of the "people who were somebody" in this "earlier generation."

During my three years in Europe, opportunities for service were everywhere. Starting as a VSer at Espelkamp in early 1950, I was soon called to Frankfurt, Germany, to work under Paul Peachey in developing the Voluntary Service program. This program provided opportunities for young people to do meaningful work while receiving free food and lodging for three to four weeks. Parallel to this work, the Korean War erupted in June 1950 and became the impetus for the development of the PAX program. The PAX men's work served to provide the down payment for refugee housing, which was probably the most significant experience for many young COs, as well as the refugees. My work in the European MVS and the emerging PAX program remains one of the high points of my work in the church.

Because of the awakening I experienced at Goshen College and in MCC, my intellectual life was ignited, especially during my three-year European assignment (1950–1952) described above. And again providentially(?) my participation in the Concern group (consisting of Irvin B. Horst, John W. Miller, Paul Peachey, David Shank, Orley Swartzentruber, and John Howard Yoder) was most stimulating. I was not nearly as intellectually advanced as the others in the group at the time, but I benefited immensely from this relationship, which helped to build my worldview. The essential insights of the Concern experience for me, which have remained indelibly, were that Anabaptism had poked a big hole in the major social construct that had obtained in Christianity for over a thousand years, namely the *corpus christianum*. Aligning politics and faith into one compound is a dangerous concoction.

Returning from Europe in December 1952, I subsequently obtained an MA in history and sociology at the University of Minnesota (1955). At the recommendation of Guy F. Hershberger, Nelson Kauffman visited me at the University and invited me to teach at Hesston College. It was this affirmation that helped cement my commitment to the Mennonite family and made me feel I could be useful. This was the first of many situations in which I was invited to serve in the church. I began teaching at Hesston in 1954. In 1955 Freda Pellman and I were married at Harrisonburg, Virginia. Our relationship, begun in Amsterdam during the Concern meetings, illustrates the power of MCC in integrating Mennonite conferences (especially in the proverbially powerful matchmaking function), for she was a member of the Lancaster conference.

Freda and I moved to Chicago where I pursued a PhD in anthropology/sociology/religion at the University of Chicago, graduating in 1959. Freda worked for one of the vice presidents to help cover expenses of my graduate training instead of pursuing her own degree. This latter cross-disciplinary study was an overwhelmingly exhilarating experience. The expansion and consequent secularizing of my worldview was very stimulating, though of course thoroughly disconcerting. The insights of the scientific worldview with its rampant positivist/empiricist emphasis—during the 50s and 60s while I was forming my intellectual apparatus—in retrospect have never been totally resolved with the heritage I called my own. I suspect they cannot be. One of our major texts by George Lundberg, *Foundations of Sociology,* confidently maintained that religion would soon be history and positivism would reign as a new religion, as I later discovered.

So I developed a double track, two paradigms of thought. I accepted the reality of "my father's house"—the unprodigal son metaphor for the safe harbor of a traditional "faith informed" community that defined one of my real worlds. At the same time I increasingly accepted the significance and value of the scientific and hence "materialist" interpretation of human existence and reality gained at the inn of academia. These "two cultures," defined by my beloved professor Robert Redfield at Chicago as the "great and little traditions," have lived side by side in my psyche ever since in a bi-polar manner always competing and allowed to co-exist in some sort of uneasy truce. I never left home fully, but the pull was always there.

The theocratic view that God was the foundation of creation and history was bedrock for me, often colloquially expressed in my Russian Mennonite folklore in the German axiom *"Der Mensch denkt, aber Gott lenkt"* ["Humans reason, but omnipotent God directs and rules the cosmos"]. The other view or perspective I understand as being basically a materialist view of history and humanity. I have never been able to reject totally the power of this perspective. I have become especially aware of the power of the economic domain in determining human behavior and ideologies. The material foundation of human life and thought (see Scott Holland's quote earlier) is best expressed by my adaptation of the axiom above, which was the result of my academic study and experience: *"Der Mensch theologiziert und philosophiert, aber die Wirtschaft diktiert"* ["Humans theologize and philosophize, but the material world defines the real world and dictates how the world runs"]. The power of ideologies such as Free Market Capitalism and various opposing forms of Socialism illustrate the colossal forces underlying the world economic engine.

This latter operating orientation did not directly dismiss the power of ideas, thought and spirit, but I became convinced that ideas and the life of the spirit (the life of the mind) are more the servant of the material world (the body, the physical, social and natural environment) than many people, even intellectuals, have wanted to admit. (Being an observer of the dust bowl and the depression in Montana no doubt dramatized the importance of the material, the environmental, and the economic reality for me. I have never been able to overcome the experiences and effects of the drought/depression background in Montana from 1925–1937.) As a corollary this tension between the world of thought and materiality has made me uneasy about focusing on either the world of thought to the exclusion of the material world or vice versa and has also made me very wary of isolating the effects of thought on the material world and vice versa. The idea of praxis has become for me recognition of this issue: life is a process, and we do not know what we do or believe until we have finished.[8]

My holding on to "my father's house" worldview was based on two motivations—one negative and one positive. Negatively, I could not go wrong in accepting that there was a transcendent world and reality (and the eternal security of my soul) even though it could not be proven (Pascal's wager). Positively, "my father's house" was so intrinsically valid, affirming and meaningful, even though restrictive in many ways, that I could live with the restrictive belief system because of the strong supportive and satisfying community. (This dynamic may appear quite different from parts of the Swiss Mennonite tradition, especially in eastern United States, which has produced considerable alienation because of regimentation regarding externals in order to retain the essentials of faith.) The necessity and reality of the human community became for me increasingly and profoundly central to human existence and its meaning, and this was corroborated time and again in almost everything I was exposed to in my subsequent academic career and experience.

Major Challenges that Emerged in Light of My History

There is no question that my intellectual interest in this issue is based on my personal exposure to pietism, revivalism and fundamentalism in my youth. Before I was about fifteen years old, I became vaguely aware of the fact that I was innocently being manipulated by psychological power games and religious indoctrination. I was emotionally torn for many years between, on the one hand, continually confessing the sins I was told I was guilty of and then, on the other hand, when I did confess my sins and commit myself time and again to Jesus at revival meetings (as stated above, I hit the sawdust trail three times before I realized I was being manipulated), of being immediately bedeviled with the terror of not having the "assurance of salvation." This paradox was trumpeted—it became clear to me—by evangelists because it served as a means for them to gain power over the faithful and keep them in constant subservience.[9]

Thus by the time I entered Goshen College I felt that many religious leaders, organizations, and functions were phony, that they were playing the field as charlatans and egomaniacs manipulating people for their own status enhancement and power. I unconsciously and unintentionally gradually became skeptical and cynical even about my own EMB heritage, which was rapidly succumbing to the evangelical fundamentalist world. It was my experience at Goshen and graduate school that helped me understand the process. As a result, a deep love and sad ambivalence developed toward my religious heritage. I rejected everything that smacked of evangelicalism/fundamentalism with a vengeance, and I still sorrow for those of my people (many are my close relatives) who were naive believers. I have stated this case in *Leaving Anabaptism*, the consequence of which was being shunned by some of my close relatives and most of the EMB community who had known me as a "grandson of a beloved EMB leader." From my perspective, that denomination has now left Anabaptism entirely.

This troublesome condition motivated me to pursue this concern in graduate school. There had to be some more objective way to look at this question and to test whether religion was really authentic or was a grand hoax used to manipulate people for personal benefit. My course of study at the University of Chicago, where I pursued a Sociology of Religion curriculum spanning the graduate departments of anthropology, sociology and the Divinity School, threw me headlong into this search.

The sociological/anthropological study of religion resulted in a number of perspectives or conclusions for me, which of course have been positions long held in the field: (1) religion is a fundamental aspect of the culture of every human grouping; (2) all religions begin as part of a cultural context, are culturally specific, and can only be understood in that context; (3) a religion cannot be transfused into other cultures without serious violence and disjuncture to both the imported religion and the recipient culture and its religion; (4) hence, all religions are relative regardless of whether or not they claim absolute and exceptional exclusivity—there is no way to construct an objective methodology that would establish the validity or "truth" of any one religion over against other religions (the methodology and philosophy of "comparative religions," which I taught many times, do not offer a very useful methodology in this regard).

I concluded that naturally Christianity had to be included in this framework unless I was to privilege it on the basis not of history, evidence, logic, or "truth" or revelation, but on the basis of exceptionalism, that is, on the basis of non-rational act, i.e., my faith tradition is absolutely unique (exclusively so) and real. Or I had to accept it on the basis of "not leaving home." I stayed at my father's house because I felt at home there, and I suspected that other religious traditions had their own share of problems.[10]

On the other hand, I became increasingly convinced that religion was a functional and inherent necessity for human existence. Regardless of whether it was man-made or revealed (i.e., exceptional or revealed), religion was the means by which a society created a moral and ethical system and provided the motivation to validate it and carry it out. If "man is by nature a religious animal," as Aristotle, Edmund Burke and many others have maintained, one of the rationales for that observation must be that consciously or unconsciously human beings have intuited that religion is a (or the?) way of assuring the survival of humanity. The very significant "social-contract" school downplayed the central role that religion plays in the creation of the social order, but increasingly religion is being given more standing in this arena. Somehow religion is not deniable, nor can it be legitimized on the basis of materialist, functionalist views alone. The dramatic eruption of a global clash between Islam and the West is one recent example. Religion is still very powerful, or even increasingly so.

Given the above insights, it became clear to me that since all peoples have been historically assigned (missionaries would often say "condemned" because of being "pagans") to a particular religion system and tradition, choice is not really an option; hence the need for missionary work. But in recent centuries through increased intercultural interaction, the awareness of religious pluralism and the ability to move to other religious systems has confronted us with the possibility (and the philosophical necessity) of choosing to which religion among the plethora available one gives allegiance.[11] Thus, as a newly-minted Anabaptist I was confronted with the challenge of choosing a religious tradition: of accepting or rejecting the Anabaptist Christianity in which I had been reared. I accepted my religious tradition and its claims in an act of faith, not because I could prove it was absolute and exceptional. In accepting the Christian faith, I remained an unprodigal son.

Thus my guiding principles began to be these: first, trying to gain a self-understanding by becoming aware of the tradition that shaped me; second, embarking on a search of whether that heritage was really worthy of my allegiance; and if so, third, encouraging my fellow believers, and finally sharing and witnessing to it in the larger world. However, I could not proclaim it as the absolute truth in light of my conclusion that I cannot claim an objective position from which to "privilege" the Christian tradition. I believe it has to be accepted by faith. As I reflect on these elements, I have discovered there is a cumulative sequence. This latter position (accepting Anabaptism) was possible because the former issues/steps were positively solved.

It would indeed be arrogant, naive or possibly even contradictory for me to say that most historical evidence points to the conclusion that the Anabaptist heritage is the movement truest to the Christian God's will for humanity (mini-exceptionalism). This argument, it seems to me, has already been suggested, even though guardedly by many people such as Ernst Troeltsch, Fritz Blanke, Roland Bainton, Earnest A. Payne, George H. Williams, H.R. Niebuhr, and recently Stanley Hauerwas, to list a few. Many of these would caution that Anabaptism was unrealistic, but all admit that the Anabaptists took Jesus more seriously as LORD than most other groups. It was taking Jesus seriously in this way that has tipped the balance for me. The one saving grace of defending this position is that Anabaptism has limited itself more to witnessing to the faith and sharing of their life through mutual aid and service, rather than promoting an exclusive system of propositional truths and consigning to hell those who resist it. (The evil of maintaining absolute truth will be addressed briefly below).

The Effects on My Life Work

With the principles outlined above as my "tool kit" of knowing, I began to "fit" Anabaptism into that scheme. Anabaptism went well with the idea of the social construction of reality since it stressed the discerning community under the guidance of the Holy Spirit and downplayed authority, hierarchy and power, and absolutism/exceptionalism, as discussed above. The approach to truth was based not on an orthodox/sacerdotal tradition but on the dynamics of everyday life as tested by the life of Jesus indicated in the scriptures and in the believing community—the discerning community, i.e., praxis.

A second aspect of this "integration" came with the discovery of the centrality of Jesus Christ in the entire faith system of Anabaptism. This is reflected in the way Menno's insistence on I Cor. 3:27 as the cornerstone of our belief has become a mantra for Mennos. "There can be no other foundation beyond that which is already laid, I mean Jesus Christ himself" *(New English Bible)*. Jesus not only challenged tradition and authority but substituted for it a new ethic: "It has been said of old ... but I say to you...." He thereby established a new Alternative Community in which the ethic was one of loving God and neighbor as oneself. The method was discipleship, that is, following Jesus, in the entire gamut of human existence, socially, economically, politically, physically and materially. I knew that Christ called me to live in the Alternative Community and to share it with others.

My response in my academic and professional career to becoming a disciple of Jesus seems to have focused on several areas: (1) concerns of material/economic justice and equality; (2) concerns for social justice focusing on power as the central problem; (3) reverence for and the preservation of creation; (4) education in the role of culture in creating as well as seducing religion. Upon reflection I discovered that most of my research and publications circle around these issues (as the titles of some of my books indicate), and these issues continue to motivate me. It would be boring to illustrate this with some of my work. Suffice it to say that my goal has been to contribute to the "Alternative

Community" that Jesus came to establish. I avoid using the term "Kingdom of Heaven" or "Kingdom of God" because of the semantic and theological problems and confusion that these terms invoke and have created. An example would be Hershberger's "Colony of Heaven," though I concur with his vision.

I have long been impatient with human tendencies to delve too far into abstract theory and thereby lose touch with reality and practice. It is here that I must mention the very important influence my wife, Freda, has been in all of my attempts to align experience and thought. She has been a balance to many of my meanderings and wanderings. This is reflected in my parallel career in the world of business. For example, in the world of economics and human existence, I have become involved in various business ventures mainly for the purpose of proving and testing for myself whether the teachings of Jesus in material and economic matters are relevant and practicable. I also became active in Church, Industry and Business Association (CIBA) and Mennonite Industry and Business Accociation (MIBA), which were the predecessors to the new Mennonite Economic Development Association (MEDA) while I was professor at Goshen College. One gratifying experience in this sector was helping to start *The Market Place,* which has become one of the leading Christian business magazines, a lay venture not sponsored by any church organization.

Freda has been a supportive critic by bringing me back to the realities of needing to put aside enough for our three boys, Bill, Ben and Fred, who needed lots of new shoes when they still "stuck their feet under our table" as my father would say of my sibs and me. My experience in the Dust Bowl and my acceptance of Jesus' teachings and life regarding our sustaining mother earth have dictated that most of my business activities and investments must be related to conservation and preservation of the environment. This is also why some of my entrepreneurial efforts ended in failure, often testing Freda's patience. I have become aware how anti-mother earth the reigning economic (and some evangelical Christian) ideologies have been. I am discouraged about how blithely fellow Christians participate in free market capitalism, which is especially destructive of the environment. This is evidenced by the empirical fact that the less concern there is for the environment, the more profitable the ventures have been in economic terms. Fortunately some reappraisals are taking place.

My View (Philosophy) of History

The idea or reality of "progress" is clearly a two-edged sword, and there is no way to determine whether it is a tradeoff or whether science and technology are actually positive or negative in their consequences. Certainly from an "ecosphere" perspective, it could well be that it has been devastatingly and tragically negative, at least as far as present indications go. A broad consensus is now emerging that indicates that the global overpopulation and pollution, atmospheric warming, destruction of species of flora and fauna, depletion of water and resources, etc., are transforming the earth with ultimately negative and threatening consequences. Incidentally, a recent review by an internationally appointed scientific panel of experts states that there is now incontrovertible proof that global destruction is real and that the challenge is now a political response to these facts. The newly released documentary, *An Inconvenient Truth,* by Al Gore is a timely and prophetic challenge to the crisis.

In spite of the environmental crisis, it may still be possible that there has been progress in human social history and existence—according only to assumptions about the purpose and goals of human life, not to materialistic assumptions. From a Christian moral perspective, using Jesus teachings and life as a guide, it is possible to say that there has been some progress, especially in the positions on slavery, murder, the equal status of women, children's rights, freedom of belief and faith in religious life and the separation of church from the domination of the state *(corpus christianum),* and finally the rejection of violence in general (this latter may be highly controversial, however). Actual practice among Christians relative to the above guidelines laid down by Jesus may, of course, be far removed from the ideal in many situations, even in Mennonite communities.

It is in this context that my belief in and adherence to Anabaptism has seemingly been vindicated; for in most of the above issues the Anabaptist tradition has been on the forefront, often being marginalized for taking specific positions of protest on particular instances. Even social science has largely evaded and ignored the great moral issues of our time, including nationalism and war, and has been increasingly critiqued in recent times for it. One recent critique of a book regarding the "nastiness" of modern war states that the book is praiseworthy for confronting social science with the fact that war and violence are integral features of advanced modernity rather then vestiges of the past.[12] This is not a very comforting thought in general, but it gives Anabaptism a vote of confidence.

Human domination of each other by coercion or violence is the key unresolved philosophical and ethical issue. No social system has solved it. Power has become so thoroughly rationalized that it has become a legitimate goal in human actions and thus seems not to be an important or relevant issue. Until this is solved, humanity will reflect a Hobbesian war of everyone against her neighbor. It is uncanny how Jesus' life and teaching modeled the true mode of using power. He told us to lay down our lives for others, to go to the cross if necessary. In His Alternative Community each will be the other's servant rather than a "lord" over the others. Too much of contemporary religion, including Christianity, is power mongering.

I am convinced that there is a dialectical process in social history. That is to say, there is always a tendency to take a principle or belief or practice to its extreme and in so doing to create a heresy. Then a reaction attempts to correct the earlier extreme, but unfortunately that does not provide a solution, only aggravating it. A "synthesis" of both extremes is also not a solution since it would transform the extremes into some compromise, which itself may divert from the possible truths contained in either opposite. For example, individualism and collectivism each contain important realities even for Anabaptism, but an attempted synthesis may negate or invalidate the truth of both. These two forces, I believe for example, can never be fully harmonized—they are inherent in human existence.

Finally, returning to the metaphors, I believe I did not (totally) leave my father's house. I believe I represent but a small link in a chain of a particular segment of ongoing human experience, and finally I believe I am the product of stopping and taking refreshment at many wayside fountains. What does it all mean? I do not have an answer. I am convinced that one of the greatest dangers of the human race is hubris, or in common parlance, mistaking our own understandings as "the truth" and imposing them on others (is this not a major human sin?). Fundamentalism is by definition the militant imposition of one's truth on others (George Marsden). Thus Charles Kimball says, "When particular interpretations of these claims (truth claims) become propositions requiring uniform assent and are treated as rigid doctrines, the likelihood of corruption in that tradition rises exponentially. Such tendencies are the first harbingers of the evil that may follow."[13] Kimball takes as axiomatic that fundamentalism plagues all religions.

Hence, I deplore fundamentalism wherever it is found. I have tried not to take myself or my "insights" too seriously, but I am sure I have failed. Here again Jesus is my model, but I leave it to others to say whether it shows. The Apostle Paul says it well: "My knowledge now is partial" (I Cor. 13:12, NEB) and it ever shall be.

October 2003
Revised April 2007

Notes

1. "Even the Postmodern Story has a Body: Narrative, Poetry and Ritual," unpublished paper, Anabaptist Sociology and Anthropology Association, June 26–28, 2003, p. 7.
2. For an excellent review of the age long debate about the relationship of nature and nurture, see Stevan Pinker, *The Blank Slate: The Modern Denial of Human Nature* (New York: Viking, 2002).
3. The "wandering" characteristic of the Anabaptists-Mennonite tradition is especially impressive if one visits some of the many "outposts" Mennonites have established around the globe.
4. An illustration: One time an officer of Goodville Mutual Insurance came to pick Jacob up for a trip from Mountain Lake to Minneapolis in the small business plane, his first plane ride. The weather was rather turbulent. When we kids asked how he had enjoyed the plane ride, Dad said, "Oh, it was all right, I guess, but I wish Wayne Martin would have flown a bit higher, since he hit quite a few rock piles."
5. This personal vignette below provides some rather specific and concrete material to the basis for the conflict and mutual disdain that the various Russian Mennonite groups had for each other.
6. This event accelerated the influences of the three metaphors in unimaginable ways.
7. I attempted to remain in the EMB conference, but the leadership (among them some of my relatives) was oriented in an opposite direction and felt I had "lost the faith."
8. The "nature " versus 'nurture" issue will ever remain—both the material and the mind or "spirit" operate in human existence. See Pinker cited above.
9. One example suffices. One of the evangelists, who had a regular schedule of leading a revival campaign in Mountain Lake, always stayed at a motel in Windom, 15 miles away. After one of his campaigns, it was discovered that he had a paramour who met him there during his campaign at Mountain Lake.
10. For a very helpful discussion of the "absoluteness" of religious truth and other problems, see Paul J. Griffiths, *Problems of Religious Diversity* (Oxford: Blackwell Publishers, 2001).

11 I am of course totally aware of the very complex interrelationships between culture and religion. But try telling that to the fundamentalists of all world religions.
12 Hans Jonas, *War and Modernity* (Cambridge: Polity Press, 2003), reviewed by Edward A. Tiryakian in *Contemporary Sociology*, July 2003.
13 Charles Kimball, *When Religion Becomes Evil* (San Francisco: Harper Collins, 2002), 41.

RAY GINGERICH

The Quest for an Authentic Faith that Engages the World

This is a narrative account of the evolution of my intellectual development and faith struggle. The struggle as here told is shared by many; yet certain parts of it may be unique and consequently not easily understood, or even alien. This is, nevertheless, my story. And in it I make myself vulnerable, for I share not merely the process of my thought, but my life—who I was and who I have become.[1]

My geography of faith as here protrayed unfortunately fails to do justice to a major series of important players in my life: my wife, my children, and many of my co-workers whose relationships are of special significance in shaping my story. Likewise, the peaks and valleys of my life are left largely unexamined. But I trust that the many anecdotes placed within the stream of larger historical events will offer connecting points of interest to everyone.

Early Years 1953–1960

On Leaving Home

I grew up in an Amish Mennonite home in Kalona, Iowa. In the early 50s, with the advent of the Korean War, the military draft was reinstated. I and an Iowa peer of mine were the first two I-W fellows to enter the Lancaster General Hospital ("I-W service" was a pacifist alternative to the military.) I had wanted to go into PAX service in Europe under MCC, but my parents resisted. The distance seemed too far, the unknowns too great. I was an adventuresome nineteen prepared to see the world. But my parents won out.

By the summer of 1955 I had finished two years of I-W service at LGH. That experience was critical in introducing me to a community of mainstream Mennonites: Lancaster County Mennonites, a people who exuded a greater certainty in the rightness of their thinking than did the Amish and the Beachy Amish, who had shaped my identity in Iowa; and also the "Weavertowners" (Lancaster Beachy Amish), with whom I continued to fellowship on Sunday mornings. The Lancaster County Mennonites added a significant ingredient: broader cultural exposure, intercourse with a more individualistic and pluralistic society in its initial stages of a breakdown of ethnic mechanisms of societal control.

Here in Lancaster County as opposed to Johnson County, Iowa, I experienced a certain inversion of practice and theology. On the one hand, those who lived in more closed communities, as was the case in my home community, possessed a communal humility (psychologically dubbed as "an inferiority complex") and had a somewhat more pliable situational community theology. On the other hand, those whose self-identity was increasingly urbane, who were in the process of rapidly moving away from the family farm, and who were engaged in mainstream professions and endowed with rapidly increasing wealth and power—descriptive of Lancaster County Mennonites—were compensating for all this "worldliness" with a theology that was more other-worldly and less relational: one that placed more emphasis on direct revelation, on individual salvation, and on doctrinal orthodoxy. They were, I later discovered, in one of the phases of twentieth-century Mennonites moving toward a more mainstream American evangelical theology that offered greater certainty for the eternal soul and was promoted as more spiritual and that at the same time called for less physical sacrifice and promised greater success in the affairs of this world.

The Lancaster Mennonites, whose hospitality I appreciated and in whose fellowship I basked, were a people who had begun to drop their overtly plain appearance and their simple way of life. They were, as well, losing their communal ethics and their structures for vocational accountability. They were doing this, at least in part, to be a more mission-oriented people, less sectarian and less tied to non-essential ethnic peculiarities. But from my perspective (particularly as I assess it in retrospect) their understanding of the systems of the larger world and of the psychological and spiritual tools essential to cope with these systems had not kept pace with the modernity and affluence that had invaded their communities. Their social mechanisms to maintain communal authenticity had failed to keep abreast of their cultural accommodations.

One more observation: Lancaster County Mennonites, as I perceived them, were "in charge." Among them I felt a breeze of freedom, of power, of having control of society, and of being the determinants of some larger destiny. For the first time in my life the Mennonites with whom I identified were extremely influential in the larger society, while still remaining a social minority. Their spirit of expansionism was most apparent, both psychologically and numerically, in their missions emphasis. These Lancaster Mennonites who were "in charge" were missions-minded. Their calling was clear. Their role in being God's instruments was unquestioned. They had in their possession the knowledge of truth, the way of salvation for all peoples. For them, this call to missions, particularly overseas missions, provided the greatest single religious legitimation for their newly acquired wealth.

The Lancaster experience, particularly because I later served under the Lancaster Mennonite Mission Board, was and remains one of the social paradigms for my understanding of the Mennonite Church regarding its institutions and its theology. Lancaster Mennonites were (and are) an economically well-heeled and powerful people, a committed people, who traversed the world with a Bible and a theology that seemed by many to be serving them well. Not until over a decade later while I was in Europe, charged with the mission to "bring to the European Mennonites those parts of the gospel which they had lost over the past 450 years"[3] (this during the time when America Mennonites were supporting the war in Vietnam through the generosity of their tax dollars), did I begin to realize how closely my reading of the Bible and my theology were aligned with the "in-charge" ethos I was exposed to during my Lancaster era and the post-Lancaster college years at EMC. The theology and the lenses through which I was reading the Bible seemed to endorse the American ethos in its major tenets of imperialism, rather than to provide the foundation for an authentic community of love and nonviolent resistance with structures of mutual accountability. Slowly, very gradually, I began to realize how little my theology had kept me from becoming absorbed into the maelstrom of the world's Super-Power Society.[4]

Comparative Cultures

The Lancaster experience provided a significant but subtle backdrop to my social and intellectual development. But it was what followed those two years, rather than the Lancaster experience by itself, that would be most telling.

Immediately after my I-W stint at the Lancaster General Hospital, I spent the summer months in New York City in several "mission churches" associated with the Lancaster Mennonite Conference. In the Bronx during the daytime and in Brooklyn at night I taught summer Bible School, harmonizing the scriptures and showing the way of God as proclaimed in the Book—knowing that the Bible, inspired by the Holy Spirit, was a tightly knit together book from God to be read just as though it had been written by a single author.

By the end of the summer, however, a chink appeared in my armor. I began to see how dependent my understanding of scripture and theology and of culture and community was on my social and political surroundings. This insight, however, did not actually come to consciousness until much later. At that particular point it was simply a befuddlement that raised doubts!

Inner-city New York contrasted sharply with the rolling green hills of Iowa, where I had cultivated the long rows of corn while memorizing scripture or working through Howard Hammer's latest revival sermon (1951). Now I spent mornings on the hot-tarred highways and trash-strewn byways, in the spaghetti-stenched, rat-infested apartments and highrises, compelling, persuading those without faith to come to summer Bible School. I held classes with African Americans in the afternoon and Italians at night. The sensory experiences down-loaded into my psychophysical hardware during those New York City summer months melded into a subconscious force motivating me to take further steps. I left that intrinsically evil but intriguing metropolitan overwhelmed, not knowing what the larger contours of my life were to be. What had become clear to me was that the world and its people constituted a phenomenon far greater and more complex than I was able to comprehend. For the first time, while still unable to verbalize what I was feeling, it seemed as though the communities that had shaped me had failed to provide the answers to some of life's most persistent questions. Sensing that where I stood determined what I was seeing, I nevertheless lacked the tools both to discover myself in the context of my surroundings and to understand my surroundings in light of the communities that had shaped me.

College and the Complexity of Reality

It was the fall of 1956. Newly married, committed to missions, committed to the Bible, committed to the church, Wilma Beachy Gingerich and I, both from Kalona, matriculated at Eastern Mennonite College nearly a thousand miles from home. Goshen College, a mere three hundred fifty miles away, was in the community from which my Mennonite mother had migrated to marry my Amish father. But GC did not enter our consideration. It was too liberal—so we were told. "EMC will make you more useful to the church." But most of our people in Iowa had serious doubts about even that. Why was I, an only son who thrived on the land, taking this interlude away from my farming responsibilities, or perhaps even leaving the farm? Sometimes in the tone of a warning, sometimes as a sincere encouragement (from adult mentors who genuinely cherished me) came the admonition not to leave the community: "You don't need an education to understand the Bible and serve the Lord, only a humble heart and the Holy Spirit."

While at EMC I had the great adventure to be introduced to differing theological perspectives leading to contrasting, even conflicting, ways of reading the Bible. Should the Book of Revelation provide our hermeneutic keys according to the premillennialists on the faculty? Or should we look rather to the Sermon on the Mount, according to those who held premillennialism as something of a Fundamentalist heresy introduced from outside the Anabaptist-Mennonite fold? Do we arrive at right ethics through the purity of doctrine? Or do we understand doctrine in the context of culture and in the service of ethics? Does Appalachian Pentecostalism offer a contemporary expression of worship equally as appropriate as a more somber liturgy with beautiful four-part singing? All this was in the EMC (EMU) melting pot of the fifties. EMC was after all founded as "the bulwark against the liberalism of the midwest."

In Biblical Theology C.K. Lehman gently nudged us into seeing that the Sermon on the Mount was meant for *now* and that the Kingdom of God (I can still see him shuffle with a kind of dignified excitement)—the Kingdom of God *was at hand!* Our daily prayer was to be "Thy kingdom come. Thy will be done *in earth,* as it is in heaven" (KJV). "Jesus," said C.K., "would not teach us so to pray if it were not God's will!" C.K. also assigned Alan Richardson's *Theology of the New Testament,* a book denying the reality of hell as a place where a *sovereign and loving* God eternally punishes the reprobates. We read it ("we" meaning Don Sensenig, Elmer Lehman, Roy Kiser, David Augsburger—all persons committed to the church and who would later each assume significant roles in shaping that church) in the last two weeks of the semester with little time to discuss and linger on the tough and politically dangerous issues. Only later did I realize that this was a deliberate strategy. But it worked! For within the Bible department it was "Brother C.K.," and only C.K., who elicited critical questions and from whom I learned that some committed Christians are also committed thinkers. It was C.K. who in brief private conversations urged me to pursue theology and who provided the model that gave me hope for the work of the church.[5]

The real "clincher" for me came in a course in *apologetics*. The text, Bernard Ramm's *Evidences of Christianity,* was an unusually clear and emphatic Fundamentalist book. The professor seldom, if ever, provided a critique. To the contrary, Ramm's "evidences" were presented as facts. I completed the course and for the first time clearly realized how far my own conservative upbringing was removed from the spirit of Fundamentalism. But the milieu at EMC was such that if one expressed this openly, it would be like wearing a scarlet letter. Equally important for my ethical life and for my commitment to the church, I realized that Jesus could not have been a Fundamentalist. All this was on the one hand a *freeing* experience, but it was also very painful—particularly so, for the alternatives were not clear—even as in retrospect, they seem not to have been clear for the Mennonite Church.

This experience of facing the solid rock wall of Ramm's Fundamentalism, his way of reading the Bible, and the "proofs" or evidences of Christianity that he provided was a landmark in a life-long pursuit of the meaning of faith and faith's relationship to epistemology. I "knew" that Ramm believed himself to know things he did not know. Much later

I would associate that claim to human-created absolutes as a form of religious idolatry, but for now it seemed more like a form of arrogance that I associated with a certain personality type.

Yet the question remained: How was it that I knew that Ramm did not know? Was the certainty of "knowing about not knowing" equally as arrogant as that of "knowing"? This remained an anomaly. Were certain ways of pursuing knowledge less prone to arrogance and idolatry than others? Were some forms of knowing more faithful to the way of Jesus than others? And more life-giving than others? With the awareness of different routes to knowing, some of them illustrated in the Bible itself, came a heightened recognition that there were different ways of reading the Bible—indeed, that within our Mennonite fellowship different ways, sometimes conflicting different ways, were practiced—but seldom openly discussed. Such differences in faith and our understanding of the Bible and the Holy Spirit served as the great "discussion stoppers."

In the community in which I grew up, how we read the Bible and constructed our theology was determined less by intellectual prowess than by the *kind* of life we lived and the community to which we *belonged*. I now began to return to that naiveté. Intellectual reasoning individually practiced, I came to see, too frequently was rationalization—an attempt to authenticate some other "reality" that lacked *self*-authentication. The Enlightenment, of which we are all children, with its near-sacral emphasis on Reason, I learned much later, had in significant ways led us down the wrong path—a conviction that was strengthened over the years as I rediscovered our Anabaptist-Mennonite heritage of discipleship.

These socio-cultural questions of epistemology and the nonviolent life of faith are what mark my interest in the Anabaptists of the sixteenth-century and the contemporary theologies of the disempowered on the margins of society. These people offer us a different way of knowing. The epistemological questions and the contrast they offer to eighteenth and nineteenth-century Protestant missions, carried out hand-in-glove with Western colonization, are what so relentlessly pique my interest in Mennonite missions. But let me return again to my story.

The "ah ha" moment with Ramm was both exciting and anxiety-filled. It challenged me to think and to act beyond the boundaries sanctioned by the communities to which I continued to be committed. It raised the threatening dilemma that the way of Jesus was not passive but came with a cost. For to love my community of faith and to be loyal to it, I had to have the courage to challenge it. In my journey of faith I began to see Jesus as a person who had the qualities of risk-taking and courage to practice it: qualities he used to serve his community, qualities that called for ultimate commitment and sacrifice. I read the gospel stories and Jesus' conflict with the Pharisees in a new light, substituting "the Mennonites" for "the Pharisees"—a practice that I have continued throughout the years.

The Middle Years: 1961–70

Missions and Anomalies

My years in Europe under the Eastern Mennonite Board of Missions and Charities (now Eastern Mennonite Missions) spurred a proliferation of questions (e.g., the nature of the biblical text and the impact of cultural context on meanings and understandings). Unfortunately, during this entire period, I far too often found myself without the presence of a hermeneutic community with whom to share, to process and to grow. In the framework of Thomas Kuhn's thought, it was a period in which the theological anomalies grew more complex but with few genuine breakthroughs. Certainly a new paradigm did not emerge. My professional role as pastor dictated not merely the content of my sermons but more and more the boundaries of my thought and the very way I dared (or was unable to dare) to reflect critically on the inherited orthodoxies of Christendom.

The Mennonite-Protestant bookstore, of which I was founder and director (made possible through the generosity of Orie O. Miller and committed Lancaster business folk), developed a somewhat sophisticated European Common Market clientele and brought me into a more socialist-Marxist milieu. On Sundays, however, I addressed a people for whom socialist thought and worship of the true God was an oxymoron. My task called for a kind of chic literalist rendition of the biblical stories. Yet the more educated in the congregation expected me to be theologically well informed; thus much of what I said needed to have the potential for at least two levels of interpretation.

I learned that the Mennonites, Protestants, Pietists and Catholics who attended the services all lived in a dual world that could be divided roughly into weekdays and Sunday. The week was controlled by the forces of cause and effect—economic, social, political and natural. What happened was within the framework of what is usually called a modern or western worldview. The normative view for the Sunday worship hour was the ancient one, the one that was common for Jews, Christians and pagans during the time of Jesus. My task, judging from the responses that I received and from the traditional piety of the congregation, was to reinforce the reality of the sacred within the framework of this ancient worldview for at least that one special hour of worship. For it was within this "thought world" and within this special hour of the week that salvation was renewed and maintained.

But was the purpose of the worship service, I asked, to provide a ritualized escape from the mundane and often harsh world of the every day? Or was it to come together to gain a new perspective on *the church in the world*—one in which the presence and power of God relevant to our everyday needs was experienced—so that as we were *scattered* into our weekday world, we could go with renewed hope and energy?

As I continued to listen to my American missionary peers in Europe and those stopping in Luxembourg on their way to and from East Africa (because of Icelandic Airlines' low-cost trans-Atlantic flights), I found none with whom I was able to openly explore faith questions raised in a trans-cultural context. (Looking back, I find this astonishing and wonder whether I failed to be sufficiently open and transparent.) Instead I identified patterns of thought that seemed to be replicas of the culture and the educational training out of which they (and I) had come. All of my missionary peers seemed to have their taproots in the culture of their childhood and their primary loyalties to the people back in Lancaster or Holmes County or Grantsville—wherever they had come from.

My American Mennonite peers working in East Africa seemed to have an even easier path than my American peers in Europe. The customs of the African natives were so dramatically different that the expectations for the expatriates were limited to selective adaptations of "cultural peripheries"; in contrast, our European hosts expected general conformity. More important for theological understandings, the worldview of the East Africans—in contrast to that of the so-called post-Christian Europeans—was much like the worldview of the first century depicted in the Bible. Hence the East African missionary experience—unlike that of the European missionary experience—seemed to reinforce the timeless and universal dualistic (this-worldly/otherworldly) cosmology of American Mennonite and Protestant-evangelical missions.

Mennonite theology—evangelical Protestant theology appended with North American Mennonite particulars[6] (the theology of both my European and East African missionary peers)—remained so thoroughly intact that a serious faith struggle, one that moved beyond the application of Christian practices, seemed seldom to ensue.[7] The single factor that did make a theological impact was the great East African Revival. That tended to push the American Mennonite missionaries into an even more pietistic, spiritualist way of reading the Bible and "doing theology"—one that corresponded with a pre-modern culture. But this was exactly in the opposite direction from the way that I was being pulled in Europe. I was looking for an integrative gospel within the cultural context in which I lived; I was searching to find a gospel that would address not merely the spiritual or individual needs of the psyche. I was struggling to find a political gospel that would speak to the community's needs and be healing for a whole people in a modern/post-modern world.[8]

Realizing that simply from a practical perspective I could not continue my work in Europe with the intense alienation I was experiencing, I decided to look for a more productive and fulfilling direction by pursuing doctoral studies in sociology in the U.S. Somewhat by chance I shared my plans for studies (not my alienation)—with Myron Augsburger, then president of EMC, in a conversation at the Mennonite World Conference in Amsterdam in 1967. Within a few weeks I received an invitation from Myron to teach sociology at EMC. He suggested that after finding my bearings in the classroom, I could then begin graduate studies. Myron was especially interested in having a sociology professor with experience abroad in the work of the church and with a strong faith perspective to bring into the classroom.

Perhaps it was my unfinished agenda with scripture and theology, or perhaps it was simply due to the awareness that at that point in my life I would be unable to bring the faith perspective to EMC that Myron was looking for, that I declined his invitation. Whatever the motivations, I wanted first to finish seminary. It was as though *I had to*. I wanted to do biblical and theological studies not primarily to gain a degree, but to find God again. And though I was urged to go to one of the more prestigious East coast seminaries, I was very consciously a seeker and *knew* that the one place where I stood a chance of finding the God I was looking for would be at AMBS.[9]

It was not that I had turned away from God. It was not that I no longer wanted to serve the church—quite the opposite. But the God whom I had served I now recognized as a human construct too puny and too much fashioned after our American triumphalism to be worthy of my continued loyalty, much less worthy of proclaiming to a needy and unjust world whether in Africa, Europe or America. I could no longer go this route. If the Christian faith was worth my total commitment, there had to be more to it; it had to play a much more all-encompassing social role than I had seen or heard. Thus at age thirty-five with a wife and four children to support, I left the "mission field" to find Jesus and to find God.

A Second Conversion

At the Associated Mennonite Biblical Seminaries under John Howard Yoder I experienced another conversion.[10] It was as dramatic and as Spirit-filled as any previous conversion. It happened steadily by jerks over the course of a year or two and with no definitive end. The anomalies, which were like single threads, now came together so that with the help of John Howard Yoder as mentor in the midst of a larger hermeneutic community, I began to weave together a whole new tapestry. I understood spirituality and faithfulness to be a quality of life, not a metaphysical perspective foreign to the primary mode of reality in our everyday lives. The earthly reality, "the paramount reality of everyday life," is the primal basis for doing theology. Ethics, rather than doctrine, orthopraxis before orthodoxy, is the determinant of faithfulness. The deadend anomalies now all began to fit into a pattern, enough so that a new paradigm, a new way of perceiving the Christian faith, began to emerge.

Central to the Gospel is the way of peace as both taught and practiced by Jesus. The model for understanding this gospel and the community that gave birth to it is Jesus of Nazareth. No longer was this Jesus one of the persons of the Godhead; were that the case no logic would allow me to emulate such a deity as an ethical model. The doctrine of the trinity was just that: a doctrine, a human construct debated, then sacralized and granted authority beyond scripture by the preeminently Constantinian church. Whatever fallacies such sacralized doctrinal constructs foisted upon us (and they continued to be significant), these were now of secondary or tertiary importance. Although institutionally I needed to lend this doctrine my respect, as a matter of personal faith I was freed from the existential burden. It could no longer be allowed to interfere with discipleship and with the necessary social constructs for faith. Life had new meaning and the scriptures held new integrity and political vitality.

My concentration in seminary was biblical studies, for the Bible, I continued to believe, provided the answers to life's eternal questions. I further held that in it was revealed the will of God for humanity, both individually and collectively. Yet as I listened to my professors in biblical studies, I began to see that *we* (meaning Mennonites *in general*) were paying lip service to the Bible with little awareness that the more powerful forces shaping our lives came neither from the Bible nor from the prophetic pacifist minorities of history. Those forces came from mainstream American culture and from our peoplehood ethnicity. The American culture shaped our *primary* identity. Mennonite ethnicity provided the particularities, largely of only tertiary political and ethical significance, but sufficiently distinctive to support the psychological illusion of being the "chosen of God."

I also began to see that we were theologizing as though the Holy Spirit had departed from the church somewhere around the end of the first century, CE, and as though what happened after the first century by and through the followers of Jesus was of only marginal importance.[11] The one clear exception, of course, was the early sixteenth-century Anabaptists, a motley third-world-like group of people whom I made the subject of my dissertation work and from whom I continue to draw inspiration and guidance. But despite the verbiage about peoplehood and history, our biblical studies took neither sociology nor the larger scope of history seriously! The operative metaphysical presuppositions always assured that the correct ahistorical (orthodox) responses would be approximated.

Too many of my mentors in biblical studies, when asked the ethical questions of the day—ranging from the militarization of our culture to issues of economic justice, life insurance, and homosexuality—positioned themselves as on the brink of a high cliff overlooking a vast void; then heaving forward (presumably exercising a wager of faith), they hoped somehow to arrive on the distant shore of twentieth-century civilization equipped with the know-how to engage the powers of the day. All too often, I felt, they had only shadowy ideas of what lay between the banks of the first century and the approaching twenty-first. I realized that biblical studies as they were currently structured would not equip me with the necessary hermeneutic tools for the church and the larger society to which the church in its mission was called to serve. Biblical studies failed to provide the tools for authentic faith. On that basis I decided that my graduate studies needed to be in the area of socio-historical theology, flanked by church history and ethics.

Later Years: the 1970s, '80s and '90s

Middle Class Pacifists or Marginalized Peasants?

In graduate school my peasant background filtered its way via intellectual osmosis into my academic studies—including my analysis of the sixteenth-century Anabaptists. It was only after I had spent time in Europe, walking where the Anabaptist peasants had walked and smelling what they must have smelled, and returned to the States, that I saw my own people through new eyes. I realized that I had grown up a peasant! What was obvious about Anabaptism had been well concealed not merely by H.S. Bender (who depicted an educated, forward-looking movement of persecuted but courageous and respectable individuals—precisely what was needed to consolidate and bolster North American Mennonite identity). A host of Bender's younger disciples continued their own versions of Anabaptist elitism in which the more mangy characters were at best fringe members. But Anabaptism as a *movement* was not the Grebels, the Mantzes, and the Sattlers, not the elitist group of students surrounding Zwingli. It was not even like the less radical Mennos. Contrary to the way middle-class North American Mennonites doing their dissertations were depicting Anabaptists—as reasoned pacifists with deep convictions, faithfully following a mostly-respectable nonresistant Jesus, but rejected by their cultured despisers—the Anabaptist movement was overwhelmingly a messy peasants' revolution. It was a movement of an oppressed people—oppressed economically and religiously—calling for structures of justice.[12]

Anabaptism was a movement with the whole mixture of calls for common-sense justice and morality that is found in every peasants' movement, whether in sixteenth-century Europe, in contemporary Latin America or in North America. At its best it was a kind of fearless uprightness that was not cloaked with political tact to appease those in ruling positions. Anabaptists, like the prophets and martyrs of the first century, did not have the luxury of seeing nonparticipation in violence as an end in itself, protected by a democracy.[13] Nonviolence was for the larger stream of Anabaptists a long time in coming through the struggle for justice. It was not some passive quality of life that had integrity as an abstraction unassociated with the struggle for justice. What I found in sixteenth-century Anabaptism, I also discovered among the motley followers of Jesus.

My second conversion was not a conversion to an ephemeral spirit, but to the Jesus who died on a cross as the price he paid for his social nonconformity. The Bible in that context took on an immensely fresh and new meaning. My hermeneutic guideline for reading the Old Testament was to read it as Jesus did. He read it through the eyes of the prophets. They, not the kings, were his models. Jesus and his followers stood in that prophetic line. The Gospel core was political and moral, rather than metaphysical, doctrinal or mystical. The earliest Christian movements were overwhelmingly composed of simple people. Jesus was a "pacifist Zealot," one who refused to hurt people or to use violence to gain Kingdom goals. That is, Jesus passionately embraced the Zealots' sense of justice (of sufficiency of goods, personal and ethnic dignity, participation in one's own destiny, and of solidarity with the oppressed) but rejected violence, which the Zealots unquestioningly assumed was essential as a means toward justice. For this political stance Jesus died.

*From Anabaptism as Mennonite Ideal to Anabaptism
as a Practiced Way of Life*

At the Associated Mennonite Seminary I developed a theological core[14] based not on dogma but on discipleship, not on supernaturalism but on the church as an incarnational presence in this world, not on salvation in the afterlife but on that which is life-giving and healing in the present life. And perhaps of greatest importance was the construction of a theological grid based on the nonviolent model of Jesus.

But it was in Nashville (where I did my graduate work) at Edgehill United Methodist Church that I experienced what Anabaptism and the Jesus-way-of-life might look like if it were practiced. After doing some church shopping, Wilma and I discovered that Edgehill was the only one of Nashville's 700 churches that had more than token racial integration. EUMC was located one block away from a large urban renewal set of high-rises, one hundred percent black, and five blocks away from a lily-white prestigious university. A dwelling house had been converted into a Methodist "church" building without a steeple. The sanctuary was a two-car garage used seven days a week for community services. When it could no longer accommodate the Sunday morning crowd, it was expanded to a four-car garage. Here was a modern version of "the church within thy house." I was being introduced to a politically active people of God whom I began to see as modern Anabaptists.[15] Jim Lawson, an earlier co-worker of Martin Luther King, was a sometime member of the pastoral team. This was in the early 70s before the days of the Metropolitan Church; but as publicly posted on Sunday afternoon, it served as the worship place for Nashville's gay and lesbian community. This was also a congregation promoting women in ministry.

The lead pastor, Bill Barnes, with whom I continue a friendship, was a Yale Divinity School graduate who had done an internship with Bill Stringfellow in East Harlem, read Karl Barth for his sermon preparations, and was a pacifist.[16] He introduced me to the Berrigan brothers, whose writings I read for my morning devotions during most of those years. And when in the midst of my doctoral studies *The Politics of Jesus* (which I had received from John Howard Yoder as class handouts while at *AMBS*) became available in published form, I began to see the possibilities of a pacifism that was linked to political action and social justice, a kind of radical nonviolent revolution—quite different from the quieter pacifism of North American Mennonites through whose lenses I had earlier read *The Politics*. I began to read the Bible again as though it were for the first time. It became a far more radical book. The existentialism of the Bultmann school, to which much of the "historical Jesus" materials continued to be theologically linked, was even more alien to me, as was also the entire corpus of Karl Barth.[17]

Questions of epistemology that had long troubled me, although I was finding some resolution in the process of shifting from a vertical to a more horizontal theology under Yoder, persisted throughout graduate school where I first began to study seriously the sociology of knowledge and the sociology of religion. If community was central to our understanding of the church and those subsequent movements of Jesus' followers (including the Anabaptists), then sociology and social history, not metaphysics and dogma, must be the tools for our analysis and interpretation. I found my lack of knowledge in this fertile arena somewhat appalling. Equally appalling was the lack of interest among the company of both Mennonite theologians and the liberal theological faculty at Vanderbilt.[18] Nevertheless, many of my intuitions regarding what we know and how we know were confirmed. The façade of mainstream Mennonite theology was further unmasked.

Slowly over a period of some years I began to grasp why the sociology of knowledge appears to be threatening, not simply to conservative and evangelical colleagues, but to my Liberal friends as well. I began to see that Fundamentalists and Liberals, contrary to popular conceptions, all draw their water from the same well.[19] The epistemological precariousness of both Fundamentalism and Liberalism (and every variation along that spectrum) became for me a driving force to discover and further develop a third way of reading the biblical texts and of doing theology. It is the quest for a life-giving faith that is ever-and-again authenticated in its engagement with a world of unfaith and determinant violence.

My Ongoing Quest:
The Follies of Being Human and the Search for a Place to Stand
Several points in my development in the sociology of knowledge and the role religion plays relate directly to my intellectual pilgrimage. I

outline these issues simply as "indicators" pointing out the direction my journey is taking me.

1. THE SOCIOLOGY OF KNOWLEDGE All "reality," as perceived by human beings, is a socio-historical construction. Sociology of knowledge reminds us that, in contradistinction to both Fundamentalism and Liberalism, we build our structures (our ideologically bound worldviews, our institutions, our rituals, our sacred texts, and our military weapons) and then, forgetting that we constructed them, we bow down and worship them.

We humans in our subconscious struggle to find security are idol builders–worshipping the gods that are not God. Even as the children of Israel in the wilderness, we today create our golden calves and then bow down and revere them by placing our trust in them. We are homo idolatrous. To understand our innate propensity for idolatry is central to grasping the nature of our human "fallenness."

The Bible, I believe, is the repository of enduring traditions of the people of God. When we make the Bible into an ahistorical Word of God, taking it out of its cultural, social, metaphoric and symbolic contexts, claiming it to be our sole authority for life (i.e., adhering to the Protestant principle of the Reformation), we have made the Bible into an idol. In our desperate search for security we claim with Martin Luther that "scripture alone is our authority."[20] In calling the Bible holy[21] we exempt it from the laws of history and from the critical appraisal of our own cultural heritage.

2. THE SOCIO-ANTHROPOLOGY OF RELIGION But what, we may ask, is the role of religion? "Theology is, after all, a religious discipline (I hear a critic respond) and dare never be reduced to the secularity of social analysis." Anthropology of religion (building on the sociology of knowledge) reminds us that the human species is most distinctive in its religious dimensions.[22] All human beings are religious. But only human beings, so far as we know, are religious. Being religious is a consequence of a consciousness that transcends the immediacy of time and space and of thing-ness and spirit, and is *sine qua non* to being human. Hence, *Homo religiosus* would be a more descriptive name for the species than the self-adulation of *Homo sapiens*.

We human beings in our "fallen," naked, guilt-ridden state scramble to do obeisance to the gods we have created. Forgetting that they are our creation, we set about to create further sacred thought structures (called doctrines) concerning the nature of these creations. These doctrines, supported by a whole edifice of lesser doctrines (and the aid of practiced rituals), are designed to enable us to deny their very source. Hence, in the case of scripture there is a powerful proclivity to worship the created book rather than the creator.[23]

To be religious is, however, not a synonym for being spiritual. We should not confuse spirituality with either mysticism (more Greek than Christian or Hebrew), or with the practice of religion—a universal human trait. Spirituality is life-giving creativity; it has the capacity to empathize and to heal. It has little or nothing to do with either mysticism or religion. There is no correlation between being a "very religious person" and a "very spiritual person." We secrete religion to help us cope with the precariousness of the human condition. It is a self-protecting, survival mechanism: partially instinctual, partially a cultural phenomenon.

Religion is the bonding material essential both to idol building and to worshipping God. The practice of religion, though a necessary and universal component of human existence, should be recognized as potentially the most deceptive in the entire range of human activities—deceptive not because it is wrong, but because it is perceived as divine, as placing us in communicative proximity (if not "in union") with the Ultimate. Religion substitutes for ethics. This, I believe, is why the harshest words of Jesus are reserved for the most ardent practitioners of religion—the Scribes and the Pharisees.

3. WORLDVIEWS Just as the sociology of knowledge and the socio-anthropology of religion (disciplines developed in the twentieth-century) pick up agenda that was not dealt with under the historical-critical method (developed in the nineteenth century but rooted in the Enlightenment), so the focus on worldviews (i.e., cultural cosmologies) picks up some of the unfinished agenda of the sociology of knowledge and socio-anthropology of religion. What we can so easily and innocently do to the Bible, namely, make it into an idol, Christians also do to the worldview of the first century in which the New Testament was written. We tend to absolutize it. We do this quite unwittingly when we assume the ancient worldview (the worldview of Jesus and the early

church) to be normative for all Christians throughout all ages and cultures. To assume that reality (e.g., spirits, demons, angels, the elements, principalities and powers) as seen through our Western eyes (perceptions acquired not primarily by choice but through the inheritance of our culture) is what the participants in Jesus' world understood it to be, is actually not to understand their reality—and is thus to fail to grasp the redemptive message of Jesus.[24]

Jesus viewed reality through the Greco-Hebrew worldview he culturally inherited. As with every previous worldview, it was culturally constructed; it was a human product. When we today in our Western world attempt to make the worldview of the first century normative for things pertaining to our faith, we create for ourselves a schizophrenic world and fail to grasp the faith of Jesus—a holistic, integrative, life-giving (salvific) mode of being. We create at least two worlds with at least two systems of reality. It makes us incapable of discerning the kingdom. For to "believe" objectively what they believed is neither to understand their faith nor the proclamation of Jesus.[25] The fundamental reality of the kingdom of God as proclaimed by Jesus is not bound to any particular worldview, but we as people are by and large limited to perception through our own culturally inherited lenses. The first-century worldview is not normative. We cannot and we need not willy-nilly change lenses, become schizophrenic[26] when reading the scriptures or sharing the Gospel or attending a Sunday morning worship service.

This has been my most freeing breakthrough within the past decade. It is, I think, one of the most significant insights for determining how I read the scripture and do theology, for understanding our mission today in a cross-cultural context, and for countering the violence and the militarization in the world in which we live. I am working to integrate my belief system and biblical understandings with my everyday worldview–not necessarily a worldview that I chose, but one that my culture has foisted upon me (even as Jesus carried out his mission within the worldview that his culture foisted upon him). I carry on this struggle not primarily as an intellectual exercise, but in an effort to be more faithful to the life-giving message of Jesus.

Finally, to work within the worldview that one has socio-culturally inherited is, I believe, the most fruitful way (perhaps the only way) to position oneself to offer a critique of that worldview and the oppressive cultural practices within it. Within this context I am seeking to lay a new foundation for nonviolence by finding the nonviolent God of the Universe—the one whom Jesus most consistently depicts in scripture.

Conclusion: Back to the Beginnings

Two anecdotes must suffice. I was in the third or fourth grade in a one-room schoolhouse when on one of those rare occasions the County Superintendent of Schools visited us. I recall nothing of what he said except one line that he carefully wrote on the board: "The more you know you know you know, you know you know the less." This was in the mid-1940s prior to the postmodern era. He was not echoing the latest philosophical fad.

Yet the Superintendent recognized that much of the certainty proclaimed in that era and in every era is an illusion. What is not an illusion is the humble recognition that whether Christian or pagan, we do not know all that we think we know. As we listen to the cacophony of voices today claiming to know the Christ, we know that many do not know what they claim to know. "Accepting Christ" and being baptized is no short cut to the hard struggle of knowing and doing the will of God—of faith through faithfulness to the way of Jesus. Surrounded by the "great cloud of witnesses," to which the writer of the Hebrews refers, we confess that together with others both past and present we continue the search to become that more perfect community of life and love and healing.

The second anecdote also comes from my early years in school. On the report cards of the rural public elementary school that I attended was a quote, all but forgotten, from Abe Lincoln: "I will study and prepare myself and perhaps someday my chance will come." I specifically remember my mother's calling my attention to this. She was the one who seemed to think that life held almost limitless possibilities for me—if at each fork I chose the right path. Somewhere in the stream of life I learned that preparing myself lay not simply in studying but in practicing; the art of "rightly choosing" was rooted in the practice of faithful living. What I do I become; the company I keep determines the path I take; and those who seek to be instruments of redemption are of all people most likely themselves to appreciate and to appropriate the gift of redemption.

My mother did not realize it, but "my chance" was not some ultimate goal or some grand once-in-a-lifetime opportunity (or epic Lincolnian battle) opening up to me for which all of my previous life was but a preparation. "My chance" was the costly providence of being born into a home where the way of Jesus was sought. "My chance" was the privilege to be instrumental in passing on the heritage of an authentic journey of faith—and here I think particularly of the years at EMU. "My chance" is the gift of participating in a hermeneutic community—sometimes weak and faltering, usually marginalized—that continues the search for truth and life in its engagement with the world. For in these searching-practicing communities we indeed have opportunity to find Jesus, and together we find life.

October 2005
Revised July 2007

Notes

1. This is an adaptation of an essay I wrote several years ago for a conference in Laurelville called "Our Journeys with Scripture." That earlier version was published as Chapter 8: "Reading the Bible in Search of Jesus and the Way" in *Telling Our Stories,* edited by Ray Gingerich and Earl Zimmerman (Cascadia Publishing House, Telford, PA, 2006). Used by permission. While writing "My Journey with Scripture" I discovered the many parallels to my intellectual and faith journey.
2. The "stories" shared in the ACRS breakfasts are not intended to be a loosely spun fabric weaving together the "entirety" of life, but rather a more focused pilgrimage of faith and intellectual evolution.
3. This is a quote from Amos Horst, Lancaster Conference bishop, who preached at my ordination service in Kalona, Iowa, April 1961. Though Horst stated this as the reason that Wilma (my spouse) and I were being sent to Europe, that was not an official statement from EMBMC, now Eastern Mennonite Missions (EMM).
4. Here, if space would allow, a series of anecdotes, ranging from encounters in the MCC European Peace Section with Marlin Miller, Leroy Waltner and David Shank to my European peers' responses to the Cuban missile crisis, would best make the point.
5. My experience at EMC, of course, stretched beyond the Bible department. Other influential persons were I.B. Horst in church history and Ruth Brackbill and Hubert Pellman in American and English literature under whose tutelage I did a second major in English.
6. The two influential Mennonite "classics" in this category are Daniel Kauffman's *Doctrines of the Bible* (Scottdale, PA: Mennonite Publishing House, 1914 and ff.) and J. C. Wenger's *Introduction to Theology* (Scottdale, PA: Herald Press,1954).
7. Another factor that played a role in the very different expectations of the hosts was the different status of the American culture and the American way of life in the host cultures: In Africa the West (America) represented modernity, progress and the promise of greater wealth with the ever emerging phenomenon of "rice Christians." Europeans, on the other hand, often envied American wealth but saw their own culture as being superior—and certainly not pagan or in need of missionaries. Many of them were inclined to see Americans, particularly missionaries, as young, generally naive upstarts.

8 During this time, Paul N. Kraybill was Executive Secretary of EMBMC (now EMM). Paul was a perceptive and personally empathetic administrator. But his location within the Lancaster Conference hierarchy and his understanding of administrative roles did not allow him to be a bridge to a larger hermeneutic community. He had to be loyal to his Lancaster Mennonite base.

9 This "need" to go to AMBS was not based on wanting to cleave to Mennonite tradition but on John Howard Yoder's presence on the faculty. At that point I had sufficient exposure to Liberal Protestant theology as well as the Bultmannian alternative to know that those theologies offered no satisfactory intellectual paradigm for my faith. I had had only minimal exposure to Yoder, including the opportunity to hear him at a conference at Bienenberg, in which Heinold Fast and David Shank were also present. But that was sufficient to let me see that he offered the possibility of a third way. Even though his doctoral dissertation *(Täufertum und Reformation in der Schweiz*, 1962) was published during my time in Europe, I had not read it.

10 There were others on the AMBS faculty who were also very life-giving and helped me to find Jesus, the Jewish prophet. Among them was Millard Lind and the late Howard Charles. But I mention Yoder for several reasons: He was the faculty person in the small group to which I was assigned; and I found his social reading of scripture combined with his horizontal theological constructs to be the most insightful and constructive in addressing my particular circumstances. Yoder introduced an "epistemology of discipleship" that I quickly realized held theological possibilities beyond the immediacy of the materials with which Yoder worked.

11 This is one of the consequences of the reformation principle of sola scriptura. The church was no longer the living body of Christ through whom God's will continued to be revealed ever anew. That locus had now been reduced to the sacred Book.

12 For an expansion of this thesis see my essay, "The Economics and Politics of Violence: Toward a Theology for Transforming the Powers" on the Peasant's War and the Anabaptists. See *Transforming the Powers: Peace, Justice, and the Domination System*, edited by Ray Gingerich and Ted Grimsrud (Minneapolis, MN: Fortress Press, 2006), 113–126.

13 This is a reference to dual-loyalty games played by North American Mennonites, who out of loyalty to Jesus refuse to go to war in person, but

in obeisance to the masters of war (and the rulers of this world) pay taxes in support of war, all the while waiting for the rulers of this world to make it legal for those of formal purity to withhold or redirect these payments.

14 For a description of this concept see Nancey Murphy, "John Howard Yoder's Systematic Defense of Christian Pacifism" in *The Wisdom of the Cross: Essays in Honor of John Howard Yoder,* edited by Stanley Hauerwas, et al. (Grand Rapids, MI: Wm B. Eerdmans Publishing Co., 1999), 46–50.

15 "Small Groups" at EUM were organized according to city precincts specifically to be the church's instrument to engage in local political action.

16 In 1968 when Watts in L.A. and 14th Street in DC were going up in flames, Bill Barnes (Caucasian) was riding up and down the African American districts in Nashville with black cops saying, "Cool it." And Nashville with all its racial heat did not burn.

17 This was despite the fact that I took an entire reading course in Barth, that Bill Barnes picked homiletic gems from Barth, and that Yoder's own thinking to the time of his death retained a significant strand of Barthianism. Discipleship—nonviolent social action of just peace—provides transcendence without necessitating metaphysical presuppositions.

18 So lacking was the interest in the Graduate School of Religion that I had to construct my own independent study with a professor who had lost interest in theology.

19 The best analysis of this phenomenon to date is by Nancey Murphy, *Beyond Liberalism and Fundamentalism: How Modern and Postmodern Philosophy Set the Theological Agenda* (Valley Forge, PA: Trinity Press International, 1996). Murphy's analysis is predominantly philosophical. An analysis from the perspective of the sociology of knowledge shedding light on this complex and often confusing problem does not, to my knowledge, exist.

20 The prophetic Catholic historian, theologian and novelist, James Carroll, said it well: "The reformers rejected the self-absolutism of the Catholic Church. Rome, they said, is not forever.... But Luther and his followers absolutized something else, the Scriptures. "Scripture alone!" they said. Nowhere is the idolatry of the Bible more obvious than in the desperate insistence that its affirmations are exempt from the laws of history, of time." *An American Requiem* (Boston, MA: Houghton Mifflin Co., 1996), 119.

21 By this I mean the whole raft of prop-up terminology—infallibility; plenary, verbal inspiration, etc.—that has become nearly second nature to many of

us reared in Bible respecting "Protestantized" homes and churches. The Bible needs none of these props to be appreciated and to be authoritative in our lives.

22 If the sociology of knowledge probes the social dimensions of our knowing, then socio-anthropology of religion probes the depth of our consciousness. It does this both sociologically and anthropologically, both in our awareness of our immediate surroundings and our capacity to transcend immediacy. We become deeply aware (with premonition and post-monition), of self and with caring and compassion for what is happening to and within others. These many dimensions of consciousness each extend to what is often referred to and experienced as the divine.

23 "Scripture" is being used illustratively because it has the capacity to communicate at a first or "initial" level. Were this being written for a broader American readership and not as autobiography for my colleagues, "free market capitalism" would be a far more appropriate category. For it is the latter that is at the pinnacle of the gods being worshipped in America.

24 This is not a novel insight. It is simply carrying forward the agenda of Hendrikus Berkhof, John Howard Yoder and, with a more evangelical spin, Jim Wallis. Each of these persons focused (and focuses) primarily on the structures ("principalities and powers") within the political arena, especially as depicted in the Epistles. My attempt is to turn the spotlight on inseparable religious-political sectors, an effort, I believe, that is more reflective of Jesus as portrayed in the Gospels. For Jesus all politics are religious and all religion is political. For Paul that seems less certain.

25 Walter Wink, within the field of biblical studies and theology, has been singularly in the forefront in exploring the arena of worldviews and relating these insights to Christian faith and practice. See his trilogy on the Powers. Especially significant for me in my journey—not only with scripture but particularly in understanding violence and power—is *Engaging the Powers: Discernment and Resistance in a World of Domination* (Minneapolis: Fortress Press, 1992).

26 Theologically this is referred to as metaphysical and epistemological dualism.

PART II

...in the Church and Community

MYRON S. AUGSBURGER

Reflections on My Journey

The words of the apostle Paul have been central in my life: "And that he died for all that they which live should not live unto themselves but for Him who died for them and rose again."

I have been given privileges of service for Christ far beyond what I deserve. Within the Mennonite church these have included pastoral ministries, evangelistic preaching, educational administration, church planting and teaching. One of the most important areas has been a meaningful family life. But not everything in my journey has been positive. My limitations have ever been before me and have drawn me to the cross. Esther and I have had many privileges and many blessings but also difficulties. At times I felt like not preaching again, but Esther continually encouraged me with these words: "Just because you can't see around the corner doesn't say there's nothing there," or again, "The last page isn't written yet; just keep on."

As I look back this November 2006 of over 56 years of walking with Esther, she has meant so very much to me, enriching my life, being queen of our family, adding dimensions in social breadth, art and missions. She is the most important person in my life. Having said this to honor her, I must also add that we have had a wonderful time as parents, enjoying our children through the years. Activities like family hobbies, raising cattle to finance numerous trips with the children, and simply sharing with one another have been most rewarding. One of the limiting factors was that our family members were not able to work together in my roles, for the nature of my roles did not immediately include them. In contrast, my parents raised five boys and a daughter on a farm in Allen County, Ohio, where we worked together and challenged each other.

Early Influences

My father's granddad was a minister, and my mother's father and granddad were each preachers; but Dad was not a preacher. However, he and my mother hosted the preachers and evangelists who came to our church for meetings. Their hospitality and these guests had a significant influence on us as a family. Also, although our church was quite conservative and strong on biblical study, it was missional; in addition to its local missions in Lima, it started a mission in Kentucky. Moreover, in just ten years, from the time I was ordained in 1951 to 1961, twenty-eight persons from that little congregation—of only around two hundred members—left for either the mission field or a pastorate.

Esther's family, having returned from India to Johnstown, Pennsylvania, moved to our community in 1945; and as teenagers we began to date. In the first year of our relationship, her folks would let us date only once a month since we were quite young. However, we sat together on the school bus every day! Five years later, in 1950, we were married.

I once took Esther on a date to a citywide evangelistic crusade in Lima, Ohio, conducted by Dr. Jessie Hendley of Atlanta. The Lord spoke to me at that meeting; and on the way home I said, "Esther, I'll be doing that some day." She just smiled and did not say anything, for, she related, she was not surprised. Of course, what I had said was about the nuttiest thing you can imagine from a quiet little Mennonite chap from a Mennonite community like ours where it was even liberal to attend that meeting in Lima. That was a time when one never talked about going into the ministry unless the church first called. We never told about that comment, but God called us into that very work. Furthermore, while we have had many area-wide interchurch meetings, we have never once asked for any; we have just responded to invitations.

At age seventeen I went to Canada to the Kitchener Ontario Bible Institute, where I studied under S.F. Kauffman, Oscar Burkholder, J.B. Martin, C.F. Derstine and Roy Koch. These professors had a great deal of influence on me; and for the first time in my life I heard people talking about an infilling of the Holy Spirit. They did not mean a charismatic kind of happening as in a later movement. They meant a personal relationship with the Holy Spirit. The next fall I entered EMC, where I wrote a paper on a Spirit-empowered witness, a paper still in my files. I did not write it for any professor but for clarity in my own mind.

In coming to Eastern Mennonite College, I was at first interested in medicine. (We even have a twenty-block sunflower quilt I pieced in my teenage years after I read a novel about a surgeon who practiced a deft touch by sewing.) Then in revival meetings here on this campus, the Lord laid hold on me and turned things around. I felt a call for another form of ministry, confirming God's earlier call for ministry. That sense of call began a new direction for my life, which has continued for these many years.

In the fall of the following year, 1948, during a powerful revival meeting on campus, the Lord touched many of us; and some weeks later I felt called to carry this revival home to the Pike congregation. I left college to do just that, and God blessed us with a significant revival. Returning to EMC the next year, I switched to a junior college program and graduated with a two-year diploma. At commencement Lowell Nissley, the president of the senior class with whom I had served as vice president, said, "Myron, you must come back to college to prepare for the work God has for you."

Fifteen years as pastor and evangelist, 1950–1965

Esther and I had planned our wedding for the evening of November 26, 1950. However, the weather changed that with a major snowstorm on the night of the 25th, which piled snow up to thirty-eight inches. We could not get married until Tuesday evening, the 28th, when the snowplows finally opened the roads and electricity and telephones were again in operation.

We intended to return to college at EMC the next fall, both of us wanting to work toward our BA degrees. Thus in March of 1951, after going to Greenwood, Delaware, to lead a Bible conference for the Christian School, we continued on to Harrisonburg to participate in Homecoming and also to look for housing. Our choice was one of the Hubert Pellman apartments.

The morning that we arrived in Harrisonburg, Truman Brunk, in Denbigh, Virginia, woke up and told his wife, "I'm not sure why, but the Lord is telling me to go to Harrisonburg today." He got up and drove to Harrisonburg from Newport News; and as he walked up the front steps of the old Ad Building, he met his brother George R., II, who was then teaching at the college.

As they stood at the top of the long stairway talking, George R. rather incidentally said, "I just met Myron and Esther Augsburger in the library and chatted a bit with them."

A sudden impression hit Truman. "That's why I'm here!" he exclaimed.

Truman came to the library and called us out for a talk. As we sat in his car, he told us about a new church in Sarasota, Florida, that needed a pastor. The Executive Committee of Virginia Conference had asked him to find a pastor, and he was quite sure that the Lord was telling him now to ask us to consider it. When we said that we had plans to go to college that fall, he responded that we could possibly do that later. After a few weeks of careful reflection and prayer back in our house trailer in Ohio, we let Truman know that we would accept this call. He asked us to go as soon as possible, issuing me a ministerial license from the Executive Committee of Virginia Conference. Thus with only a hundred dollars, we left for Florida early in May in our small Pontiac coupe filled inside and on top with our earthly possessions.

Several years earlier I had registered for the draft; and filling out the forms, I had written across the front in bold letters, "I am conscientiously opposed to participation in war. Please give me an interview." I had had no response from the Draft Board even though many of my friends had been called up for service. Now I sent the Board a letter telling them of my move to Florida and assuring them that I would make the trip from Florida if they offered an interview. Several weeks later I received a letter asking for evidence of my license for ministry, and in turn they sent me a 4-D classification.

Many things happened in those first years of ministry in Florida that helped to shape our future work. One was interacting with the large number of persons from other denominations who attended our church. Also, I was quite conservative: we did not even have a radio, and I was somewhat critical of radio preachers. Another change began when Jake Yoder, an insightful bearded Amish man, came to where I was working one day, expressly to talk to me.

Jake said, "Myron, I need to talk to you. I've served my generation, and you've got to serve yours. You ought to buy time on the radio and start preaching to the public." This opened a new area for me, and in a few weeks I did just that.

We began in the Florida church with nineteen charter members and forty people in attendance in May 1951. I worked part time as carpenter and the once a month offering gave us $65. Amazingly by January 1952 we had nearly 500 people attending, several hundred of whom were not Mennonites. I well remember the time an Episcopalian couple came down the isle to take communion. I had announced carefully that we practiced "closed communion," and we were holding the service on Sunday evening to avoid any problem with the many non-Mennonites attending mornings. Jason Weaver, a senior visiting minister who was standing beside me as we served the emblems, saw how nervous I was as these friends came closer in the line. Pondering and praying about what to do, I glanced at Jason, who smiled and nodded; and I concluded that he meant that I was to serve them, and I did.

From that setting I was asked for meetings in various places outside the Mennonite Church, including the Billy Sunday Tabernacle at Winona Lake, Indiana, the Moody Bible Institute for Moody Founder's Week, and the Grace Bible Institute.

At Moody Bible Institute Dr. Culbertson introduced me saying, "Myron is a Mennonite, but he's one that preaches the Gospel."

Thus when I got up to speak, I said, "I speak for hundreds of Mennonite preachers who preach the Gospel even though many of them are not known beyond our circle." Further, I said, "I'm glad to be here and stand in Moody's tradition as an evangelist." Then I added, "But there is another thing I must say, that I am in agreement with D. L. Moody when he said, "When it comes to the matter of war, I am a Quaker." Those and other early experiences kept pushing us to more openness and relationships with other groups. I carried the conviction that the larger Christian church needed to be confronted with our Anabaptist values.

During those first winters, I invited the Brunk brothers to come to Florida with their large tent meeting. As you know, the Brunk Tent Revivals started in 1951 with a major meeting in Lancaster. I invited them to come to Florida twice, in the winters of 1952 and again in 1953. Those were good meetings, and they touched the larger Sarasota community.

Henry Brunk, Senior, a businessman in our congregation and a good friend, made a new commitment of his life to the Lord during those evenings. Later he came to me and said, "I'll buy a tent and put it on the road with you as the evangelist if you just let me go along and manage the tent."

I thanked him for his affirmation but said, "No, Henry, it has to be a call from the church." He then went another direction in mission.

Most important to us was the birth of our two sons in Florida, John Myron in 1952 and Michael David in 1953. After these several years in Florida we faced a difficult decision. President John R. Mumaw asked me to come to EMC as the campus pastor. My answer was, "Well, not right away." But with his persistence and after thought and prayer, Esther and I felt inclined to make him a proposal. I responded, "If I can serve half time and finish my college degree by studying during the other half time, we'll come." Thus Esther and I moved north to Virginia with our two little sons, John and Michael. I made an exchange of position and housing with Paul Martin from the Bible faculty. He served as the interim pastor at the Tuttle Church in Florida while I served at EMC. In spite of a very small house to live in with our family of four and a half-time salary of $95 a month, we enjoyed a busy but happy family life.

It was during our second year at EMC that Howard Hammer, the evangelist for Christian Laymen's Tent Revivals, decided to terminate and go to Brazil as a missionary. In the fall of 1954 he drove to Harrisonburg to ask me to substitute for him in the tent in Johnstown, Pennsylvania, as he wanted to spend time with his son in the hospital with leukemia. Later that fall he and the executive board of Christian Laymen's Evangelistic Association asked me to become the evangelist for the CLEA in Howard's place. This was a call from a church group, which was different for us than an individualistic decision. After some time of counsel and prayerful reflection we gave our answer, "Yes." I then went to J. Mark Stauffer, a friend on the faculty, and asked him if he would team with me and serve in a ministry of music.

After graduating with my Bachelor of Arts degree at EMC in the spring, we held the first crusade in Berlin, Ohio, for two weeks—a wonderful happening, with an attendance around five thousand. Following this were two-week crusades in these cities: Goshen, Indiana; Quakertown, Pennsylvania; Baden, Ontario; Lancaster at Gap, Pennsylvania (with the larger meeting of the summer with 7,000 attending); and Plain City,

Ohio. It was a wonderful summer of preaching to thousands of persons; if the figures of the high night in each of the six series had been added, the total would have been well over 35,000.

At the close of the Ohio meeting early in the fall, Esther and I went back to our pastorate in Sarasota. Here we started the Shekinah Bible School, at which about 250 young people registered for the winter period of study. We fully intended to continue the pastoral ministry in Florida while taking out time in the summer months for the tent meetings.

The Shekinah Bible School added another stimulus. However, early that winter President Mumaw came again and said, "We need you at EMC. The young people need you more at the college than the older people need you down here." After considerable counsel with our Bishop, Truman H. Brunk, and other pastors, as well as our own heart searching, we felt that I needed to pursue seminary studies. With this in mind I proposed to President Mumaw a pattern of service/study similar to the previous one. Thus in the late spring of 1956 we left the pastorate at Tuttle, spent the summer in Crusades and then returned to Virginia. For the next two years I served as campus pastor on half time and completed two years of seminary study. Each summer, June through August, we were out with a full summer schedule of tent meetings.

When I graduated from the seminary in 1958, I went to President Mumaw to say that I needed to resign my pastoral role at the college in order to go somewhere for another year of study to get my Master of Divinity. In response he recommended Westminster in Philadelphia rather than Goshen. He said, "With the bias of the East, if you go to Goshen, there will be no future for you at EMC."

I visited Westminster and interviewed professors such as Dr. Cornelius Van Till and Dr. Young in theology; but not liking some of the emphasis, I came back home undecided. A few days later Harold Bender called me and invited me to come to Goshen. He offered to give me a college class in evangelism to teach to help us financially while I was in seminary, and we made the decision to go there that fall, 1958. I was in a late summer tent meeting in Lewisville, Pennsylvania, when we needed to move to Indiana in time for our two sons, John and Michael, to begin school. It was therefore Esther, pregnant at the time, who moved us, driving to Goshen with our two boys in a very loaded car. Settling into the house we had rented, she enrolled the boys in school while I finished the meeting and came a week later.

During my studies, I took a few speaking engagements in churches, and the honoraria were a real help with our living expenses. In early April of 1959 we held a citywide meeting in Constitution Hall, Hutchinson, Kansas, with the churches of the city. The Mennonites were fully involved, but the leaders of other churches were skeptical about their involvement in counseling. When I arrived, they asked me whether these Mennonites knew about the assurance of salvation. Our Mennonite separatism had caused a limited understanding of us.

A week after my return from Kansas, Esther was in the hospital for the birth of our daughter, Marcia, a wonderful event of pride and joy for us and our sons.

We so often thank God for the remarkable experiences we enjoyed as a family in Goshen and Elkhart. Persons like Harold Bender, Paul Mininger, John Howard Yoder, Guy Hershberger, John C. Wenger, Laurence Burkholder, William Klassen, and others became friends, not just names. The J.D. Grabers, long-time missionary "aunt and uncle" to Esther, and the Russell Krabills were helpful to Esther in my absences. And I had a great year in seminary with John Howard Yoder as a mentor.

In the spring near my graduation Harold Bender called me into his office to ask, "What are you planning to do next year?"

I said, "I've applied to Princeton for a doctoral program and have been accepted. We plan on going there. I would like to work on a doctorate."

He replied, "Oh, I don't think you ought to do that."

I asked, "Why not?"

He said, "I'm afraid you won't come out an evangelist, and we don't have many evangelists in the Mennonite church."

When I asked why Princeton would change this, Bender answered, "Because nobody else has come out an evangelist."

I said, "They didn't go in as evangelists."

He said, "Nevertheless, I don't think you should do it."

His words shook me up, especially when President Paul Mininger repeated the same lines a week later. I then drove to Princeton, where I spoke with Dr. Homrighausen, the Dean. He agreed that I could take a "rain check" and come later. We stayed in evangelism and moved back home in Harrisonburg.

But the matter of further study kept eating at me, especially because by now I had moved to interdenominational citywide meetings. I felt that with only a Mennonite theology I needed further study to be more understanding of the many other people attending. Study would also help me to be sure that I was representing Mennonite theology clearly.

Thus one evening while at home in Harrisonburg between meetings, Esther and I inquired at Union Seminary, Richmond, and found that the Dean, Dr. Lewis, was in Staunton on a summer break in the Valley. We called and went to meet him. After listening, he said, "We closed the admissions back in March for this school year; but we just had an international student bow out, and I was going to invite the next person on the list to be admitted. If you really want to come, I am willing to recommend you to the committee." And that is the way God led. In two weeks I was admitted at Union Theological Seminary, and we moved to Richmond that fall, where I began graduate studies.

After finishing the ThM degree the first year and passing my language exams in German and French, I continued the second year in the ThD/PhD program. As I pursued those studies, I was not aiming for college administration but for integrity and effectiveness in the work of evangelism. During that time, I was invited on several occasions to educational positions, one explicitly for a college presidency in the West, another for a seminary deanship. I turned them down, saying that my call was evangelism.

When we moved back to Harrisonburg after I completed my residency, I promised our children that I would spend more time at home with them. Dean Ira Miller negotiated with me an arrangement to teach part time and accept speaking engagements part time. In this style I taught at EMC for several years, sharing an office with Grant Stoltzfus. After two years the board even gave me the rank of professor by counting the four years I had served earlier on the faculty as campus pastor as part of my qualification. Thus I was on campus when the board moved to elect the fifth president of the college.

I would like to flash back to the days in the interchurch crusades. It was a new thing for a Mennonite to go into citywide meetings on an interdenominational basis. I wore the plain coat; I never hid being Mennonite; and I shared a theology that was Anabaptist, presenting the meaning of why we believe in peace as disciples of Christ. In Denver, Colorado, while attending the National Association of Evangelicals in the early 1960s, I had a good interview with Billy Graham. In the discussion I said, "Billy, I'm a young man, a Mennonite, starting out in interchurch evangelism. What advice do you have for me?"

"Well," he said, "I have two things. You might begin by changing that coat," and we laughed. Then he said, "Seriously, you have to distinguish between the *kerygma* and the *didache*."

When I reported this later to my major professor at Union Theological Seminary, he said, "I'm glad that Billy knows about *kerygma* and *didache*." Well I knew what Billy meant, that I should leave my Mennonite doctrine (*didache*) out of the evangelistic message. I said, "Billy, that sounds good except for one thing. You must recognize I cannot preach the cross without preaching love for our enemies."

My response did not turn Billy off because later he had me lead a retreat for his staff in Miami, Florida. He also invited me to serve on steering committees for several of the World Congresses on Evangelism. Years later I invited him to speak at a vesper service in Washington, D.C. When I presented him, he stepped up to the pulpit and began by saying, "Now I'm not a pacifist like Myron here," and everybody laughed. Then he surprised the group with these words: "But I want to tell you that I have become a nuclear pacifist." You must recognize that this was back in 1982 when Reagan was pushing for strength to counter Russia. Billy said, "I just came back from Russia, and there is no way that as Christians we can think it is right to nuke those people." (We had other conversations about this, but I wanted to share this one vignette.)

In the years of my interchurch-preaching missions I became known as a "discipler," calling people to walk with Jesus in life. Invited to speak at the Billy Graham Congress on Evangelism at Minneapolis, I spoke on "Evangelism as Discipling."

Fifteen years as the president of EMC, 1965–1980

When the board of Trustees of EMC interviewed me about the presidency, I well remember telling them, "If you want an educator who will bring his theology and evangelistic emphasis, then I am willing to be considered. But if what you want is primarily an educator, not so involved in theology and evangelism, then go to another candidate." There were other reasons why I was hesitant about being pursued further. However, after various conversations and broader counsel, when the board came with the call, we accepted.

Today we can almost block our lives off in fifteen-year periods: fifteen years as pastor and evangelist, 1950–1965; fifteen years as president of EMC, 1965–1980; fifteen years, 1980–1995 (with nine months at Princeton) in inner city church-planting in Washington, D.C., which included six years as president of the Council of Christian Colleges and Universities; now we are in the midst of this fifteen years in busy retirement with seminars, international teaching, preaching missions and interim pastoral service.

The fifteen years here at EMC were especially rewarding as we were enriched by so many wonderful persons on the faculty and in the student body and by many families and guests. Let me focus on a few things about that service in administration. I sought to emphasize a Christian mission in education, discipling people as they studied from a Christian perspective. What had motivated me in the first fifteen years was sharing the Gospel beyond our ethnicity and yet sharing it with fidelity to our heritage and faith. Now in education, I asked how we prepare a generation to understand the relation of the gospel to their field of study and to share this gospel beyond our ethnicity. While I did not work at this question as adequately as it deserved, I worked at it diligently and I think creatively.

One of the first things we did was to look at how to integrate the meaning of our Anabaptist Christian faith into the whole of our academic program. In the summer of 1965 I went to Dean Ira Miller with this proposal: "Why don't we shorten the first semester to fourteen weeks instead of the traditional sixteen (as it was then with two weeks coming after Christmas), and let's take the two weeks after vacation and do an all-school seminar?" To make it short, we did that with the theme

"Discipleship in a Brave New World." The whole student body, around 600 at that time, divided up into small groups with a faculty or staff member in each group to discuss the lectures of the day. We all listened to the same lectures, read the same books and did journaling. I arranged for speakers from a variety of denominations to come one each day, ten of them for two weeks. The seminar was an academic experience of oneness. At the tables in the dining hall we could all talk about the presentations and issues as we were all in the same class, having the same experience. That was a unique and significant program, which we carried out in the first year of my presidency.

Also that year I held an interdenominational conference at EMC on global mission and our Anabaptist emphasis on peace. I brought a variety of speakers, including the following: Dr. Paul Reese of Evangelical Covenant; Dr. Akin Taylor, a Southern Presbyterian; Dr. Carl Lindquist of Bethel College and Seminary, a Swedish Baptist; Dr. Harold Ockenga of Gordon-Conwell; Dr. Lloyd J. Ogilvie of the Presbyterian Church from California; and others. We had a good group of Mennonite scholars as well, including Dr. John Howard Yoder and Dr. J.C. Wenger. At the beginning John Howard Yoder commented to me, "You've got the wrong crowd here. These evangelicals don't talk about peace."

I said, "That's why I wanted them. I have been working on this, and we need to hear each other, what others are saying."

I invited Akin Taylor to speak in chapel. Addressing the chapel audience, he said, "I was an officer in the marines, and I killed a lot of people; and I know that war is wrong and that killing is a sin. But you can't live in our kind of world without sinning, so you have to ask God to forgive you and go on from there."

I was sitting there as moderator, pondering how to respond. After his conclusion I got up and said to the audience, "Now you understand clearly the difference between the Protestant position you have just heard and what you are being taught on this campus." That was enough of a rebuttal.

We went to work that year on a new program, redesigning the whole curriculum. We developed what we called IDS, Inter-Disciplinary Studies. The planning committee that I appointed included John A. Lapp, Laban

Peachey, the late Herbert Martin, Catherine Mumaw, James Bomberger, Jay Landis, Hubert Pellman, Dean Ira Miller and myself. While it was my idea, it was this group who developed it, redesigning the whole educational program. What we did was pretty radical. First, we developed seven courses, one for each semester in the first three years and a final course for seniors on Christianity and Ethics. The overall theme was Christianity and Civilization. Each course was taught by five professors from five disciplines, serving as a team in each class, all present together in the same class. At first we had 80-minute periods for those classes. The plan was for the faculty to begin with input; the five would then interact with each other and finally open the discussion for student interaction.

I could give accounts of the impact of this IDS program far beyond EMC. Few colleges were working systematically on what we now take too much for granted—interfacing faith with the liberal arts. Several years before this, in August 1964, we held a faculty conference at Goshen, the year before I became president, which included the three faculties—those of Goshen, EMC and Hesston. The planning committee brought a Lutheran as the key lecturer, and he spoke of the need for the integration of faith and learning. One of the problems for colleges is that most faculties secure their graduate education at secular universities, and, unless they work at an integration of faith for themselves, it does not get done.

When I discussed this vision with Goshen College President Paul Mininger, he was very supportive but saw the difficulties. He asked me, "Do you know what you're trying to do with such revisions at EMC? Are you sure you can carry this off? Are your faculty ready for this?"

I answered, "No, but we'll never be ready unless we learn to do it in practice."

Later Laban Peachey took some of these ideas along with him to Hesston and formed the Foundation Series. John Lapp took some of these ideas to Goshen as an added stimulus in their curricular revision. I was asked about the IDS program by several deans of universities. One dean from Pittsburgh, where one of our alumni went for graduate studies, asked, "What in the world is happening down there? We expect graduates to excel in science or math, but your graduate has such high marks in general studies." Another, the dean of Rutgers, called me to ask questions, wanting to know about the IDS program we had developed.

About that time the Danforth Foundation came out with a study of Christian colleges in which they listed a group of colleges as "Defender of the Faith" schools. Some ten of us presidents engaged in conversation about responding to this, including Everett Cattell of Malone College, Ray Hostetter from Messiah, Carl Lunquist from Minneapolis, Hudson Armerding of Wheaton, and a few others as we wanted to challenge this listing. We met together in Arizona, drafted an outline appealing to the Danforth Foundation to designate another category, "Faith Affirming Colleges." That was the beginning of the Christian College Consortium. Adding several other college presidents, together we formed the Consortium, which became chartered by thirteen member schools. Some years later, since other colleges wanted to be included, the Christian College Coalition was formed. (The Consortium continued its work while also belonging to the Coalition. It had already begun to cooperate in financing and now published a paper on faith and learning with an editor based at Wheaton.)

The next years here at the college were demanding financially. We were growing, and for those times we were doing a lot of building. We had just constructed the science center, for which President John Mumaw had previously had plans drawn, and now the development staff and I raised the money for this building. I was able to get a Federal Title III grant. Since there were some questions about this from government personnel who said they could not fund anything used for religious happenings, I made trips to Washington and to Charlottesville. I remember going to them and saying, "Look, we won't use this as a chapel; we have a chapel. But when the faculty meets, we pray. I want to know if that's a problem or if we can go on with this grant?"

They said, "You ask too many questions."

We got the grant, but they told me that this Title III program would run out in a couple of years and if we wanted another grant, we had to ask for it soon. Therefore, I applied for a grant for a new library. James O. Lehman's report in the October 1971 *EMC Bulletin* tells the story in exciting detail. Briefly here, that Title III grant of $388,629 for the library was approved; but to receive it, we had to raise at least a matching amount by December 11, 1969. Actually, by that fall Sam Strong, Robert Messner and I, working like beavers, had raised well over a million dollars, including the grant. Meanwhile, the EMC Trustees had set the same deadline for enough cash commitments to begin the building process. By December 2, a Thanksgiving student drive had brought in $22, 950.74, but we still needed $126,005 in fewer than ten days. I asked for prayer in chapel, and then I left for a previously scheduled fund-raising trip.

The most amazing event then was the second student fund drive just when we were really "up against a wall." When I returned to the campus, I was dumbfounded by what was going on. More money had come in, but on Friday, December 5, we were still lacking $111,000. Thanks to Truman Brunk (the campus pastor) and some student leaders, an amazing student drive was under way. Students were soliciting funds, getting jobs in the region to work for money for the library, and collecting things for an auction. Just a few days later, on the unforgettable night of December 8 people crowded into the gym for an auction. There, with an old dinner bell ringing for each new $1000, around 1:40 a.m. we reached the goal for the needed $111,000, and in Lehman's words, "bedlam broke loose in a standing ovation."

The next morning in chapel, Dewitt Heatwole, Chairman of the Trustees, and Sam Shrum for the Nelson Corporation, signed the contract in front of the students in chapel. This remains one of the high water marks in EMC history. It is not something for which I take credit; I present it here in honor of the students and to review with you this bit of history, which, in a time of much negative student protest, hit the national news with this positive student action.

Beyond that, there were important but lesser projects. For the first time at the college, we added musical instruments to the campus and curriculum. (The first president was forced to resign because he refused to give up a piano!) We added several dormitories to meet the increase in student enrollment. We negotiated for the old industrial arts building from the high school, buying little Park School and trading it to the high school for their industrial arts building behind the administrative building, which we renovated, and which became the first location for the seminary. Several years later we renovated the chapel, using clouds in the ceiling so that the music could reverberate adequately and also make possible the installation of a new Reuter's Pipe Organ.

When I came in office in 1965, among the things that were problematic were three well known ones: we did not dress for athletics, we did not have musical instruments (publicly), and we did not use drama. I do not know if the faculty understood quite what it meant for the president to walk a tightrope between very conservative people on the one side, who were watching us, and progressive persons on the other, who wanted to see EMC grow in academic relevance. I had good friends like Bishop Lloyd Horst who was on the Religious Welfare Committee for the Trustees, a wonderful brother and advisor, who helped me to hear what the more conservative people were saying. At the same time I needed to keep us moving in directions that would help us to offer a fuller program of excellence in education. We also needed to meet the expectations of the Southern Educational Association and increase our association with other schools. These challenges called for creativity, diplomacy and empathy.

I feel so much gratitude to the faculty, especially some of the older ones, who were supportive of this young president with different ideas from the norm—my interchurch associations. To my knowledge, no one other than a Mennonite had ever spoken in chapel prior to 1965 except a Brethren in Christ guest faculty member from Messiah College. Thus when I started bringing persons from other groups to address us, it was a change and needed to be done selectively. Several bishops told me that my brotherhood was too broad. Also, I can pull from my files letters from several church leaders against my use of musical instruments and against our engaging in athletics. I made numerous trips to Lancaster and met with the bishop board to talk about what we were doing. Their concerns included the fact that the girls were not all wearing the covering at EMC. I commented that it is amazing what happens between the time they drive out of their setting in Lancaster and the time they arrive in the Shenandoah Valley.

A major issue in the late 1960's was the general criticism of the VietNam war. I called a friend in D.C., and he arranged an interview for me with Melvin Laird, Secretary of Defense, at the Pentagon. I drove over and we had an hour of discussion as I called for a higher honor than what he and President Nixon were speaking of. At the conclusion he said, "Myron, I couldn't be Secretary of Defense with your philosophy, but I must say that it makes more sense to me than that of those preachers who come to Washington crying for victory at any price. When he asked me to lead in prayer before I left, I did so, praying that God would give us each the humility to rethink our positions.

The deeper things that we were working at on campus were an application of an Anabaptist faith to contemporary things in education. I am grateful for persons of influence like Paul Peachey and Irvin Horst, who had taught here when I was a student and who were strong voices along with numerous others for the Anabaptist faith. We also gave considerable attention in faculty conferences to meeting accreditation expectations, to reviewing our organizational patterns, and to acquiring improved relational patterns. Since our salaries were so low, numerous persons with special strengths whom I invited to our faculty were not able to accept the invitation. This situation was especially frustrating to me.

While I spoke often in many Mennonite congregations, I also held a limited number of citywide preaching missions, using these occasions to promote the college and to build a greater support base, including among non-Mennonite churches. Loren Swartzendruber worked for me at the time and served as the coordinator for such meetings. I remember coming back from such interchurch missions and meeting C.K. Lehman at the back of the chapel—who would say, "Myron, tell me about the meetings. What happened? Tell me of persons who came to the Lord." Then after my comments he would look at me with his little twinkle and say, "Now remember, the Apostle Paul did a lot of things away from Jerusalem that he didn't do in Jerusalem."

I began putting some things in writing because people began asking for the materials I was sharing in sermons. Earlier, upon completing my doctorate at Union with my dissertation on the theology of Michael Sattler, I had called the Institute of Mennonite Studies (then at Goshen), wanting to offer a section of my dissertation for publication. However, when I talked with Guy Hershberger about whether a part of my dissertation and Sattler's materials could be published, he was apologetic: "Myron, we just engaged John Howard Yoder to translate Sattler's works for a book on *The Legacy of Sattler,* and another publication may not be timely."

I commented, "Yoder knows German better than I do, so his translation would be more accurate." But I felt that the full story needed to be shared because in the 1960s scarcely anyone was talking about Sattler. Urged by my crusade secretaries, Janet and Elizabeth Kreider, to write this story, I finally produced the historical novel entitled *Pilgrim Aflame,* which has been through three editions and made into a movie. It is amazing how many people beyond Mennonites circles have come to a peace position through reading this book. Certainly more persons have read it than would have read a publication of my dissertation.

Fifteen years in inner city church planting, 1980–1995

When in 1978 the Board at EMC elected me for a fourth term, Esther and I agreed that I should take only two years of that term. What I did not tell them or anybody else was that I was under negotiation for the presidency of another school (a seminary). I had gone through major interviews and a psychological test, had met the faculty and student leaders, and knew that the search committee was ready to recommend me to the Board. When I accompanied the search committee to the meeting with the Board, on which occasion the committee were going to give their recommendation, the chairman of the board "jumped the gun" and asked the board how they would feel if the next president of this seminary was a pacifist. Three board members had a problem with this.

I listened to the discussion and finally spoke up: "Gentleman, I wouldn't have come here to try to force everyone to be pacifist, but neither will I come here if I can't be honest and share my convictions." That was a really difficult happening, and this account is too brief to tell you how deeply this negotiation had involved us.

The question now was, having resigned from EMC, I and Esther wondered about our next step. But in God's providence Dean Arthur Adams and President McCord of Princeton Theological Seminary invited me to come there as resident scholar for a year. I had known Dr. Adams for a number of years on the board of the Presbyterian Minister's Fund and respected him highly. Hence Esther and I left EMC in the summer of 1980. Our children had married, and it was just the two of us making this move. We both went to Oxford University in England for a summer school session, took some Presbyterian friends from the search committee mentioned above on an Anabaptist tour of Europe, and returned to Princeton for a year. While there, I wrote the commentary on Mathew for the *Communicator's Commentary* series, and Esther did editing. She also wrote some articles on art and worked on producing sculptures, among them the bronze of Jesus washing Peter's feet.

Early in our time there in late October, Ray Horst and another Mennonite Board of Missions representative came to see us. At that point I was moderator-elect of the General Assembly of the Mennonite Church; and when they brought their proposal, I thought they were asking my advice. They sat with us and talked about the need for an additional witness in Washington, DC, to engage the Mennonite church more fully in the heart of the city. This was not a reflection on the work of others, but it was to say that an inner-city approach was needed in that setting. I said, "That sounds good to me, go for it." Having been in and out of Washington, preaching at the National Presbyterian Church in the summer for some years, we had friends there and I recognized the challenge. The men responded by saying that they believed that the Lord wanted Myron and Esther to do this.

After some weeks in prayer and reflection, we finally said we would go for a couple of years and get a work started. We re-crafted the Inter-Church Board to include a representative from each of the four "sending" groups—the Mennonite Board of Missions, the Virginia Conference, Allegheny Conference and Lancaster Conference. We were affiliated with the General Assembly of the Mennonite Church for the first years; later the congregation became affiliated with the Virginia Conference.

We went to Washington on May 10, 1981, after finishing at Princeton. The first weeks we met people, studied the city, negotiated a meeting room at the Lutheran Church on East Capital, and planned our first service. Since Curt and Judy Ashburn were going to come to Washington to work with John Stagers, I invited Curt to become associate pastor of a church that did not yet exist. Because they could not arrive until June 20, we scheduled the first service for that Sunday. Around forty people came, among them numerous visitors from the city. We met in the educational wing of the Lutheran church, where we continued to gather during the summer months.

In the next weeks I began negotiations with the Potomac Development

Corporation for a closed church building on the corner of 9th and Maryland Avenue N.E. Late in the fall we bought the Keller Memorial Lutheran Church building, which had been closed by the New York office of the Lutheran Church after the racial riots in DC In the next several months we did a total renovation with many people donating time. Trennis Yoder coordinated this work, and by his tabulation people gave over 3,000 hours. With Esther's care we were able to save and repair several large stained-glass windows, which added considerably to the beauty of the facility. People came to help from the Virginia, Lancaster, and Allegheny Conferences and beyond, including some young Amish fellows. Bernard Martin, a director in Mennonite Disaster Service, brought workers, commenting, "Myron bought a disaster in Washington, so let's go and help him." Two of the antique chandeliers were missing. Everet Suter came, took one of the existing ones down to copy and crafted two, which cannot be distinguished from the original!

We enjoyed the congregation as it emerged. I stated early on that we would bring an Anabaptist theology without bringing Mennonite ethnicity. We affirmed that we wanted to hold the evangelistic and the social dimensions of the gospel together. Being in the inner city, we designed our sign to read that we were "A Church for All Peoples;" we crossed the racial and status lines as both homeless people and government workers came. My approach in a city so conditioned by partisanship was to be an advocate of "The Third Way," neither rightist conservative nor leftist liberal but one seeking the way of the Kingdom of Christ. Esther and I named the church "Washington Community Fellowship" with the subline reading, "affiliated with the Mennonite Church."

The early pastoral counsel worked to develop a membership covenant for the congregation, which the charter members studied and approved, with a pattern of multi-denominational membership. People rallied who had been praying, totally unknown by us, for a new church on Capital Hill. As the congregation grew, at least some 80% were from a variety of other denominational orientations. They included many people who at first did not have any idea what it meant to be Mennonite. However, it was amazing how the Lord worked through this developing congregation, enabling us to find a spirit of unity with diversity. We benefited from the strong leadership of persons like Rich Gathro,

Miriam Mumaw, Jerry Herbert, later Phyllis Miller, and others. We had a number of women in leadership; and although the several women mentioned above came from our EMC background, all were elected by the congregation to be elders.

I have frequently said that I would not take a million dollars for those fourteen years of experience in Washington. We enjoyed the creative developments in the congregation, the remarkable interchange with other church leaders, and the cultural benefits of the city. We had the privilege of working with persons such as Dr. Richard Halverson, Dr. Samuel Hines, John Staggers, Tom Skinner, Doug Coe, and numerous others in church work. We shared closely with Senator Mark and Antoinette Hatfield, who attended our church for a considerable period. We also shared with a few other senators and congressmen, the latter including the dedicated Christian, Tony Hall. Our friend Senator Hatfield brought George Critten of the CIA to the church; and after about six months of attending, George came to me saying, "Myron, I've quit my job. I am ready to apply for membership." He became vitally involved and remains a very special friend who continues to promote pacifist convictions in California.

In 1988 John Dellenbach resigned from the presidency of the Coalition of Christian Colleges and Universities, and the board invited me to take his place. After a three-month teaching assignment in Pune, India, which we had promised before knowing we were to go to Washington, we said yes to the Coalition. I adjusted my role at the church to serve on the pastoral team as a minister of the Word, preaching once a month. Now we had a fine associate pastor, John Hays, who became the primary pastoral director for a period; and then we called Dennis Hollinger from Elkhart to serve as lead pastor.

I had six wonderful years with the Coalition—nearly 100 colleges from across the country. All seven of the Mennonite colleges became members, including of course EMU. President Shirley Showalter of Goshen became very actively engaged and served on the board. Bluffton became a very active member, and President Lee Snyder became an effective participant. The interesting thing about the Coalition is that it gave opportunities in many settings for conversation or dialogue about a peace position. Many had looked at pacifism simply as "a position of left-wing liberals." Here, in this mix they came to meet Christian people who had an evangelical faith and who were also deeply committed to a peace message based on the teachings of Jesus and our relation with Him as disciples.

Going back to my opening statement as I conclude, what has guided me in this variety of settings has been the search for ways to share the gospel beyond our ethnic communities and to do so by interpreting the gospel with integrity and with a perspective true to the Anabaptist faith.

Sola Deo Gloria.

September 2004
Revised November 2006

EDWARD B. STOLTZFUS

Jesus, Where Are You Taking Us? Tradition, Vision and Culture

> *Jesus went before [the disciples toward Jerusalem] ... they followed ...amazed...afraid (Mark 10:32b). And when they saw him [Jesus], they worshiped [and]...doubted (Matt. 28:17 KJV).*

"I bet you can't hit the ball as far as the school's steps," dared my friend Willie as we walked toward the school entrance.

"Bet I can. Here goes!"

The ball rose up and up. To my horror and panic it crashed through the second floor office window of our school superintendent, Mr. Graham. Broken glass sprinkled down on the kids going into the building.

"Run, quick! Go in the basement's side door over there. Hide!" Willie urged.

I tramped through the broken glass and the startled stares of fellow students up one flight of steps and turned right up another flight straight into the office, where a shocked secretary and superintendent were picking their way through shattered glass.

"I'm sorry, Mr. Graham. I did it."

"What happened?" He looked up at me, forehead wrinkled, eyes angry. "What'd you do?"

"I hit a ball." My lips trembled, and I felt my eyes fill with tears and fear. "It went through your window."

"Why did you do it? Didn't you know there's a rule against playing ball at the entrance of the school?"

"Yes, I knew that."

He looked at the floor. No words. Just the sound of the secretary's scratching of glass off his desk and chair. He looked up.

"Your dad's my friend. He wouldn't like this. Your people don't do such things. Well, you're inside the school now. Go to class, and on the way find the custodian and tell him to come to my office."

I never told Dad about this accident. Mr. Graham didn't either.

But his words, "your people don't do such things," ricocheted through my mind. What did he mean, "your people"? We were Christians, but he couldn't mean only that because *he* was a church member of the Aurora Congregational Christian Church, whose members also didn't likely "do such things" as break windows. I guessed he was talking about the whole religious, ethnic tradition of us Mennonites there in Aurora, Ohio. Our way of living was different. I imagined what he was thinking from hearing him elsewhere: *Your people are law-abiding citizens. They have good values and behavior. They work hard, mind their own business, and are honest. They care about family life and don't aspire to fancy living or wear showy clothes. Their women wear white caps to church, and their men won't go into the army. Their kids do okay here in school. They don't break windows. You're a part of that tradition. Why are you breaking my window?*

In a dimly reflective way I thought, yeah, he's right. Mennonites are different. We have our own idea of who Christians are and the way they should live. This way of life has been built up by religious teachings, beliefs and rituals that have come to be embodied in specific ethical practices and patterns of group relationships. These are "my people," my family; yet, I am a little embarrassed when my classmates think we are sort of odd or strange. I do not know. Maybe that is the reason I broke the window; I wanted to try to prove I could be one of the buddies at school. Maybe that is why I am not going to tell Dad; I certainly do not want him to know how I smashed our tradition's good name. I felt surprised, a little afraid, and also uncertain of what my real reason was.

Mr. Graham spoke sternly: "You're in school now. Go to class." I did as he directed, but my questions about "my people" and "other people" stayed with me.

Later Dad said, "I don't think you enjoy Aurora High School very much. Would you like to transfer to Eastern Mennonite High School for your junior year?"

"I don't know," I replied.

He went on, "John L. Stauffer, its principal, is passing through our area in a couple weeks. We can talk to him about it."

I liked EMHS. It had a tighter sub-variety of my home church's Mennonite tradition, being more self-contained and more insulated from worldly traditions; but that didn't bother me. After all, I now knew "my people" at Aurora were my real cultural and religious home. Also, the classes were okay, the kids were great, I could play any sport (which I couldn't do at home), and J. Mark Stauffer chose me to sing the David role in the cantata *David the Shepherd Boy*. But there was something else. The spirit of Christian love, joy, and trust in Jesus abounded and made me glad. It was that spirit that sparked my interest in memorizing Ephesians, a book that deeply affected my thinking. It was that spirit that moved me later to tell Bob, my brother, while we were milking cows one evening at home, "If Dad gets home while we're doing chores" (he was away for church work), "I'm going to leave the barn and talk to him about being a Christian and a Mennonite."

When he came home, we did talk. Our first topic was being a Christian. He read from the third chapter of John and said things that I already knew because I had heard them many times at church and at EMHS: "God already loves you. If you confess your sins (that smashed window came to my mind) and trust Jesus, you are his child and part of his separated people, part of his kingdom people. Do you believe that?" he asked.

"Yes, but I don't understand the separate kingdom idea."

"It means that we try to obey Jesus."

"Well, don't other Christians obey him?" I asked. "Why are we different from them?"

"Well, we try to follow Jesus in the pattern of our tradition. We think that this tradition is true and right and good, and we witness to it by the way we live and speak."

The conversation ended, but I still wondered, "How does one know our Mennonite tradition is what God wants?"

However, I am getting ahead of my story. At Plain View, the name of our home congregation, I had already heard a key word in our Mennonite worldview discussed in Sunday sermons. It came while we boys were sitting on the third bench from the front of the church on the right side and watching the grandpas in the Amen Corner sink into restless slumber. The word came from Daniel Kauffman, the main Mennonite leader in the 1940's: "We Mennonites are nonconformed to the world; we're *separated* from it. We're in God's kingdom; we're God's people."

Well, okay, that's what Dad said, and that's what they said at EMHS. But what does this "separation" business actually mean? How are we in another "kingdom," God's? This question seems tied to Mr. Graham's "'your people'" comment, but it does not make sense. We are part of the Aurora community. We buy groceries at the A&P and clothes at the department store in Kent. We own farms and businesses; we sell milk and wheat. All kinds of men join together in our threshing and silo-filling circles to help each other. We go to school and study the same stuff everybody else does. We are not separated. Is he saying all non-Mennonites are sinners, and we should stay away from them? That cannot be right.

Yet Dad said, "We are separated in the way we live our lives. Our actions demonstrate the Jesus' way, and our words interpret those actions. That's why we are different from the world, but we live for the welfare of society and of the world."

Umm. So in our separation from the world we are in continuous jousting. We are all mixed together with other people in the social structures of society and yet try to communicate a different loyalty. The smashed window flashed into my mind. What kind of communication was that?

After completing high school, I studied at three colleges (EMC, Kent State University, and Goshen College), six seminaries (Goshen Biblical Seminary, Hamma Divinity School, Princeton Theological Seminary, Chicago Theological Seminary, Chicago Divinity School, and McCormack School of Theology), and the graduate division of three state universities (Ohio State University in philosophy, the University of Iowa School of Religion, and Notre Dame University). During these years, part of my thinking roamed and wrestled with "my people's" worldview and its relation to the worldviews of other Christians and secular people. Much of this time I was not only a student but also a pastor deeply involved in the bureaucracy of the Mennonite Church. Sometimes, as I walked along with Jesus, I was amazed and afraid, and still am; I doubted and worshipped, and still do.

I became intrigued by secular worldviews and by subvarieties of Christian ones. Their reasoning rested on human rationality as an interpretation of the will of God or on the laws of human experience or on formulas of scientific verification. Most claimed to be definitively true. It seemed to me that the "my people" tradition of my cuddly Mennonite Christian world was also largely a socially conditioned worldview, that it had developed in the mill of limited human thought within specific social and religious settings. Then the real question for me became, "Does 'my people's' tradition really have a Christian worldview or is it a cultural fossil that needs revisioning?"

About this time I began thinking about *how* we communicate with each other, not *what* we communicate.

Slowly I perceived that all types of communication are symbolic, that the immediacy of every reality is always mediated through a created form. I noticed that we are a little like broadcasting stations sending many types of signals to communicate with each other. I noticed that Zip, my best dog pal, and I communicated some things to each other really well, though with only a few symbol signals, while people can and do use many more. We utilize sounds and written marks. We use words, signs, facial expressions and gestures. We communicate through the things we create: by the buildings we build; the institutions we found and the technologies we develop; by our music, art and drama; by all our actions and styles of life. Using these symbols humanizes us. But all these symbols seemed to me to be only instruments, pointers to "realities" behind them. They are not those realities, but those realities could not be formed and known without the symbols. In human communication I noticed at least four components: the idea, the person or that symbolizing the idea, the symbol itself, and the person receiving and interpreting the symbol in the complex neuronic and synaptic processes of the physical brain. I noticed that symbols both reveal and limit the realities they point to; they open and conceal the interpretation of the idea behind them. The possibility of error in interpreting our symbolic communication is great; but of course the reward of some genuine communication, some understanding, is greater still. These symbols of communication can stand alone; but more frequently in combination they supplement, modify, clarify and enrich understandings.

Language is a fabulous invention by us human beings. While studying as an English major in college, l noticed that word sounds are very important symbols for us humans. When they are joined in extended phrases, sentences, paragraphs, essays, poems, stories, and books, they extend and enrich ideas enormously. And when those ideas are sprinkled with figures of speech (metaphors, for example), they stimulate the imagination's interpretation even more.

Words and language are important symbols for Christians because they reach out as a human creation to suggest symbolically and imaginatively transcendent reality and God's relation to creation and man. I noticed that there are not any divine words, just human ones. In fact, in earlier centuries theology was called *symbolics.* This fact is a built-in humbler for theologians and for all religious people who talk of spiritual realities. No, the revelation and knowledge of the mystery of God's creating, saving, and consummating grace is not apart from human symbolization, as the great Protestant theologian Karl Barth believed and taught, nor, as Paul Tillich said, as something "residing in" the word-symbol.

But then the big question began haunting me. How does the invisible transcendent reality impinge on created reality, on us humans? How do we know God's presence? As an answer in process, I decided, we construct our knowledge of God just as we construct our knowledge of anything else. Our brains receive stimuli from our senses and interpret and process them in light of our worldview, and we interpret this material on the basis of a previous faith in God.

Then I noticed something else. Since symbols are absolutely necessary, many genuinely religious people have tended to divinize the symbol itself. These folks identify God with the symbol. It looked to me as though this can and does happen with the worship of idols of pagan peoples, with the sacraments of Roman Catholicism, with the icons of orthodoxy, with books like the Torah, the Bible and the Koran, with the creeds or even the acts of preaching and praying. What a problem! On the one hand, symbols are absolutely necessary in the formation of our religious experiences; on the other hand, in utilizing them, we are inclined to absolutize and worship them and not God himself.

This point is acutely important in Christianity, which posits some kind of transcendent reality. What or who is this God and how do we talk about him? According to the second commandment, Israel was to make no graven or carved images of God. How does this prohibition of images apply to word symbols for God? Our scriptures use many titles to identify God: some from inanimate nature, e.g., God is a rock, a fortress, a wind; some from human political and social relationships, e.g., God is king, Lord, creator, judge, father; some from a superlative extension of moral attributes, e.g., God is perfect righteousness, love, goodness; and some from the powers of nature, e.g., God is Being, light, life. All these titles arise from our human experiences and descriptions, but the mystery and glory of God is not limited to any of them; they engulf all of them and more. For Christians the mystery and glory of God and his grace and truth appear most clearly in the man Jesus of Nazareth, who is received as such by those of faith who have eyes to see and ears to hear. He is above, below, around, and within our living, within our tradition; some symbolic aspects of the tradition are better at communicating God's love in Christ, some are poor, and some are deceptive. Is the cultural tradition of "my people" what it could and should be?

Walking across the Goshen College campus one day, I doubt I was thinking these thoughts when a figure stopped me with these words, "Why are you wearing such flashy socks? They're worldly. You know better than that. A Mennonite congregation won't like that." Dumbfounded, I looked into the no-kidding, half-grinning face of Dean Harold S. Bender, one of my teachers. Though only halfway through seminary, I had watched him turn the tattered pages of his lecture notes in the eight-hour Church History course, in the History of the New Testament Church class, in a class on Anabaptism, and in the seminars on discipleship and eschatology. Now I was soon to become a minister at Bethel Church, West Liberty, Ohio, where he was scheduled to preach the ordination sermon.

Oh, boy, I thought. Why is he picking on my socks? Well, I know why. He wants me to be accepted as a Mennonite minister even though I have been to seminary. He's afraid my colored socks may deflect from that acceptance by the congregation and maybe even hurt the good name of the seminary. After all, the style and color of clothes remained a sensitive issue among Mennonites in the 1950's. He had never mentioned clothes in class, but now he must have decided that since I was going to Bethel as a minister, I should smarten up on the color of socks I wore.

I was not particularly close to Dean Bender, but I think he trusted me. He knew that my linear ancestors, the Stoltzfuses, went straight back to one form of Anabaptism in the Palatinate and earlier still to a priest who had worked with Luther in the Wittenberg area. I do not think he knew that my mother's line, the Lenharts and Casebeers behind the Beechys, came from England. He knew very well that I was part of Mr. Graham's "your people" group. He knew that I had listened and appreciatively absorbed his revisioning of the Mennonite Christian worldview in light of his reading and reinterpretation of 16th century Anabaptism.

So what did I hear from him before his challenge to my haberdashery?

In short, he said that the church was to be a fellowship of believers in God through Jesus of Nazareth, a fellowship who, in taking on the character of Jesus, which Bender called discipleship, continued the incarnation of God's forgiving grace and love for all.

To come to this vision, he carefully selected these three components from the wild 16th century Anabaptist movements in revolt with other 16th century European peoples against a long-standing social, political, cultural and economic worldview controlled by medieval Catholicism. He carefully shaped them so they could elicit support and bring vision and inspiration to 20th century Mennonites and beyond. His vision juggled Christian realities involving Jesus, the early church, medieval Catholicism, major reformers' ideas, Anabaptism and 20th century Mennonites. The vision involved a major adjustment to medieval Catholicism's worldview of Christian reality in the world and to the critiques other reformers were giving it. The Anabaptist debate swirled around the question, "How does God's grace create and recreate all things?" His selective analysis—inaccurate in some ways and incomplete in others—opened unresolved questions for Mennonites already involved in remodeling their sense of identity and tradition. Nevertheless, it was a wonderfully generative, fruitful and inspiring vision for people like me, thinking about "my people's" tradition.

To the question of the identity of the church, medieval Catholicism had said it was a divine-human institution with Christ as its unseen spiritual head. The church was led by bishops in apostolic succession and headed on earth by the pope. This hierarchy controlled and communicated God's grace, authority, truth and life to all things on the earth. Therefore, the church had universal, theocratic hegemony over all nations, peoples, and creation, according to God's intentions *(de jura)*, though in fact *(de facto)* this was not fully realized. It communicated the grace of God sacramentally by virtue of its operation *(ex opere operato)*, though the validity of mystical experience outside the sacraments was acknowledged. The pattern of Christian living for common people was to confess their sins in the confessional, share in the other sacraments, repeat the Lord's prayer with certain other texts, and participate in holy vigils, pilgrimages and the adoration of relics. Those in monastic orders swore to a life of obedience, celibacy and poverty to Christ under the Abbot's direction.

In contrast, Bender said the church in "the best" of Anabaptism was a gathered voluntary assembly of committed believers in God through Jesus Christ. They were led by God's Spirit through their charismatically accepted leaders in the fellowship who guided the social processes to nurture the group's identity and Christian solidarity. The church was a separate political order, controlled neither by Catholic hierarchy nor by civil rulers wielding their power for social control by the sword, nor by both acting together. Most Anabaptists downplayed the idea that any forms communicated God's grace simply *opere operato*. Rather, God appeared as mystery and gift, as grace and power, and as light and life when people loved God with all their heart, soul, mind, and strength and their neighbors, even their enemies, as themselves, as Jesus had directed. Anabaptists gave witness to their beliefs forthrightly to non-members and to the social structures of society, including the civil/church structures, most of which did not try to control them.

Bender developed his vision of the shape of Christian reality in the world through his studies of the early New Testament church and his opposition or reaction mode to both medieval Catholicism and other reformers. He envisioned these theological principles in Anabaptism and the NT church as principles that could renew Mennonite "peoplehood," but he let those principles become self-generating ideas. He himself did not work out the changes these forms or symbols might or should take in the reordering of the 20th century Mennonite symbol system and practices except in nonresistance or pacifism. I noticed that he gave his genius to a perpetual whirl of activity in starting, nurturing and maintaining institutions—chiefly educational and service ministries.

Bender did not engage deeply in the dynamic character and content of theological development between the early church and the 16th century or in the theology of the enlightenment or post-enlightenment periods, except to sidle closely to orthodox perspectives. He discussed God and redemption for the church, but not God's providence at work in creation and in the movement of the human enterprise in culture. He emphasized the church as fellowship, but did not discuss how the church as a complex socially structured institution operates in the dynamic institutional power relationships within itself and with other social structures, except in its relation to the religious/civil orders, a major concern of the Anabaptists. He did not discuss how leadership ministry operates in a fellowship where each participant is equally Spirit-gifted for Christ's ministry. He did not comment on how God is with us, except to infer that it is at the point of obedient response of love in action. He did not discuss how to determine the actions of love, except to say that love does not kill other humans. However, he did say," Change your socks." He meant that church begins where Mennonite peoplehood is located. *Wear socks of peace, and proceed just as the first disciples did; follow Jesus in trust and worship, though the following is mixed with fear, doubt and amazement.*

What else did Bender's seminary give me? It introduced me to the biblical languages, which helped me peer into the way earlier peoples in the biblical narrative thought about transcendence and God's ways with man. The seminary introduced me to inductive Bible study, a disciplined probing of the text to discover its meaning in its historical context. This I found extremely helpful. It introduced me to Jesus as a historical human figure who symbolized God's grace, love and truth in human flesh. And the faculty members became role models for me. I was able to see how educated, dedicated Mennonite churchmen and educators go about interpreting Christ's way in their work and lives.

I suspected that Bender was not overly worried about my socks. He was probably more concerned about whether or not I was going to get married. "A Mennonite minister needs to be married," he said. He knew I had been working in this direction because his house and Mildred's family's house sat side by side. But he did not know how persuasive I was trying to be.

Mildred would say, "I don't know, I don't know." Then one time she asked, "If we did get married, where would we live?" Then I knew I had won one of the greatest victories in my life. For fifty years, as of last July 31st, we have loved each other and worked together. Her love, wisdom, Christian faith, patience, hard work, good judgment, and wise management have made our union and our family experiences a wonderful trip. I think Bender would be glad about that.

After seminary I was headed for work in a congregation. Mennonites in the 1950's were in the throes of rapid change in the character of their peoplehood. Congregations were receiving early return waves of multiple influences from major institutions established earlier: the Mission Boards, the Publication Board, the Commission for Christian Education, which worked with congregational life, and the Board of Education.

The patterns of congregational leadership were changing the most dramatically. Churches began calling younger men instead of older men to be ministers and persons from outside the congregation instead of those who had grown up in the congregation; they elected their ministers by congregational vote instead of calling them by lot. Also, they called one pastor to serve with a church council or elders instead of having several ordained persons—a bishop, a deacon and one or more ministers forming a bench of leaders. There was change from self-supporting farmer-ministers to some (partial, rarely full) financial support, from leaders who embodied the total ethnic Mennonite Christian tradition and helped the congregation conserve it to leaders from outside who could not embody that tradition either because of their youth and inexperience or because they did not respect the congregation's peoplehood tradition in relation to their own vision. There was movement from exclusive male leadership (except in the Sunday school and WMSA, the women's organization) to the first imaginings of women leaders in other leadership roles.

So, I wondered, "What does Bethel expect of me for half-time support? What should I do?" There was no list of duties. I had some awareness about these questions because as a boy I had watched my father work as minister in our congregation, as a conference leader, and as a successful businessman farmer.

Before I arrived at Bethel, two ministers, devoted men each one, were silenced by the institutional structures of the Ohio Mennonite Conference; and forty members left the congregation. Why? Not because the ministers could not talk together as Christians. They talked and talked. Not because they did not study the Bible. They studied it. Not because they rejected God's grace or did not want to walk in love. They just could not interpret the tradition in the same way.

These were the things I worked at slowly as I made my own way as a half-time supported pastor. I thought about the advice given to a medical doctor beginning to practice medicine, "Do no harm." I did not feel called to break any of the congregation's heritage windows or force any new change, even colored socks, if it was an irritant. Instead, I did the following: planned worship services; preached regularly (and rather poorly, as I noticed when I reviewed some of my sermons recently); led Bible studies; started a weekly bulletin; worked with the people during the special occasions of births in the family, sicknesses, weddings, other celebrations, and death; listened to persons grieving over the pain of the congregation's recent troubles; carried out a birthday visit program to every person related to the congregation to discuss how each felt about our congregation and his/her Christian pilgrimage (this one-to-one contact was of incomparable value to me and, I think, appreciated by the congregation); helped plan special meetings; worked closely with our church council and Sunday School leaders in planning our congregation's life and work; and helped develop and put in place a reorganization of the congregation.

Bender's theoretical (theological) Anabaptist vision underlay my ministry. The Bethel congregation as God's "people" worked wonderfully well together, and I believe we slowly allowed implications of that vision to settle upon us and through us as a renewing power in the practice of our changing ethnic Christian, Mennonite tradition.

During the first two years, I finished my seminary work at Hamma Divinity School, a Lutheran Seminary (ELCA) attached to Wittenberg University in Springfield, Ohio. Here I began a serious reading of theology under T.A. Kantanon, a major theologian in ELCA circles; I took courses in pastoral counseling, congregational administration, and preaching—all of inestimable, immediate value to me in my work—and I added courses in other specialized areas. I learned that Lutherans, not just the Mennonites, practice their own distinct heritage of "peoplehood."

When I had completed my program, I asked Dean E.E. Flack, "Shall I receive the Master of Divinity degree from Hamma or transfer to Goshen?"

He replied, "You've been a fine student. We would be very pleased to have you graduate here, but I suggest you transfer your work back to Goshen Biblical Seminary. I know Dean Bender there. That's your Mennonite School, and you're serving 'your people.' Do as you wish." Here were the words "your people" again from another non-Mennonite school administrator. I transferred my credits to Goshen.

If Bender thought that I should buy other socks, I did, too. To add to my halftime salary, I painted buildings for Forest King, wrote adult Sunday school lessons for Herald Press, edited the *Ohio Evangel* (the Ohio Conference's monthly publication), and accepted speaking assignments. Mildred worked as the treasurer of the Mad River Valley Milk Producers Association, besides getting our four children on their way to school and later working as a substitute teacher at the public elementary school.

At Bethel I learned that the relationship between a congregation's Christian identity (the church issue), its pattern of discipleship (ethics), and its ministry and witness to Christ's love in the world are complex elements that are in need of continuous review. Christians and their congregation work with, in, and around many social structures. A church fully supports some practices in the social structures of society, encourages change in others, criticizes still others, and totally rejects some, like participation in war.

I also began thinking of God as a God of all of creation and the human enterprise in history. This interest drew me into studies in the graduate philosophy department at Ohio State along with continuing work in theology, especially Believers' Church theology. I had a seven-year period at Goshen College scattered among three assignments: interim pastor to students, a teacher in the Bible Department, and a representative of the Seminary in Church and Seminary Relations (this latter an assignment that did not suit me at all because I did not want to be away from our family so much). Then in the 70's I went as pastor to First Mennonite Church, Iowa City, Iowa and in 1979 to Virginia to teach at Eastern Mennonite Seminary.

But all that is another story. If I could talk to Mr. Graham now, I would say, "Thank you for identifying me with the ethnic Christians you called '"my people."' And if I could see Dean Bender, I would say, "Thank you for introducing me to the Anabaptist vision, for your concern that I wear socks of understanding and appreciation for the character of our Mennonite ethnic tradition, and for your steadfast conviction that Christ walks with us in our amazements, fears, and doubts as he continuously creates and recreates his people on the earth."

October 2004

JOHN R. MARTIN

A Life of Twists and Turns

In this brief story of my life I will focus broadly on three themes: formative experiences, education, and ministry. It is a story of many twists and turns.

Childhood and Grade School, 1928–1942

I was born in September 1928 on a small dairy farm in south Park View. The sixth child in a family of nine children, I ended up with four brothers and four sisters. In those days Park View was a small mostly Mennonite community. In fact, to many in the larger Harrisonburg community, it was Mennonite Town. We were frequently reminded of this view during World War II.

My earliest memory stems from an event on my third birthday when the family was seated around the large dining room table. This was an extra special day because of the birth in our family of a new baby boy. After supper I was handed a small wrapped gift. Tearing it open, I was delighted to see a beautiful red tractor. (In a novel it would have foreshadowed my later love of farming.)

Someone asked, "John, which do you like best, the tractor or the baby brother?" "The tractor," I replied instantly. Hearing the roars of laughter, I knew I must have made the wrong choice, but that was the way I felt.

Throughout my childhood my strong interest was in farming, not the ministry. However, I do recall the Sunday we could not go to church because of a snowstorm. We younger children planned a church service, and I was the preacher. My sermon was about the Apostle Paul and all that he had suffered on his missionary travels. According to my sermon, his suffering included the time he was in a train wreck!

My public commitment to Christ took place at the Lindale Mennonite Church, my mother's home church, when I was twelve and S. G. Shetler, the father of Sanford Shetler, was conducting revival meetings. I clearly remember my sense of guilt and need to surrender my life to Christ. A wonderful peace followed my prayer of confession and commitment.

High School and Beyond, 1942–1950

During these years, since my love of farming kept growing, my favorite class was agriculture. There I developed plans for my future farm operation. The farm I wanted eventually to buy was along Linville Creek and north of Lindale Church. I sketched a dairy barn and estimated the number of cows I wanted to milk, the number of hired men I would need, and the amount of money I would have to borrow.

While in high school, I milked cows twice a day, bottled and delivered milk in Park View to many (of the then Eastern Mennonite College) faculty members, and hauled feed from Harrisonburg. With my older brothers in Civilian Public Service (CPS) and my father away much of the time, I was fortunate in being able to get my driver's license at age fourteen. The only problem was that since I was only four feet and ten inches tall, I needed to sit on a large pillow to be able to see over the dashboard of our 1939 Buick, which we used to haul feed and deliver milk. The farm work left me little time for studying, but I did not mind. Schoolwork was not my real interest.

My first sense of a call to the ministry came during a chapel service at EMC in which the speaker challenged us students to give our lives in missions. For some reason I felt that God was calling me to mission work in the South, and I was actually both excited and frustrated. Operating a dairy farm had been my dream, but it now looked as though God had other plans for me.

I proposed my becoming a farmer-preacher like many Mennonite ministers, but God seemed to be calling me to full time ministry. I then told God that I was needed on the family farm because my father was depending on me to do the farming and because surely the faculty members needed milk. God did not seem impressed with this argument either.

After a period of inner struggle I heard God's quiet voice in the scriptures in one of J. Mark Stauffer's Sunday school classes. Our passage for study, Mark 1:16–20, told the story of Jesus' calling four of his disciples. One of them was a man named John. That was my name. He was working in business with his father. So was I. When Jesus called him, he left his father and his hired men to follow Jesus. Suddenly I saw God's answer to my problem. A hired man could keep the dairy in business. That Sunday morning I breathed, "Yes, Lord."

After graduating from high school I continued to work on the farm, but the long-range direction of my life had changed. This new direction was nurtured by a number of important activities. First, I took on several responsibilities at the Chicago Avenue Mennonite Church. Second, I began singing in a men's quartet to help in the summer activities of the YPCA while the college students were off campus. For six years we sang at street meetings, the county jail, weddings, funerals, and evangelistic meetings; we sang, also, as part of Gospel Teams and as Bible School teachers in West Virginia.

Third, I decided to take two particular college courses. I believed that Personal Evangelism and The Christian Life would meet my academic needs. However, as I finished them, I was beginning to realize how much I did not know.

Fourth, I had an important conversation with B. Charles Hostetter. It was with a lot of apprehension that I told Charlie that I sensed a call to the ministry but did not know what to do about it. Charlie listened, assured me of his interest, and encouraged me to test the calling by being involved in Christian service. I left that meeting with a great sense of relief. I had shared my inner secret and found it not only understood and respected but also encouraged.

Fifth, in November 1949, after the end of World War II, I and seven other Mennonite fellows sailed (in what was known as a "cattle boat") from Newport News to Israel with 740 Holstein cows. Witnessing to the "pagan" sailors and traveling in Israel became life-changing experiences.

College, 1950–1954

During the spring of 1950, I began to consider going to college. However, since four years seemed much too long for me, I decided to enter the two-year Junior College Bible program.

The discussion of this possibility with my father was difficult for both of us. I knew he was counting on me to operate the farm because none of my brothers was interested in farming. Yet, although my father needed my help on the farm, he also wanted to encourage my interest in the ministry. The decision was for me to begin college but to help as much as possible on the farm. Eventually my father decided to sell the milk route and the cows, and he gradually reduced the size of the farm by selling building lots.

My biggest reservation about entering a degree program was my fear of English Composition, a requirement. I knew how poorly I wrote and doubted that I could pass the course. Considering what topic to choose for one of the early assignments, an essay about an important personal experience, I decided on my opportunities for witnessing on the cattle boat. To my surprise Hubert Pellman, the professor, felt that it should be submitted to one of the church papers. In time it was published in *The Youth's Christian Companion.* My first article! Seeing it in print was deeply encouraging. Yet after I took a standardized test, the professor who interpreted the results said that I might be able to go into mission work but that I should not consider becoming a pastor. Still, at the end of the first year I decided to switch to a four-year curriculum with a major in Bible, but I doubted that I would complete all the requirements for a degree.

Following my sophomore year, I spent most of the summer in Voluntary Service in the MCC Unit at Gulfport, Mississippi. My activities included teaching Bible School in black churches, doing community service, and helping in a mission church. Several biblical truths that opened up to me were life changing. First, God's promise to replace our anxiety with his peace was real (Philippians 4:6–7). Second, the message of Romans 6 on dying to the old self and being alive to Christ was good news to be accepted, not a message on sinless perfection to be rejected. Third, the New Testament teaching that Christ lives in the believer was a reality to be claimed, not simply nice sounding words. I began picturing myself as a pencil in God's hand for him to use as he wished. For me, the Christian life had taken on new dimensions.

During college I participated in the Intercollegiate Peace Fellowship. At one of our annual meetings Calvin Redekop spoke on the possibility of Mennonites witnessing to the government. His address caused considerable discussion and created urgent questions. Should we or should we not witness to government? The answer came to me in an unexpected way several years later.

Singing in the quartet and touring with the college choirs enabled me to observe many congregations. I noticed that where there was strong pastoral leadership, the youth tended to stay in the church. Many also went to college and on to various areas of missions. I began considering the pastoral ministry and maybe one year of seminary. I realized I could contribute to the total mission of the church by being a pastor.

My years of high school and college were a time of radical transition as my focus shifted from farming, to missions, and to the pastoral ministry. My attitude toward formal training grew gradually from no college, to two part-time courses, to junior college, to full college, to seminary. God's ways are amazing. He changes us at our speed.

Seminary and Student Pastorate, 1954–1956

I began to consider the possibility of some seminary after determining that God wanted me in pastoral ministry. At that time the Goshen Biblical Seminary offered a ThB degree, which required one year beyond a college degree if one had a Bible major. I felt one year of seminary would be valuable pastoral preparation and looked forward to studying under church leaders such as H.S. Bender, J.C. Wenger, Howard Charles, Guy F. Hershberger, and Paul Miller.

That fall Paul Miller asked me to assist at Fish Lake Mennonite Church, a mission congregation located about forty miles west of Goshen. I spent many weekends there, doing visitation, teaching and preaching. With my studies going well and the coming of an invitation to be licensed for Fishlake, I switched from the ThB program to the BD degree, which would require two more years.

At Fish Lake the last Saturday evening in October 1955, I received a phone call from Harold Eshleman, my home pastor in Harrisonburg, with tragic news. My older brother Robert, his wife Mabel, and one of my younger brothers, Sanford, plus two other persons had been killed in an airplane accident near Harrisonburg. I was to return to Goshen, report the news to Ralph, my younger brother who was then a student at Goshen College, and drive to Harrisonburg the next day.

Ralph, his wife, and Marian and I (we had just announced our engagement) arrived in Harrisonburg Sunday evening to find our family and the Harrisonburg community in a deep state of shock. All of us struggled with the *how* and *why* questions.

The *how* question was never fully answered but seemed to include engine failure. The *why* question was partially answered for me by Isaiah 55:8: "For my thoughts are not your thoughts, neither are your ways my ways." Also, I changed the question from *why* to *what:* What could I learn from this experience that would be useful in the ministry?

For my father the loss was especially heavy. Robert, Mabel and Sanford were key persons in the stove business that he was operating in Harrisonburg. To help, Ralph decided to drop out of college and return to Harrisonburg. I would complete the fall semester at Goshen and transfer back to EMC for the winter semester. Life had suddenly become unsettled and unpredictable.

Yet Marian and I decided to get married that spring. She was from Blooming Glen, Pennsylvania, and we had met at Goshen College, where she was a student. I am a firm believer in having a college and a seminary on the same campus! Also that spring I was invited to become the pastor of the Woodridge Mennonite Church in Washington, DC. We decided to accept the invitation for a two-year period, even though this would delay our return to Goshen for me to complete a BD degree and for Marian to complete her bachelor degree.

Washington DC, 1956–1959

In a step of faith Marian and I, a newly wed couple, moved to Washington to pastor a young congregation with 35 members. Not everyone was in favor of our decision. Shortly before we went to Washington, J. L. Stauffer met me in the hall at EMC.

"I hear you are moving to Washington," he said. "That is a very wicked city." Shocked by his comment, I replied, "Yes, I know. That is why I am going." The conversation ended.

I was employed half time at the church. For the first six months I also worked half time in a lumberyard. Then a half time position opened, Associate Executive Secretary of the National Service Board for Religious Objectors (NSBRO). My primary responsibility was to assist conscientious objectors who were not able to get a CO classification and wanted a Presidential appeal. I also worked with persons in the military who had become conscientious objectors and now requested discharge on the grounds of conscience. The work involved contacts with key persons at the National Headquarters of Selective Service, the Pentagon, and the Navy Annex. I was also the MCC representative in Washington. This variety of contacts opened doors to a number of unique experiences. One special activity was our attempt to get Congress to release the Frozen Fund. Amounting to over one million dollars, this fund had been earned by CPS men; it was intended for relief work but was kept by the government. We failed.

I began working at NSBRO with Cal Redekop's question about witnessing to government still hanging in my mind. One day while pondering Cal's question, I suddenly realized that this is what I was doing: I was witnessing to government officials about the conscientious objector position and why some Christians chose this position. This work seemed necessary and right. The question was answered with a big YES.

My work at NSBRO was exciting, but it challenged my commitment to working in the church. I automatically compared the power and size of the government agencies to the small congregation at Woodridge. In particular, the government program of international aid impressed me. I wondered if I could accomplish more for the needs of the world by working for the government rather than working for the church.

God gave me his answer unexpectedly. One afternoon I was walking from the office to Union Station to get a commuter train to my home in Hyattsville. While I was waiting at a traffic light and facing the Capital building, God seemed to say, "You see all these grand buildings and power? The day will come when these will become dust and ashes, but the church will last forever." My response was a renewed commitment to ministry in and through the church. This commitment guided the rest of my service and ministry.

In January 1958 my youngest brother, Ralph, became ill with cancer. He was given X-ray treatments, but his condition did not improve. He died in May. The loss of three brothers and a sister-in-law in three years caused me often to reflect on life and its meaning. The question, "Why am I still alive?" was one I could not fully answer. Apparently God still had work for me to do.

Because of the legal problems connected with erecting a new church building, we stayed in Washington three years. The last six months I switched from working at NSBRO half time to being the Eastern Representative of the I-W office at Elkhart. This change was in preparation for my becoming the Director of I-W Services when we returned to Goshen.

Back to Seminary and the Mission Board, 1959–1961

When I took the job in the I-W office, the plan was to work one year, terminate when I graduated, and return to Washington. However, the Mission Board invited me to continue full time after graduation and to make some major changes in the I-W program. They wanted me to develop an orientation program for the men entering I-W Service and to organize a I-W Council with representatives from each district conference. After consideration Marian and I decided that I should accept this invitation.

An unexpected part of my work at the Mission Board was teaching several classes in the Voluntary Service orientation sessions. I was amazed at how much I enjoyed teaching and began to have thoughts of teaching full time some day.

By the summer of 1961 the new I-W programs were operating well and I was considering returning to the pastoral ministry. Bishop O.N. Johns approached me about becoming the pastor of the Neffsville Mennonite Church in Lancaster County.

Before Marian and I made the trip for a weekend visit, Harold Bender called and said, "John, I understand Neffsville is inviting you to become pastor. I think you should go." When I asked why, he said, "Some in the congregation want to become an independent congregation, and I think you could help them stay in the Mennonite Church." This was a strong affirmation from a person I highly respected.

Neffsville, 1961–1971

The weekend at Neffsville went well, and we said yes to their invitation to the pastorate. When we visited the church before moving, the people seemed very friendly. On the surface it appeared to be an ideal congregation to pastor, but under the surface there was a lot of pain and some anger, the result of a period of struggle and conflict with the previous pastor. He had left the congregation to start another church, taking a small group (ten to twelve) with him.

Another concern was relationships with Lancaster Conference leaders and congregations. For many of them Neffsville was an unacceptable Mennonite congregation because it was a member of the Ohio and Eastern Conference and too liberal. In addition, the founding group had left the East Chestnut Street Mennonite Church after the Brunk tent meetings. I had worked with some of the Lancaster Conference leaders in I-W activities and felt we had a good relationship. I wanted this to continue. I decided to reach out to Lancaster Conference people whenever there was an opportunity but not to force cooperation. Eventually many of the walls came down.

Life in the congregation was good. The members worked together well and welcomed many new members, and in time we needed to build an addition to the church building. Our children had a good congregational experience and developed wholesome attitudes toward the church. As a congregation we adopted the New Testament church at Antioch as our model and emphasized evangelism, nurture and mission. We agreed that our goal was to be a "Winning, Training, and Sending Church." It was thrilling to see God call members to move to other locations to assist mission churches. Some went to New Jersey and some to Maryland. Neffsville youth who are today leaders in the larger Mennonite church include Ron Byler, Richard Kauffman, and Everett Thomas.

One of the most unique ministries of the congregation was hosting a busload of military men several times a year from Ft. Monmouth, New Jersey. These were men in the signal corps who came from twelve to fifteen different countries for special training. We started the program at the request of a Presbyterian church, which had a similar program with another army base. The men would come to Lancaster on Saturday morning, tour the Amish country, stay in our homes Saturday night, attend church Sunday morning and return to New Jersey Sunday evening. Most of the men were respectful and supportive of our peace stance. We hosted a captain from Vietnam in our home several times. After his return to Vietnam the last time, he wrote asking if we would adopt his eight children. We declined.

During the late 1960s, one of the spiritually enriching opportunities was the visits of Bishop Elam Stauffer, a retired missionary from Tanzania. He spoke at Neffsville on a number of occasions, emphasizing our walking in the light and relying fully on the grace of God. In one of his messages he said that many Christians begin the Christian life by grace and then switch to works. Some weeks later the Holy Spirit showed me that this was indeed true of me. As I had grown in my Christian life and ministry, I had unconsciously begun to think that I no longer needed the grace of God as much as I had when I became a Christian at the age of twelve. My renewed reliance on the grace of God brought a fresh touch to my spiritual life. As Elam used to say, "No need, no grace; much need, much grace."

During the years at Neffsville, I also became involved in conference and denominational work. In addition to pastoring, I served as overseer for a number of congregations, was active for several years in the leadership of Ohio Conference, and was a member of the Board of Directors of Mennonite Broadcasts and also a trustee of EMC.

In the late 1960s Myron Augsburger began talking with me about my possibly teaching in the Bible Department at EMC and eventually teaching at the seminary. He encouraged me to work toward a Master's Degree. I enrolled at the Eastern Baptist Theological Seminary in Philadelphia, to which I commuted by train one day a week. I enjoyed this arrangement because I could read while traveling.

Eastern Mennonite College, 1971–1978

Accepting the invitation to teach at EMC meant a major change for the family and me. I had considered teaching at some point partly because Jacob Enz at AMBS had told me I should consider the teaching ministry. For the family it meant a change of roles.

I found my first year of teaching extremely heavy. In the fall semester I was assigned two sections of a course called The Christian Worldview, which had been taught by Linden Wenger and reflected his interest in philosophy—not my field. The huge sections—90 students in one and 100 in the other—met in the large lecture hall in the science building, S106, and the two sections were scheduled back to back three times a week. In addition, I taught two other courses. Being a pastor seemed less demanding.

When Christmas vacation arrived, I began writing my Master's thesis. (I had completed my course work before moving to EMC.) Working day and night, I was able to complete the thesis in time to graduate in the spring. J.C. Wenger was teaching at EMS that semester. Since my thesis related to divorce and remarriage and he had written on that subject, I asked him to read it. He returned it with a page of editorial corrections, some supportive comments, and these large letters, "Ought to be published." I had not written for this purpose but submitted the manuscript to the Mennonite Publishing House. It was published under the title *Divorce and Remarriage, A Perspective for Counseling*. Since the subject was so controversial, I expected to receive a lot of negative mail but did not. What I did receive were numerous invitations to lead congregations in studying this difficult subject. Out of these experiences I received some important insights into dealing with controversial issues in a congregation.

During the last several years of teaching in the college, I developed and directed a program called Church Work Practicum. It was a college version of supervised ministry for college Bible majors. Partly because of having developed this program, I was invited to the seminary to serve as Registrar and to develop and direct their field education program.

Seminary, 1978–1994

Fitting into the new roles at the seminary was not difficult. There were new tasks to be learned; but the seminary was small, the faculty and staff helpful, and the students patient.

During the fall of 1979, I began working on a writing project that I had been considering for several years. As a result of my pastoral experience and seven years of working with college students, I was convinced that many Christians found the Bible a closed book and seldom studied it because they did not understand it. I felt a book on Bible study that was solid in content yet simple in language could fill a real need. I saw a potential audience in the church and also in the general public, who might buy such a book on the Choice Books racks. Herald Press agreed to be the publisher, and *Keys to Successful Bible Study* was released in 1981. A number of copies were sold, but it was too expensive for the Choice Books market. This was a disappointment.

With the arrival of my first sabbatical I began a Doctor of Ministry program at the Lancaster Theological Seminary the summer of 1981. I chose this seminary because it offered the schedule and subject flexibility that I was looking for. My focus of interest was discipleship and discipling.

For some time I had had an interest in spiritual renewal, and I was enriched by programs such as Faith at Work. However, some aspects of these programs were not compatible with my Anabaptist beliefs. I reasoned that if the Anabaptist movement was as spiritually dynamic as we said it was, why could not the Anabaptists' beliefs and practices become a guide for spiritual renewal in the Mennonite church today? I saw this as a real need because I sensed that many Mennonites had a limited understanding of discipleship and had seldom been discipled in a systematic way. I became intrigued with the dream of a discipling relationship between seminary faculty and students.

In my doctoral program, it was agreed that the doctoral project would be the development of a handbook on discipling for use at EMS and in congregations. In my background studies I focused on Christian spirituality, discipleship, spiritual direction, and related areas. I also did a major inductive study of "The Anabaptist Concept of Discipleship and Its Application in Discipling."

I began the Anabaptist studies with the assumption that the Anabaptists had a planned program for effective discipling. My findings only partially supported this assumption. Yes, they did have many effective methods of discipling, but they did not have what I would call a planned program for discipling. Rather, the intense form of their congregational life provided instruction in discipleship and nurtured their spiritual lives. Their corporate view of the church and of the Christian life resulted in the congregation's becoming the center of spiritual development. This was their program. The content focused in three areas:

(1) personal aspects such as "walking in the resurrection," and "the obedience of faith;" (2) corporate expressions such as "communion and community," and "admonishing one another;" and (3) societal applications such as "children of peace," and "ministry to human need." The handbook that I organized around these three areas was later published by Herald Press with the title *Ventures in Discipleship*.

By the summer of 1982 I had finished the background studies for my doctoral project, which I anticipated completing over the next two or three years along with working full time. However, my family began talking about the fact that in June of 1983 all three of our children would graduate: Don from medical school, Lee from EMC, and Ann from Messiah College. I was tempted to join them.

From the summer of 1982 until March 1983 I studied and wrote evenings and weekends. Marian faithfully typed as I wrote. We slaved away month after month. By early spring the project was approved; and, if I passed the oral exam, I too could graduate in June.

I passed the exam but then encountered another problem. In checking the calendar, we discovered that three of us had commencement exercises on the same day. Ann's commencement at Messiah was scheduled at 10:00 AM. Mine at Lancaster was scheduled at 11:00 AM. Don's in Richmond was scheduled for 2:30 PM.

What was the solution? We first attended Ann's graduation at Messiah. Then we were driven to a nearby airport, from which we flew by chartered plane to Richmond, arriving two minutes before the starting time for Don's graduation. The following Friday Dr. Freeman from Lancaster attended the EMS graduation and presented my diploma to me. And the next Sunday Lee graduated from EMC. We four graduates then presented Marian with a booklet honoring her as the "closet graduate." In the back of the booklet was a diploma awarding Marian a Doctor of Family Education degree from the John Martin University.

During the course of my studies, I developed the Formation Course sequence for the seminary's curriculum. These three core courses became required of all students: Formation in Personhood, the first year; Formation in Ministry, the second year; and Formation in Discipleship, the third year.

For a number of years *Ventures in Discipleship* was used in the latter course. My dream was that students going through the discipling experience would then disciple their church members when they became pastors. I did lead several groups of ministers through the studies at off campus locations, but the book has not been used as broadly as I had hoped. It seems that the experience of Spiritual Direction, as valuable as it is, has more appeal than the experience of being discipled. I am grateful that the book has been printed in Spanish and is still available in English. The book has twenty-three lessons, each one on a discipleship theme. These themes are developed with biblical teaching, quotes from Anabaptist writers, quotes from contemporary writers, journaling exercises, spiritual disciplines, and discussion questions for discipling partners.

Not long after offering Formation in Discipleship, I was a discipling partner with Wendy Miller, a student. I soon discovered her deep spiritual interest and gifts in teaching, and I recommended to George Brunk that upon graduation she be invited to teach courses on prayer and spirituality. She agreed and has since developed the variety of course offerings in Christian Spirituality.

During my time at the seminary, I was privileged to serve in a variety of ministries, such as the Board of Congregational Ministries and the Ministry of Spirituality Committee at Elkhart; also, I served as Moderator of Virginia Conference.

In the year 1988–89, my second sabbatical, my writing project was to develop a plan that could be used by congregations to discern and call gifted members to the ministry. The motivation was my observation that while our church had discontinued the use of the lot, it had never replaced it with another way of calling ministers from the congregation. Also, the number of students coming to seminary who had never tested their call in a congregation concerned me. In 1990 the Mennonite Publishing House published my study under the title *Calling the Called*. At that time the denomination was not focusing on calling ministers as a major emphasis. I am grateful that the concern is now covered in *Culture of Call* and that many of my concepts are being promoted.

Reflections

What are my thoughts and feelings at this stage of life? I am overwhelmed by the goodness of God, and I have the feeling of having been born at just the right time. I am old enough to have lived through world-shaping events such as World War II and to have known church-shaping leaders such as J.D. Graber, Orie Miller, H.S. Bender, J.C. Wenger, and C.K. Lehman. But I am also young enough to enjoy life, my family and some types of ministry.

I have been blessed with unique and enjoyable ministry opportunities. They came to me. I did not go seeking them. In the various roles I always felt like a generalist, not an expert in any one area. My self-image is being more a pastor than a professor. Yet I have the arrogance to believe that if all Mennonites would work through *Ventures in Discipleship*, they would have a fuller understanding of our Anabaptist roots, of the meaning of discipleship, and of an enriched spiritual life. And if every Mennonite congregation would apply *Calling the Called*, our pastoral shortage would be solved.

What has been occupying my time since retirement? Most of it has been as a volunteer—at the Park View Mennonite Church, the Virginia Mennonite Retirement Community, and Turner's Mill Restoration Committee. Also, I serve as instructor for the Pastoral Studies Distance Education series, entitled "Leading God's People." This is a correspondence course designed for pastors without college or seminary training. I work with Unit V, "Tending God's Flock." In addition, I review books for Choice Books. Of course, time with our seven grandchildren is important. They will be young only once.

As I reflect over the past years, I can see a shift in what I felt was most important for the ministry. It requires knowing, doing, and being. If these are viewed as the three sides of a triangle, all are important; but one must be at the base of the triangle. During seminary, I thought *knowing* should be at the base; and I studied diligently. When I began the ministry, I thought *doing* should be at the base; and I worked diligently. In recent years I have discovered that *being* really should be at the base, and I am giving more attention to this aspect of life. I wish I had made this discovery earlier. I would have been a better servant of Jesus Christ.

September 2005
Revised March 2006

TITUS W. BENDER

A Journey toward Embracing God's Wider Family

Perhaps more than I have realized, my parents shaped the values I have come to hold so deeply. My father was a pastor, bishop and sometimes Conference Moderator in the Conservative Mennonite Conference. I admired his focus on a God of love who reaches out to every person and expects us to do the same. My mother also had a deep impact on the direction of my life. Her influence was on the very personal level. I remember the anguish she could not hide when anyone in the church or community was treated as a second-class person.

It is no mystery to me that from my early teenage years I expected to become involved in the leadership within the church. Experiencing affirmation from my family and some fellow members in my congregation, I enrolled at Eastern Mennonite College in 1953 and focused my attention on biblical studies and courses in the social sciences. There I met Ann Yoder. From the day we began to see each other regularly, we have continued to grow more deeply in love.

After getting married, in 1958 we became the VS leaders in Meridian, Mississippi, with the Conservative Mennonite Conference. Later the Peace Section of the Mennonite Central Committee asked me to serve part time as their representative in the South. Little did we know that our eleven years there would so profoundly shape the way we came to see our faith in relating to people at the personal, community and state levels. Even more than before, we came to identify with those who have been excluded by the community, too often with the collaboration of the organized church.

The Role of Eastern Mennonite College in Our Journey

From my four college years and one year in the Bachelor of Theology program at Eastern Mennonite College, I particularly recall two of my professors who have been frequent attendees at these ACRS breakfasts. I remember when Dr. Paul Peachey returned from a trip to Alabama during the time of the Birmingham Bus Boycott. It was clear, as he discussed this experience with our class, that he had been electrified by Dr. King's commitment to nonviolence. It was also clear that Dr. King had impressed him as a person. Paul Peachey's influence on me as a student at EMC was profound.

I was also deeply affected by Dr. Irvin Horst's History of Christianity course during my year of seminary training. I will never forget the day when we discussed a major thesis of one of our texts, authored by a Baptist historian, Kenneth Scott Lattourette: The validity of a Christian movement is demonstrated by its ability to attract adherents. Dr. Horst suggested a possible alternative Anabaptist thesis: The validity of a Christian movement is demonstrated by its ability to elicit the "fruits of the Spirit" in the lives of its adherents. This perspective has grown in me ever since.

During this year in seminary, I had a conversation with Mark Peachey, Paul Peachey's brother, who was the Secretary of the Mission Board for Conservative Mennonite Conference. He told me that the Board was interested in developing a Voluntary Service Unit in Meridian, Mississippi. I was eager to visit there to get some feel of the city I might be calling home for the next number of years; and during Christmas vacation that year, my father accompanied me to Meridian. Enroute, we stopped in Americus, Georgia. I suppose most of us know something of the history of Koinonia Farm in Americus. Dr. Clarence Jordan and like-minded people had purchased a parcel of land on which they worked the farm and shared their finances in common. They invited people into their community of faith without excluding anyone on the basis of race or other forms of bigotry. That inter-racial community of faith suffered hostility from the surrounding people, who could not understand those who refused to practice racial exclusion in the church. I had been inspired by the courage of Clarence Jordan and his family.

When we arrived, he welcomed my father and me warmly, and I was warmed by his message the next day at their worship service. There he was, preaching from a Greek New Testament with no English text in sight, making the life of Jesus come alive. There was no pretense; he was just a Baptist minister and his family, joining hands with others to be a living witness to the call of God in breaking down walls of bigotry. (It was at Americus that Millard Fuller later met Clarence Jordon. Like many others who spent time with Jordon, his life was transformed. Fuller eventually spearheaded the birth and development of Habitat for Humanity.) Now my visit with Clarence Jordan on this trip became the preamble to my family's later sojourn in Meridian, Mississippi, and afterward. He gave us several tapes of his messages, which, when our VS group reached Mississippi, we initially played behind closed doors. This secretive attitude soon gave way to just being ourselves as we sought to live out that same kind of spirit.

When I returned to EMC from Americus, Georgia, and Meridian, Mississippi, my priority was to see my future wife, Ann Yoder. We decided to share our lives together and to have a serious conversation with Mark Peachey about Meridian, Mississippi. Mark invited us to serve as leaders for initiating the new program in Meridian. We accepted the call.

Walking With People

Ann and I feel fortunate to have been born into families who saw God as a parent of mercy and nurture, rather than as an almighty being who would turn to revenge if he became angry with us. We also see ourselves as blessed by our Mennonite tradition, in which God is understood as always pursuing us with love. That is the theology for which we are thankful. Admittedly, in daily life, personal and denominational actions sometimes do not reflect this; but for the theological tradition of love, peace and justice, we thank God.

While Ann and I have a deep appreciation for our faith tradition, at the same time it has become important for us to avoid Messianic illusions that God has already made clear to Mennonites (or Evangelicals) everything God is doing in this world. One antidote for us has been to walk with others who are quite different from us in theology, as well as with those who share a similar theology.

Initially we saw ourselves going to Mississippi to "share truth." Surely there was some degree of legitimacy in this. However, this view can create the danger of assuming that "They need answers; we have these answers." Gradually we came to see ourselves as *walking with* persons we learned to know, and having an ongoing *two-way conversation*. Sometimes these conversations have been vigorous; but we believe that unless we are able to understand the deepest passions of those with whom we walk, they will not feel safe in our presence.

For at least three reasons we came to believe in this two-way conversation in relating to others. First, it keeps us from judging others too severely. From the Native American tradition we are reminded, "Don't judge a man until you have walked two moons in his moccasins." Also, the persons with whom we walk may learn from us. The third reason for this two-way conversation is that the persons with whom we walk may teach us truth we need.

I want to share with you the stories of a number of people with whom we have walked in Mississippi and since and whose experiences changed us. Most of these persons were ordinary people although some were more powerful. None were perfect. Some had visible faults. Some struggled with alcohol abuse while others struggled with nicotine addiction. These people, who helped us mature, taught us truth about God that goes far beyond technical theological correctness. This walk with them changed our lives forever.

My vocational pursuits in Mississippi and since have been important in my journey. I will let you in on some of them this morning. But the reason I plan to use the stories of people whose faith helped shape me is that my vocational pursuits have been inextricably intertwined with my journey *with* people.

Our *journey* in Mississippi and since can be divided into six chapters. Our first five years were in relationship with the organization that sent us, the Conservative Mennonite Conference. The next two years, 1964 and 1965, were in deep relationship with Mennonite Disaster Service and the people this brought to our door. Chapter three began in 1966 when Edgar Metzler, head of the MCC Peace Section, invited me to be their Mennonite Representative in the South. Chapter four was our 36-month transition to a new vocation at Tulane University in New Orleans. Then there was the four-year University of Oklahoma chapter. The sixth chapter began with our return to Eastern Mennonite College/University.

Four Families Who Helped Reveal God's Face to Us

Our first challenge as VSers was learning to share our lives with the residents and employees at East Mississippi State (mental) Hospital, where we were employed, while inviting them to do the same with us. During October of 1958 and several months following, nine of us in the VS unit arrived and entered into the life of the mental hospital and the surrounding community. We learned to know the ordinary people around us: white, African American and Choctaw (The Choctaw tribe is the predominant native American tribe in Mississippi.)

The Pratt Family (a Caucasian couple)

Mr. and Mrs. Pratt worked at East Mississippi State Hospital with persons in our VS group. Mr. Pratt and I worked in the "B Building." He was in his 60s, and I was 26. We worked on the night shift, when we each cared for twelve elderly men who were limited to their beds and/or chairs. Most of them had a significant degree of dementia. Mr. Pratt and I sat beside each other in the hallway, just outside the doors to the two wards, where the twelve men under the care of each of us slept. We watched them through the night and tried to answer their requests for help. As we attempted to soothe them through the fears and pain they faced, Mr. Pratt and I learned to know each other well.

There is no way Mr. and Mrs. Pratt, who both worked in that mental hospital with us, could have missed the whispers among some of the staff about the "Yankees who wanted to change Meridian's way of life on the race question." As VSers we were about as inconspicuous as elephants walking down Main Street in Harrisonburg. We were young people among comparatively older staff; the women of our group wore prayer veilings; we had northern accents; and we carried the name Mennonite. Mr. and Mrs. Pratt never asked us about these rumors. They simply responded to us by inviting Ann and me into their home, where they served us authentic Mississippi country cooking, including butter peas from their garden, and we helped them paint the inside of their modest home. Ann painted the trim, and I painted the walls. It was important to the Pratts that we stop our work every afternoon and listen to one of their favorite TV programs, *As the World Turns*.

The Pratts were members of a church they called "Hard Shell Baptist," to which they invited us for a worship service. They even practiced what other Baptists around them viewed as old fashioned, foot washing. From their worship service I gathered that the core of their theology was summed up in the song they sang with gusto (a cappella, by the way), "The Old Account Was Settled Long Ago." To us it seemed the pastor was centering his efforts on maintaining the conviction that their one-time experience years ago was authentic enough to seal their eternal fate.

The Pratts did everything they could to help us feel welcome in a community where "Yankees" were expected to prove themselves for a significant period. Clearly their faith was real. We came to believe they had a personal faith beyond their congregation's theological understandings. (The reverse side of this dynamic is also true, of course. Some of us are less mature than some of our theological statements.) Walking with the Pratt family helped us understand that theological beliefs sometimes tell us little about the depth of a person's faith.

Nettie Henry and her Family

We also became acquainted with Nettie Henry, a Choctaw woman who worked in Meridian but who returned to her rural community whenever she could. We rented a van one rainy day and took her to her family, who treated us to their favorite food: hominy grits and black-eyed peas cooked in fatback and pork. Although we got stuck that rainy day on the slick red clay roads of rural Mississippi, our friendship with Ms. Henry was our introduction to the Choctaw community.

Two years later my parents came to the Nanih Waiya area, a few miles from Philadelphia, Mississippi, where my father became the pastor; and from that time on, our lives became deeply intertwined with the Choctaw community. Their ancestors had survived the "Trail of Tears," when Andrew Jackson helped force their journey to Oklahoma in the cold of winter, and now the understated smiles and warm hearts of Nettie and her fellow Choctaws reminded us of the attempted genocide perpetrated on their ancestors. The people who did this to them had claimed the name of God in their practice of "manifest destiny," the right to own whatever lands they could conquer. Even in the 1960s fresh scars continued to be created. During my father's pastorate there, these people were to survive three dynamite destructions of their place of worship, the Nanih Waiya Mennonite Church, which was about 40 miles from Meridian. My parents became brother and sister to them. My sister and brother-in-law, Emma and Glenn Myers, and my sister Mildred soon joined them. We owe a great debt to Nettie Henry and the Choctaw people of faith with whom we walked.

T.R. and Verna B. Hill and their Daughter Velma White and her Family
We have traveled a life-changing road with T.R. and Verna B. Hill and their children on to the fifth generation. We first met Mrs. Hill when we visited a local Baptist church, where she was a member. Her pastor was Sheriff Morgan, who served in the dual role of sheriff and pastor. It was public knowledge that he regularly carried his Bible on the dashboard of his official sheriff's vehicle. He had seen people with the problem of alcoholism and decided it was his duty to run for sheriff on the platform of enforcing Mississippi's law against any beverage above a two percent alcohol level. The Meridian community had elected Rev. Morgan but was not serious about his prohibitionist ideas. During the church service, Pastor Morgan introduced our group of VSers to the congregation. Mrs. Hill met us at the rear of the church, and from that day on we were friends.

I will never forget the first cup of coffee Mrs. Hill made for Ann and me when we visited her. It was strong and black with about three teaspoons of sugar. I drank it, thanked her and told her I enjoyed it. She began to tell her neighbors she had discovered, on the first try, how I liked my coffee. I never asked her to change her recipe when she served me coffee. I drank it for Turkish coffee.

We walked with Verna B. and her husband, T.R., and their extended family. Some neighbors did not know what to do with Christians who crossed racial barriers and who came to Mississippi in lieu of military service. However, the extended Hill family reached out to us. They became our intimate friends, and paid a price for it.

T.R. and Verna B. had three daughters. Velma, the oldest, was married to Robert White, whom we all knew as "Dusty." He and T.R. taught me the occupation of roofing houses. We discovered a building a block from the Hill home and remodeled it for a place of worship. Verna B.

and her daughter Velma and her family became increasingly important in the life of the Mennonite Church in Meridian. Velma called me "T. Titus," and I returned the favor by calling her, "V. Velma."

Velma and Dusty had five daughters; and Velma and her daughters became the bedrock of the Fellowship Mennonite Church, Velma rapidly becoming a major influence in the life of this congregation in Meridian. In the early days of our congregation I was optimistic that Conservative Conference leaders would recognize the authenticity of the faith of the White family and others fellowshipping with us. I will return to the White family later.

The Cross Family

Ida and Mac Cross, who had two sons and a daughter, welcomed us into their modest house. We found out later that one of Ida's very close friends was African American. After all, they did have a lot in common: both had come from the "wrong side of the tracks." However, Ida certainly did *not* think of herself as a community changer. Out of fear she actively avoided being seen as bucking the tide of segregation in Mississippi. She sometimes babysat our children. While both she and Mac had a problem with an overuse of alcohol, we knew she would never drink alcohol while she had our children's lives in her hands. In fact, when our family needed to totally relax we would go to Ida and Mac's house.

Ann and I will never forget one Christmas Eve when we stopped in to see them with a small Christmas gift to wish them a "Merry Christmas." They were just getting up from the table where they had eaten with relatives who were visiting from about thirty miles away. Some food was still sitting on the table, and Ida insisted that we eat the last bite. Later we discovered there had been no food in the refrigerator for Christmas the next day. Also, we found out that, as roofers, the Cross sons had had a rainy couple of weeks and there was no money for Christmas presents. For people in Meridian this was painful. As you can imagine, our pangs of guilt were severe when we realized we had cleaned them out of food that Christmas eve. If our roles had been reversed, Ann and I would have been tempted to hide the leftover food. Not Ida. She watched with obvious pleasure as we ate.

Ida Cross seldom used religious language, but walking with her shattered our stereotypes about persons labeled as "losers."

Freedom Summer and Church Burnings

In 1964 Ann and I faced a kaleidoscope of experiences that changed us forever. That was the year Dr. Vincent and Rosemarie Harding and Michael Schwerner came into our lives almost simultaneously. On February 25–26, 1964, the Mennonite Central Committee Peace Section convened a Conference on Race Relations in Atlanta, Georgia, where the Hardings were leaders of a voluntary service group who lived at Mennonite House. I particularly remember Dr. Harding's address, "Decade of Crisis: 1954–1964," which dramatized the immediacy and urgency of this problem for Ann and me. He swept away our defenses for avoiding involvement by "sticking to religion" in our witness amid the injustice in our communities.

Vincent had also invited C.T. Vivien from the Freedom Movement to speak to the Conference on Race Relations. The response among the representatives from the various church communities across the southeast was mixed.

One somewhat dubious Mennonite pastor asked, "Are not civil rights activists stirring up hatred?"

Vivien replied, "If you stir a glass of water with a spoon and the water gets dirty, there must have been mud in the glass before you stirred it."

Vincent and Rosemarie Harding

The two who most profoundly changed us were Dr. Vincent and Rosemarie Harding. Ann and I came to realize we had not treated the scourge of racial bigotry and exclusion as the paralyzing sin it is. We were part of a denomination that was still too often ignoring the devastating results of racism on so many lives, especially the lives of little children. Vincent and Rosemarie knew we recognized our complicity as part of the larger church in the South, which had been too casual about racism. Sometimes the church even stoked the fires of racial injustice. We recognized we were also part of the culture of selfishness in American society, and we knew we were guilty of not having done more to be a part of the solution. They reached out to us with generosity and forgiveness.

Three months after the conference in Atlanta, on May 30 and 31 Vincent and Rosemarie came to see us in Meridian. Ann and I will never forget that weekend with them in the VS House. Soon after they arrived, the Hardings and our VS group sat down for dinner. Next door lived the Salvation Army Captain and his family. Several times during our dinner, the Captain's 12 year-old son came to borrow some small food-related item such as salt. He would take a good look around the table, leave, then return a few minutes later to borrow something else. The twinkle in Vincent's eye kept getting brighter as he clearly enjoyed the stir made by this scene of African Americans and whites eating together. Indeed, one of the virtues that made Vincent and Rosemarie's role so powerful in the Freedom Movement was their ability to retain a sense of humor in the midst of bigotry. They understood that God was behind the movement for freedom and justice, and they trusted that in the end that movement would be victorious. Vincent and Rosemarie became Ann's and my mentors from that day forward. I will return to them again, to show how heavily our family depended on them as we tried to make sense of our Mississippi experiences.

Michael Schwerner

Three weeks after the Hardings' visit, late at night on June 21, 1964, five days before my 32nd birthday, James Chaney, Michael Schwerner and Andrew Goodman were murdered by members of the Ku Klux Klan and buried in a dam near Philadelphia, Mississippi. Michael Schwerner had come to meet us in our home several months earlier. My walk with him was too short.

Unaware of what had happened the night of the murder, Ann and I had planned to leave Meridian early the next morning for a visit with Ann's family in Ohio. A news brief on the radio startled us. Several "civil rights workers" were missing. I thought of Schwerner but told myself, "Surely not him." I had been with him just a few days earlier.

As soon as we returned to Meridian, Rita Schwerner called me, asking if we could meet. The station wagon in which her husband, Chaney, and Goodman were riding had been gutted with fire and abandoned on a fairly well traveled road that passed near a Native American community in the area where my father and mother lived. Rita wondered, and I tried to find out, if anyone who lived in the vicinity had seen anything suspicious or heard rumors of the whereabouts of the three freedom workers. I could find none.

For the next forty-four days we heard spiteful speculation by some white Mississippians, including law enforcement officials, that the three missing men had left the state to create a sensation. Then on August 4 the men's bodies were recovered from the dam where they had been buried. Freedom Summer of 1964 was off to a tragic beginning.

Five civil rights groups had joined hands to plan for hundreds of college students from all over the country to come to Mississippi for several months that summer. (The movement would challenge the very foundations of legally enforced segregation in Mississippi.) They worked under the umbrella of an organization called Council of Federated Organizations, which became known as COFO—for many white Mississippians an obscene word. Robert Moses, the coordinator of the program, had invited Michael and Rita Schwerner to Meridian about six months ahead of the students, who were coming in June. The Schwerners worked alongside their colleague, James Chaney and other local African Americans to initiate several "Freedom Schools" in the Meridian and Philadelphia areas. There they prepared citizens to register, since voting was essential if discrimination on the basis of race was to be ended.

Schwerner and a local African American, Preston Ponder, knocked on the door of our unit home one evening several months before the death of the Chaney, Schwerner and Goodman. They told me someone had assured him it would be "safe" to come to see us. Being the direct person he was, Michael asked me what we could do to help them.

I returned the question, "How *can* we help?"

He told me his secretary, Sue Brown, hoped to go to college the following year. I offered to try to help get her accepted at EMC and to enlist financial support. I was corresponding with EMC, and her admission seemed likely. Then Chaney, Schwerner and Goodman were murdered. At that point Rita Schwerner, devastated over her husband's death, encouraged Sue to apply to a school in the North, which she did.

I knew Michael as a person at peace, kind, yet courageous in pushing for justice, and one of the most non-violent persons I had ever known. I frequently visited his small upstairs office in downtown Meridian at 2505 1/2 on 5th Street. Mickey was Jewish. In those days I was more confident about my sense of urgency for others to agree with my Christian theology.

One day I said to him in what I considered to be a non-threatening way, "Mickey, Why don't you recognize that Jesus represents the justice we are working for and then continue with your work?"

In a totally non-judgmental way he responded with a smile on his face, "Think so?"

Within several months he was murdered by Klan members, many of whom claimed to be "born again." My theology has never fully recovered. Mickey had reached out to me. My faith had grown. Today, I wish I had him back for *a two-way conversation.* I would tell him he taught me a lot about faith. Ann and I came to recognize that God will be close to and work with anyone God chooses without our permission or the permission of any church or theology that might claim otherwise. For our short walk together, far too short, I am so thankful.

Three months after the death of Chaney, Schwerner and Goodman, on September 19, the Nanih Waiya Mennonite Church building where my Father was pastor was destroyed by dynamite. Vincent and Rosemarie's concern for our extended family and for the Choctaw people helped us survive without losing our way. They helped us discover how pain can either make us bitter or enable us to walk with others who experience pain.

Permit me an anecdote that indicates the storm of conflicting emotions swirling around us at that time in Mississippi. The day after the dynamiting of the Choctaw church building, my father, my brother-in-law Glenn Myers, and I were at the site. Sheriff Rainey and his deputy, Cecil Price, came by, ostensibly to investigate the ruins. We were convinced that both had been involved in the murder of the three freedom workers three months earlier. As Rainey and Price walked around looking at the ruins, they laughed boisterously. To say I was irate is an understatement, but I tried to keep an appearance of outward calm.

As we moved closer to them, I said to my father, "Let's begin rebuilding the church within a week." There were mixed reasons for my comment. I *did* believe it was urgent that with our actions we assure our Choctaw friends that violence could not destroy the church. There was a less noble reason. I wanted to look into Sheriff Rainey's face and refute any suspicions he might have that we were afraid of him.

The burning of church buildings was gaining momentum, as told in the movie, *Mississippi Burning*. In my recollection about 70 churches were burned or dynamited in the 1960s, most of them in 1964 and 1965. Mississippi's denominational leaders, African American and white, organized to raise money to contribute to African American congregations for rebuilding their places of worship. They called themselves Committee of Concern.

Lawrence Scott

Enter the picture, Lawrence Scott. In order to understand this Mississippi chapter of Scott's life, it is necessary to know a bit about this courageous Quaker, who lived in the tradition of A.J. Muste. Simultaneously he exuded calmness and restlessness in struggling for justice done. Earlier he had actively opposed nuclear testing. He had been part of a group who moved their boats into the immediate vicinity where nuclear research was being conducted in out of way ocean areas. Scott and his colleagues did this illegally and at great risk to themselves in order to help stop the madness of the nuclear arms race. After leaving Mississippi, he was deeply involved in the voyage of the Phoenix, a ship taking medical supplies to the harbor at Haiphong, North Vietnam, because of the medical devastation from the Vietnam War. Although the U.S. government blocked the delivery of their medical supplies for some time, it is my understanding that they were finally able to deliver their cargo.

However, in 1964 and 1965 we were graced with Lawrence Scott's restless presence in Mississippi. Having heard of the Klan-related burning of places of worship, he came to our state to enlist volunteers to work along with deacons and other church members whose places of worship had been destroyed. As any creative Quaker would do, he talked to Mississippians who were working at the same problem, and the leaders of the Committee of Concern asked him to join them. Believing that more than money was needed, he wanted this Mississippi organization to make room for people of all races to work side by side with the church members. If African Americans and whites were to work together to rebuild destroyed church buildings, their actions would send a message that burning churches was unacceptable to whites, as well as to ethnic minorities. In consultation with the Mennonite Disaster Service, Scott asked the Committee of Concern to add me to their group, which they did. Thus, Mennonite Disaster Service became a crucial part of the movement for rebuilding. Over a period of four to five months, about ten MDSers at a time, many of them trained carpenters, spent an average of one month each, helping with the rebuilding. More than forty MDSers did a significant amount of work on ten church buildings together with church members and other volunteers.

Scott decided to move one step further, inviting college students from the University of Mississippi and Millsaps College in Jackson, Mississippi, to participate as volunteers. Then he invited students from other parts of the country to help. Our VS home served as a meeting place for most of the forty plus MDSers, students from the University of Mississippi, Notre Dame University in South Bend, Indiana, and Queens College in New York City. We also shared our home with many Quakers who had been active in justice issues, a retired Presbyterian missionary from Korea, and several persons for whom organized religion seemed to hinder more than it helped in the crisis of injustice in the '60s. After meeting at our unit home, many went to motels throughout the state or to other private homes for housing.

The first MDSers arrived at our unit home on December 9, 1964. This was the beginning of a steady stream of persons who did their part in turning the pain of attacks against churches into some modest, but authentic, actions of reconciliation.

I will highlight one group of MDSers who arrived on February 5, 1965, to help rebuild the Mount Pleasant Church building near the town of Collinsville, a few miles north of Meridian. I decided to reserve motel rooms in Meridian for the workers. (Out of appreciation for the deep friendship that developed between him and the MDSers, I will use a fictitious name, Mr. Byrd, for the owner of the motel.) Within several days of the beginning of the MDS work, he became aware that we were helping to rebuild burned African American places of worship; and he responded with immediate respect for the MDSers. Although I did not know this at the time, Mr. Byrd was in the process of leaving the Klan, a dangerous act for him. He warned the workers they were in danger. Yet he admitted he had hated Mickey Schwerner as an outsider who had meddled in Meridian's "private business." He told them he would have killed Schwerner himself if someone else had not beaten him to it. He was a man troubled by his past, yet not far removed from his old approach to conflict. He spoke violently about his former colleagues in the Klan, using language sure to anger them when they began to see him as a turncoat.

At the motel one night after dark, while the MDSers were sleeping, someone who had just rented a motel room called the office to tell Mr. Byrd that the plumbing system was not working. He went to check the room, and when he opened the door he saw three men in white sheets. It was too late to run. They beat him mercilessly. Eventually he left the state.

For a moment let me jump ahead more than a decade. Floyd Bender of Springs, Pennsylvania, had been part of the MDS group in Meridian. To his surprise, one day someone looking a bit familiar stopped at his home. It was Mr. Byrd, who had seen the name Bender on the mailbox and stopped to see if this Floyd Bender was the same man who had stayed in his motel a decade earlier. Mr. Byrd had moved north and become a worker on a crew that maintained the power lines. The lines of human relationships and the influence of MDSers reach far and deep.

Another event that occurred during the reconstruction of the Mount Pleasant Church building will explain how walking with Lawrence Scott changed my life. Feeling the tension in the community rising, I asked Scott to come and help with communications. I clearly remember our visit to a local country service station, which had a small food store attached.

Scott's approach was direct: "Some volunteers have come to help the church members put up their church building that was burned. We are not troublemakers. We are just going to help. We need *your* help. Please pass the word around in the community."

It was clear to me that they had been "passing around" the word, the wrong kind of word. However, within days I could feel the tension lessening. Scott believed that if we hide from people what we are doing, they probably imagine the worst. He believed it best to be up front with our convictions and intentions. He taught me the value of transparency.

1964 was not the first period when a stream of people came through our VS home, but at that time Lawrence Scott helped bring together a wide variety of people with a wide variety of theological persuasions, even some with little theological persuasion. I distinctly remember one Monday evening when thirty-three people had gathered in our VS home for dinner. Among them were VSers, Mennonite MDSers and Norman Walsh, a Quaker teacher from New York. Present also were eight students and two faculty members from Notre Dame. Father Alcuin, the local chaplain at St. Joseph Hospital, was also there. Today I can still see him, dressed in his ministerial robe, lying on the floor playing with our daughters Anita and Maria, who were one and four years old.

That same week rumors circulated that the Notre Dame students, who were helping rebuild churches, had really come to join a march from Selma to Montgomery, Alabama. Our phone rang frequently with less than friendly messages. My greatest challenge was keeping the irate callers on the phone long enough to help them understand that the students—and we—did not have horns. Some callers ended up being quite civil.

In 1964 and 1965 a miracle seemed to be occurring before our eyes. For a brief time we were able to move beyond our religious and political differences. MDSers, college students, and a growing variety of volunteers put their bodies on the line to rebuild what had been destroyed by the fires of fear and bitterness. These volunteers, cooperating with the Committee of Concern, worked as a team to heal wounds. In some small way all of us helped make Mississippi a bit safer and a more just place to live. Had it not been for walking with Lawrence Scott, our family would have missed these deep relationships with a wide variety of people who, in their own ways, cared deeply about a better life for all people. Scott helped our family believe we could dream and work alongside others without first untangling all of the theological differences that could have torn us apart.

It was inevitable that as our family's relationship with the Freedom Movement and more intimate relationships with people of various races and religious persuasions grew, tensions would arise. To relate with people as equals without social barriers was seen by some as threatening their way of life.

Our family experienced this in 1964, during what seemed to us to be just an everyday natural human event. The property that would later become Pine Lake Fellowship Camp near Meridian had been purchased by a number of persons. It had a seven-acre lake and an amphitheater-shaped spot at the front of the property that was ideal for picnics. One

Saturday a close friend, Rev. Porter, a local African American pastor, offered to bring meat to barbecue for our two families in the picnic area. While we were eating, two local teenagers—part of our youth group at Fellowship Mennonite Church—came by with their mother to swim in the lake.

We saw them walk by, but more significantly they saw the Porter and Bender families enjoying a barbecue together. I expected *some* flak because their mother had made racist remarks, but I was unprepared for what happened the following day. By then she had contacted all the local persons who attended Fellowship Mennonite Church, filling their minds with doubts about us. Except for the VSers, only one native Mississippian came the next day to the church service. She was Kathy White, the daughter of Velma and "Dusty," of whom I spoke earlier. To our relief, the members and most of those who were part of our regular group returned in due time.

(Incidentally, Rev. Porter was Gerald Hudson's pastor at that time. Gerald was a former student and faculty member in the Social Work Department at EMU. He is now a pastor in his home city of Meridian.)

I seldom felt fear of physical danger in Mississippi, but sometimes I did experience a great deal of stress over the possibility that white persons who had confidence in us would withdraw because of fear and misunderstanding. Standing with people who have been marginalized—when others whom one loves disagree—caused me to have a recurring dream of preaching in our church with nothing on but a very short T-shirt, behind a skimpy pulpit. I kept trying to make my T-shirt reach.

MCC Peace Section "Representative in the South"

In November of 1966 Edgar Metzler invited me to be the "Peace Representative in the South" for the MCC Peace Section. For the rest of our Mississippi years I spent part time as the pastor of the Fellowship Mennonite Church in Meridian and the rest of my time with the MCC Peace Section. I also became a member of the Advisory Board of the Delta Ministry, sponsored by the National Council of Churches. Those associated with this Ministry had come to Mississippi to work alongside participants in Freedom Summer in 1964 and had remained to stand with the ethnic minorities in their struggle for justice in achieving voting, economic, educational and political rights. Their sense of call to challenge injustice in the larger society stimulated us to broaden our view of God's call for us.

Before taking leave of the Mississippi era of our journey, I must return for a moment to Vincent Harding's role as my mentor. He helped our family understand that every injustice is unavoidably related to every other injustice. For example, soon after a book by Felix Greene, entitled *Vietnam, Vietnam,* was published, he gave Ann and me a copy. Atrocities, which were far too common in that conflict, were made graphic in that photograph-filled book. Our hearts sickened; we resolved to do our small part to see that war ended. Vincent believed one in good conscience could not work against racism in Mississippi and ignore the fact that African American young men were being recruited for Vietnam because there were almost no other opportunities for them in Mississippi. They were sent to do violence in Vietnam in the name of "freedom" while those with greater economic privileges often avoided being drafted. Even after our move to Virginia, Vincent and Rosemarie continued to be crucial in our lives. They came to EMU several times to share with the campus community. They sent occasional books that stimulated us profoundly. Octavia Butler's *Parable of the Sower* was painful to read because of its reminder that unless justice becomes available for everyone, eventually all of us will pay a tragic price.

Then in 1996 Brother Vincent sent us a copy of his new book, *Martin Luther King: The Inconvenient Hero.* In the book he described Dr. King as having moved well beyond focusing on desegregation in public accommodations. He recognized that without economic justice there would be no lasting change. Racism and class were part of the same cancer in our communities. I never met Dr. King. However, through my brother Vincent, my life was profoundly changed by the spirit and beliefs of Dr. King.

Our family had intended to spend the rest of our lives in our adopted state of Mississippi. However, the Conservative Conference was not ready to accept local families such as Velma White and her extended family, who had put their lives on the line, as potential leaders in our congregation. It seemed clear to us that the Conservative Mennonite Conference dream of a "transplanted" church would not be a congregation where Ann and I could be true to our faith. Only because of Mark

Peachey, Secretary of the Mission Board of our conference, were we able to serve at Fellowship Mennonite Church in good conscience as long as we did. He understood our convictions far better than many of his contemporaries in the Conference.

It was during our eleven years in Mississippi and experiences since that we found our deep appreciation for our Anabaptist roots faced with a challenge. Church-related institutions, like all institutions, feel pressures to search for "smooth sailing." Potentially this can lead us in the name of peace to resist Jesus' call to justice for all until a "more convenient time."

Subsequently our family moved to New Orleans, where I entered the Tulane School of Social Work.

Three Tulane Years

I intended to get a Master's degree in social work and then to move back to Mississippi where Ann and I would work according to our convictions at the community level. One of my professors at Tulane was Kate Mullen, a former nun, who had worked in the field of probation before she came to Tulane. I remember telling her of my disappointment with some aspects of the Mennonite denomination, aware that I was speaking with someone whose journey with the Catholic Church had involved some stress. Her question to me was teasing, "If your church was so bad, how did you turn out like you did?" Did I forget to tell you she was biased?

She encouraged me to continue for my doctorate and prepare for teaching in the field of social work. She also gave a boost to my growing interest in the area of corrections.

Four Years at the University of Oklahoma

At the university in Norman, Oklahoma, I accepted an offer to teach in the graduate program in the School of Social Work. The reasons? I trusted the Dean, and I wanted to begin teaching where there was a large, diverse faculty from whom I could learn. Among about fifteen full-time, on-campus faculty members in our School, Ronald Lewis was Cherokee, Elgie Raymond was Sioux, Danny Ho was Chinese and Nadine Roach was African-American. In addition to teaching, I worked with the Dean of the School of Social Work at a satellite program in a Cheyenne-Arapaho community.

Another experience kept us in Norman four years longer than we had anticipated. Nadine Roach, the faculty colleague I just mentioned, invited our family to her church in nearby Oklahoma City, where Ann and I not only ended up singing regularly in the choir with her, but we also became members of that congregation, Trinity Mennonite Presbyterian Church, which had about an equal number of African-American and white members. It had a full time Presbyterian pastor, Jim Defriend, and a half-time Mennonite pastor, Stan Smucker. The dialogue was sometimes vigorous, yet respectful. I was ordained an Elder, which for Presbyterians is a lifetime call.

While in Oklahoma, we felt a strong pull toward a stronger relationship with our roots through an unexpected source. Our family went to see the movie *Fiddler on the Roof.* You may remember the scene in which Tevya struggled with the issue of accepting his third son-in-law to be. He and Tevya's third daughter wanted Tevya's blessing for their marriage. However, this future son-in-law belonged to the Russian Orthodox Church, a church that was persecuting Tevya's own people, the Jews. In a style that for him had become routine, Tevya began his soliloquy, "On the one hand...but on the other hand." Suddenly he stopped in his tracks and shrieked, "No, there is no other hand. If I bend any farther I will break." *I heard him!* I asked myself if I was having more tolerance for Tevya than for my fellow Mennonites.

I came to believe that in my teaching I dared never purposely encourage a student to abandon a religious position lightly. While holding to a belief that has served as a "rock on which to stand," one dare not step off that rock until finding a more secure one. I resolved to urge students to find a more secure basis for conviction before abandoning ways of believing that had kept them from losing their way.

By the same token this stance faces a faculty member with a dilemma. What if sometimes in my teaching I would be expected by my community of faith to accept a position that would cause me to participate in what I was convinced was oppression. Might I lose my inner soul? This is the paradox Ann and I have needed to learn to live with from our days in Mississippi to the present.

At Eastern Mennonite University this dilemma came into sharp focus. In the early 1980s I became closely acquainted with lesbian and gay students who experienced rejection by the institution at which I taught.

My and Ann's choice became clear, walk with them as fellow travelers of faith or turn our backs on everything to which we had given our lives.

Our Harrisonburg and New Hope Years

I returned to teach at Eastern Mennonite College/University in 1976. We moved to Harrisonburg, wanting our children to understand their roots from the perspective of living in a "regular" Mennonite community. For Ann and me our vocations and our fellowship with colleagues and fellow members at Lindale Mennonite Church have been rewarding. In one sense our whole family felt as though we had come home again. However, we intended to return to Mississippi after a few years.

In Virginia our vocational calls found fertile soil for making some small contribution in the community. Ann has worked to strengthen community-based services for older persons so that they can stay as involved in the community as long as feasible. My focus in the field of social work has been to help create community-based services that enable incarcerated people with addictions to re-enter the community successfully. For this to happen both residents of the program and community members need to learn to reach out to each other.

In addition, both Ann and I have found ways to relate to the political arena for the purpose of planting seeds that will grow in making our communities more healing places for vulnerable people to live meaningful lives. Some feel the call to work for change at the national and international levels. We have found our niche at the state level. Gemeinschaft Home now has seven to eight years of experience as a pilot program with The Virginia Department of Corrections. The Department welcomed independent research to test the proposition that a transition home in a welcoming local community will enable a greater percentage of ex-prisoners to stay out of prison, save funds in the long run, and result in restored lives. From the cooperative research between James Madison University and the Virginia Department of Corrections, the Department has become convinced that Gemeinschaft Home is effective. The "ripple effect" has already given rise to a similar program in the Roanoke area. To me this seems Anabaptist. Lighting a candle in one place can encourage the lighting of candles in other places, which gradually helps transform a revenge-oriented response to addiction into one based on restoring human relationships that have been broken.

Epilogue

As I look back over our family's journey from Mississippi, to New Orleans, to Norman, Oklahoma, to Harrisonburg and New Hope, Virginia, there is a thread that ties our family's journey together. We have become sisters and brothers with a wide variety of persons and groups who invited us to share their lives. In walking with them, we have been transformed. We constantly relate what we learn in this walk to an ever-emerging understanding of who Jesus of Nazareth was and how Jesus calls us to live today in love, justice and peace.

Sometimes these persons with whom our lives have become intertwined have been those whom we saw as being treated as less than full human beings. Each situation began with specific persons who invited our friendship and understanding and gave us theirs. They stretched our hearts and changed our lives. Arenas of exclusion have been on the basis of a wide variety of issues. These have included ethnicity, differences in income levels, religious differences, homelessness, incarceration, supposed "physical attractiveness" or the opposite, same gender sexual orientation, or differences in formal educational level. To us the presence of oppression always feels the same. It comes as a "slap in the face" whenever and wherever we encounter it.

As in the lives of many of us, walking the path of opening our hearts to those who seem very different from us can sometimes feel risky. We have come to believe that we are taking Jesus of Nazareth seriously, only if we walk that path.

April 2005

PART III

...in the University and Society

SAMUEL L. HORST

Reminiscences of an Eighty-six Year-old

Paternal and Maternal Background

My Swiss-German paternal ancestors migrated to the province of Pennsylvania in English Colonial America in the 1730s and settled in the Groffdale area of the Conestoga Valley of Lancaster County. As agrarian people they sought land to continue their way of life.

Ancestor Henry Horst moved to Franklin County, Pennsylvania, in the 1830s. His son, my great grandfather Levi Horst, married Anna Lehman of Franklin County. Levi was an active Chambersburg Mennonite Church layman in the mid-19th century. Their daughter Catharine witnessed and wrote the story of her family's Civil War experiences, including her father's confrontations with Confederate officers when their troops moved into the Cumberland Valley in 1863.

My maternal ancestors, also of Swiss-German origin, migrated like my paternal ancestors to the province of Pennsylvania in English Colonial America in the early 18th century, settled in Lancaster County, and proceeded to continue their agrarian way of life. Andrew Hershey emigrated in 1719, and it was his descendants who later settled in the Pequea Valley of Lancaster County. One of Joseph Hershey's (1816–1891) children, Catherine, was my grandmother (1847–1918).

Parents

My father, Elmer Kuhns Horst, was born in Franklin County, Pennsylvania, near Chambersburg on September 29, 1890. He along with some other Franklin County Mennonite young men spent time in the Denbigh-Fentress area of Virginia, where George R. Brunk, I, and other

Mennonites, including Mennonite young women, attracted them to this Tidewater region. However, several of these men, including my father, later went to Lancaster and courted young women there. Catherine (Hershey) Buckwalter, a widow whose sons had died but who had four surviving daughters, moved with them to East Orange Street in Lancaster. My father's favorite was Katie, the youngest of the four; and on May 14, 1914, the two were married. I never knew my maternal grandmother, Catherine Buckwalter, since she died in 1918, more than a year before I was born on July 18, 1919.

In January 1921 my parents moved from Lancaster to a small farm just across the Lancaster County line into Berks County, Pennsylvania. My oldest brother, Irvin, remembers the cold day that we moved. He tried to keep warm by sitting between Father and Uncle John Lehman on the team-wagon seat for the twenty-four miles from Lancaster to the farm just beyond Adamstown. Mother, Aunt Amanda (her oldest sister), my older brothers Paul, Elmer and I traveled by trolley car to our new home, an old log house on the old Mosemann farm. The trolley line between Lancaster and Reading was down the road and across the creek from our new home. Sadly, my brother Elmer drowned at the age of three in this creek. Joy came, however, with the birth of six more children, first three sons, then two daughters, and finally another son. Kathryn died when she was also three, leaving her younger sister, Orpah, to fend for herself among seven brothers.

Childhood and Youth

Work and Recreation

A farm always has work to do, such as plowing, hoeing, cultivating, doing chores in the barn, picking raspberries and cherries, and turning the milk separator. Our truck farm produced market crops and butter, eggs, cottage and cup cheese, and *fasnachts*, all of which we took to the Reading Bingaman Street Market. I keenly remember rising very early to go to market on Tuesday and Saturday and sometimes Thursday mornings of these depression years. I often went there with Abe Gehman, a neighborhood baker, to help unload his freshly baked wares or with Lemon Youndt, a local town butcher, to help him unload his fresh meat. I also remember going with Noah Musser on his Friday peddling routes to Reading's suburbs. I remember especially well our own peddling of products, which we sold in nearby Adamstown.

We boys did have time for recreational activities, such as fishing and swimming in the nude in the pond behind the bushes, where father sometimes joined us. I went trapping regularly for fur bearing animals, especially skunks (the less white the more valuable), muskrats, weasels (on which there was a bounty) and the least valuable, possums. We would skin the carcasses for their pelts, stretch them over boards to dry out, and sell them to the fur buyers who stopped by. When I later related such experiences to my children, they could hardly understand how their gentle father could be so cruel to these animals. How could I?

School

I began attending elementary school at age six in 1925 in the one-room Stavers School in neighboring Lancaster County, where Cora Harding was my teacher for three years. We children respected her as a good teacher. Unfortunately, however, she gave me the only punishment I ever received in school. She paddled me one day when I was, I believe, in the second grade. With her permission I had gone to the outdoor toilet. Somehow she saw me making gestures that I had observed other students make but the meaning of which I did not understand. My next younger brother, who died less than a year ago, told me that I had not been the only one who cried; he had also. His comment gave me a better feeling about him.

Because we actually lived in Berks County, we were eventually required to change to a Berks County school. In those years we had never heard of school-bus transportation. We walked the two miles every day to and from our one-room Trostles School, where for the fourth grade and beyond I had three different teachers. The one I had for the last three years was elderly Cyrus Fasnacht, who frequently spent time talking about his deceased wife. He was the least effective of my elementary school teachers. Still I learned enough to receive the highest score on the Brecknock Township's final examination for my school and the second highest in the township's six one-room schools. High school, however, was not in the cards for me since my father did not favor my attending a public high school.

Finding My Way

Factory Work and Night School

By 1933 we were deep into the Great Depression. Although we always had ample food and adequate clothing during the early depression from 1929 to 1933, when I was fourteen I was expected to bring home money to help support the family. I began by getting employment at the Fein & Glass shoe factory in Reading and started at twenty cents an hour. After three months I was put on piecework, where I usually made less because we soon worked ourselves out of steady hours, especially as the factory orders declined. Not until the foreman, Joseph Knutt, chose me as his handy man did I have more steady work and income. The factory seemed almost empty at times as I threw shoe lasts into size bins and completed other assignments.

It was on one of these days when the floor was empty and even the foreman was out that a recent employee of Greek background suddenly came in. He had noticed that my older brother Paul, who had formerly worked at Fein & Glass and was now working at Berkshire Knitting Mills, was continuing to go there to work even though a strike was in progress (being what was called a "scab"). The young Greek man, who was now a striker there, assumed that I like my brother would also come to work during a strike. Actually by this time Paul and I were forming different views about strikers during the depression. I was beginning to have more sympathy for the strikers' cause than my brother Paul and may likely have not persisted in coming to work as he was doing. The young Greek had no patience for my explanation but immediately socked me in my face and ran out of the building as fast as he could go. When my foreman returned and saw my swollen face, he asked what had happened. Hearing about my experience, he wanted to report the situation, but I urged him not to. I was apparently already serious about my pacifist beliefs, although I may not have felt so peaceful toward my brother.

When I was seventeen, through the help of May Knauer, a city member of our Reading Mennonite congregation, I secured work at the Nolde & Horst Hosiery Mill, where I made slightly higher wages. I worked there for another two and one-half years, frequently parking the car I was driving in front of Reading's Socialist Mayor Stumpf's simple row house on Oley Street. While working at Nolde & Horst, I began taking classes at the Reading Standard Evening High School and eventually rented a room located between the mill and the school. It was a convenient arrangement although during successive winters I missed many class sessions because of repeated attacks of bronchitis.

After my employment ended at Nolde & Horst, I continued to attend night school sessions, driving into Reading from home. Another of our city church members, Margaret Curtier, was also attending night school; so I dropped by the private home in the suburb where she worked and took her along. I never dated this young, devoted Christian girl, who, as I look back, no doubt wondered why my brothers and I seldom dated and never married any of the girls who were converted and joined our church in Reading. We surely valued them as "converts" but never considered them as candidates for marriage. No wonder Margaret later joined a Church of God congregation and married a member there.

Faith Development

I was already finding my way as an individual by entering employment and resuming school. I remained within the parameters of my church and background influences, although I hesitated making a personal commitment to accept Christ and become a church member until I was fifteen. One Sunday evening at a regular church service, rather than in a revival series, I took the plunge when our pastor, John W. Hess, gave the invitation. I stood in response without pressure and all alone. I did not find it a highly emotional event, but it was a decisive step in my spiritual journey, during which I had at times doubts and fears as well as reassuring faith. From this time on I felt free to be outgoing concerning my faith in my own limited way in my employment and educational situations.

As a member of what was then our city mission congregation, I was active in various church service roles such as a Sunday school teacher, superintendent, and committee member. In fact, I was placed in the lot for minister. Fortunately, the slip was not in the book that I chose. I never regretted that a younger brother was ordained instead of myself. Although the Reading Mennonite Girls' Home matron, Margaret Horst, pressed me to consider leading a small Mennonite congregation in Montana, I declined. I was really interested in acquiring a college education and teaching.

During the years after factory employment, I sold Fuller brushes and was a night watchman on a Chester County, Pennsylvania, turkey farm. (Yes, I did carry a gun to shoot at prowling animals.) Later I was a wholesale truck driver for Royer's Bakery in Denver in Lancaster County. I little relished the brush-salesman role although it provided more income than before. My younger brother Leon got into it through me later, and his more enterprising style enabled him to enjoy it and to make it more profitable.

World War II

World War II broke out in 1939. I was working in Chester County in 1940 when I was required to register in the first draft of the war, which I did in October. Although I was hoping to attend college, the draft registration caused a delay in such plans as I waited to be called. However, as the months in my second year of waiting rolled by without a call, I decided to begin college and enrolled at EMC in September 1942. Then, two years after my registration, the call came, which required me to report in mid-October. Since my Christian commitment eight years earlier had directed me to register as a conscientious objector, I received a 4E classification. Dean Chester K. Lehman offered to get me a deferment if I chose to pursue a college Bible major. However, I decided against this choice and reported instead to my draft board at Phoenixville, Chester County.

My railroad travel to the Civilian Service Camp on the Blue Ridge above Luray was blocked by raging floods, which had washed out bridges below Hagerstown. I stayed with nearby relatives until Mennonite neighbors improvised travel via automobile to get all of us who were on that stranded train to camp. I arrived there on October 17, 1942. Living in the camp dormitory provided opportunities to become acquainted with other CPS men, and working in the natural environment had advantages. However, hearing about the urgent need for men at hospitals, I gradually sensed that National Park Service work was hardly as urgent. I requested a reassignment and was sent to serve at the Greystone Park State Mental Hospital near Morristown, New Jersey.

This was indeed a needy place. Assigned to the Reception Building, I began working without any orientation. There I aided in the admitting of incoming patients in varied conditions. Sometimes I worked on Ward 8, the male disturbed ward, where Mr. Gleason kept tight control over potentially violent patients. Most frequently I served on Ward 10, the regular admission ward, where ambulatory and some bed patients were temporarily placed before their assignment to a more permanent ward in the institution. During the day, most ambulatory patients sat in the large day room, where we employees were expected to oversee them. Most appeared relatively relaxed, although we needed to be ready for any eventuality. On this ward we actually worked hard at tasks that included carrying bedpans and cleaning up after incontinent patients. On the whole, I thought my efforts at this hospital were more urgently needed than working along the Skyline Drive and clearing mountain trails.

One day as I was walking out of the day room, a disturbed young man in a camisole came up from behind me and kicked me extremely hard in a sensitive spot with his pointed shoes, forcing me to report to the Clinic Building for medical care for a day or two. Upon my return I spoke with the calmed down young man and asked him why he had attacked me. He replied that at the time he had thought that I was the devil.

After nearly two years at this indoor work I realized that my respiratory weakness called for my return to outdoor work, so I requested a transfer. I was assigned to the Soil Conservation Camp at Grottoes, Virginia. Eventually an appeal was made for men to volunteer to transfer to the National Forest Service camp at North Fork, California, to be available for fire fighting. Sensing this as a more urgent task than digging post holes in Virginia, I agreed to accept the assignment to be the leader of the first of two Pullman car-loads of men to make the transfer to the Sierra Nevada camp above Fresno. Sometime after arrival I was assigned for the summer to a two-man side camp higher up in the mountains along the San Joaquin River below its sources at Huntington Lake for standby fighting of lightning fires in the high Sierras. We could stay there only until September to avoid being caught in the later mountain snows that would prevent our return to North Fork. Gradually we moved down toward base camp as we fought fires and checked deer brought in by hunters. Back in base camp I worked at the experimental plots near the camp and at Bass Lake. Later, when the North Camp was to be closed, I was assigned to the camp at Powellsville, Maryland, to serve my remaining time in CPS. I was released on April 13, 1946.

Romance and Family Development

I had noticed Elizabeth Good, who was employed at a Wyomissing upper-class suburban home, when she came to Sunday church services at Reading. Her personality and demeanor continued to attract my attention. Early in 1944 when I was home on furlough from my CPS duty in New Jersey and working at a local greenhouse, I called her to ask for a date. She agreed, and we met at her place of employment. She proved to be a delightful friend, was patient with me as a slow suitor, and was a faithful letter writer especially when I was transferred to California. After I had worked through the remainder of my CPS service at Greystone Park, Grottoes, North Fork and Powellsville, we were happy to be with each other more regularly. Since she also had college in mind, we came to EMC together for the 1946 to 1948 college years. We were engaged in the summer of 1947, and Elizabeth completed a two-year program by the spring of 1948.

Immediately after commencement my friend Lowell Nissley proposed that we travel to Florida to purchase house trailers for sale from people who had wintered there. We filled our cars with friends, including Ivan Magal, a student from southeast Europe who had fled via Budapest, Hungary, to the U.S., and Ada Zimmerman, the Dean of Women. It was a fun trip just prior to our wedding. Elizabeth and I traveled in one car and Lowell and his wife Miriam in the other while the others settled into the remaining passenger seats. Ada Zimmerman "let her hair down," so to speak, and became one of us. However, even though it was convenient to have trailer homes for the summer, it proved unwise of us to pull them to Pennsylvania and west to Goshen, Indiana, to where Lowell also was moving and where there were trailer factories.

Two weeks after we returned from Florida, Elizabeth and I were married on the open lawn at Elizabeth's home; and we moved across the road into our trailer, which her father and her brothers had helped to set up before our wedding. The day after our wedding we headed out on our honeymoon to a delightful private lake site in southern New Jersey, owned by some of Elizabeth's uncles.

When we went swimming the first day, Elizabeth dived in first and swam out into the deeper water. Suddenly in trouble as she tried to turn back, she began to sink and waved at me desperately. Meanwhile, thinking these were just friendly signals, I, still on the bank, simply waved back. Only when it dawned on me that she was signaling for help did I dive in to rescue her. Don't ask me how I succeeded in doing so. I only remember that I did bring her safely to the shore. However, our remaining honeymoon days were delightful as we went boating and fishing and hiked along the lake.

We returned to our trailer home and after the short summer pulled it out to Goshen College. There we worked and studied through the academic year and the summer session, and I graduated with a BA. During our time there, when President John R. Mumaw was on campus from EMC, he asked us to come to EMC for me to teach in the High School Department. We decided to accept his invitation and took our trailer back to Virginia, where we situated ourselves in Park Woods among other house trailer neighbors. Then, needing a little more space after our Kenneth was born, we sold the trailer to Walter Hartman and rented an apartment in the home of Betty Mosemann.

I left teaching after two years; and we moved to the attractive Oley Valley, where I carried on a self-operated business in which I was able to improve our family income. At the same time I appreciated learning about the rich history of this valley, where Moravians and French Huguenots had settled in the 17th century. There our family grew with the birth of our first daughter, Hannah, and we enjoyed working with the local Mennonite congregation.

Intellectual and Career Development

Pressed to return to EMC in 1954, I was assigned the same high school classes that I had taught earlier. I relished teaching and had good success in these classes. I fondly remembered one of my three required senior American Government sections, in which I had several of the more intellectually endowed seniors. It was a delight to carry on discussions at a higher level and to have one of them stay after class to request more reading than I had required.

I was soon able to pursue graduate studies in the summers toward an MA in history. My 1961–62 sabbatical year gave me the option of continuing my MA studies at the American University in Washington, DC. Here, taking residency courses on campus and at the university's downtown center near the White House, I was close to the rich resources of the National Archives and the Library of Congress. My desire was to search Confederate military records to dig out all I could find on the Virginia Mennonites in the Civil War years, an interest encouraged by guiding professor, Arthur A. Ekirch, who approved this subject for my MA thesis.

I want to note that in all of my graduate studies we as a family moved together. Elizabeth's letters to her family reveal our interesting family experiences and hold our fond memories of these sojourns.

We moved back to our country home in the Valley in August 1962, and I resumed teaching. I took every opportunity I could to travel to Washington to press on with my research, usually staying two or three days at a time, working through stacks of Confederate military records and walking over to Library of Congress to search relevant materials. I spent many days reading the individual claims made to the Southern Claims Commission by individuals as the endnotes to my 1967 published book, *Mennonites in the Confederacy: A Study in Civil War Pacifism*, revealed. A second printing followed in 1969.

It was the notes in which I cited the claims made by numerous individuals to the Claims Commission that led David Rodes and Norman Wenger to proceed to obtain all of the claims made by Rockingham residents for publication. I remember their concern about not getting the kind of support they needed to get them published. It was at this juncture that I appealed to individuals who were organizing the Valley Brethren-Mennonite Heritage Center and urged them to hear David's and Norman's appeal. Their appeal was eventually heard. However, the strenuous work of these two men continues as they travel and work away at this laborious and on-going task in their spare time.

As a college history teacher I broadened the perspectives of history to make students aware that the term *American* is, in its real sense, much broader than the traditional scope of study, which begins with the coming of Europeans to South and North America. I included a study of the civilizations and peoples of much earlier centuries in South and Mesoamerica, as well as in North America, and emphasized the life and culture of reds and blacks as well as whites. In these years I planned many special required class trips to Philadelphia for Colonial America, to Washington, DC, for 20th Century America and American Government and Introduction to Politics, and to other sites for Nineteenth-Century America and Afro-American History and Culture. Often we took in an appropriate play or movie. These were the good old days in the old Administration Building, where some of us took packed lunches to the large room in the north end of that building; and along with Anna Showalter, Anna Frey, Grant Stoltzfus, John Lapp and others, we ate, told stories and laughed together. I can still hear John Lapp's unique laugh sounding through the hallways. Some of our classes met in the south end of this old building, many of them in the large room with windows on the west side, surrounded by our offices on the east and south sides.

In 1967 I applied for David Donald's offer of a Fellowship at Johns Hopkins University and was accepted. Moving as a family to Baltimore, we settled in on the edge of the racial divide and within walking distance of the university. That same year Mary and Carol began first grade with both black and white students in the nearby public school. Our other children were also attending public schools in various parts of the city. I remember keenly that as Carol and Mary would tell us about their school day, we parents waited with some anxiety to hear them identify their individual friends by race; but at first we did not ask. Finally, when we did question them about whether a specific child was white or black, we discovered that they did not really know their classmate's color. Thus we learned a much-needed lesson from our youngest children.

Professor and Fellowship Director Donald greeted me with a copy of my just published *Mennonites in the Confederacy* for me to autograph. The well-endowed Fellowship was for a full academic year and was later extended through the summer. Of the twenty selected Fellows, ten black and ten white, from southern states, I was the only one from Virginia. We were there for a reading-discussion program led by Professor Donald. In addition, he brought in top scholars in the field of racial and social history of the eighteenth and nineteenth century USA. We were also encouraged to take another university course, and I took one offered by the leading eighteenth-century historian, Professor Jack Greene. Tragically, during our time in Baltimore, Martin Luther King was murdered in Memphis. Riots broke out in the city, and restrictions were imposed on leaving from and arriving into the city.

My hope was to study in a PhD program with Professor Willie Lee Rose at the University of Virginia. She had produced her award winning *Rehearsal for Reconstruction: The Port Royal Experiment*, a model study of black reconstruction during the Civil War. I was interested in researching a similar subject on Virginia's blacks. Since Professor Donald's recommendations for my study at UVA were effective, as were my contacts with Professor Rose, we moved from Baltimore to Charlottesville for the next four years, September 1968 through August 1972. There, studying for my graduate courses, learning the two required languages, and preparing for my oral examination were a challenge.

Meanwhile Elizabeth was attracted to a program managed by a member of the Mennonite congregation, a program that provided work for disabled persons. She enjoyed relating to these people until the manager consented to take on a project making tiny parts for missiles. This Elizabeth could not conscientiously do since she would as she stated it, "be teaching disabled persons to make parts for missiles that would disable more people." She was dismissed by her Mennonite employer and maintained a clear conscience. I was very proud of her. Fortunately, Byard Deputy, another member of the congregation and UVA professor of dentistry and now VMRC resident, was instrumental in securing Elizabeth a position as a home economist in the University's Children and Youth program, which she filled ably.

As my oral examinations loomed closer, I diligently prepared for them. When that crucial evening arrived, three professors in my several fields and Professor Rose sat in the room with me and probed me diligently for a few hours. Then I stepped out and paced the hall while they discussed my fate. I was aware that several candidates had recently failed. Although not overconfident, I felt reasonably secure, although at this point I was hardly at ease. A load lifted when they called me in to inform me of my success. Of course, the task of writing my dissertation was still ahead.

We then moved back to the Valley after our five-year absence, where I continued working on my dissertation as much as I could while resuming teaching. Most of our daughters returned with us. Kenneth was attending UVA, and Hannah, Goshen College, while Sylvia was about to begin at EMC. In 1977 I sat for the exam on my dissertation and later received my PhD in absentia since at that time Elizabeth and I were traveling with the Schleitheim discussion group to Anabaptist places in Western Europe. In our hotels we carried on discussions on the significance of Anabaptism, and those of us from a Swiss-German background had our insights broadened by the intense informal and larger group discussions with group members from a Russian-German orientation.

Post Graduate Teaching, Study and Writing

My further studies and the Schleitheim group experiences broadened my teaching perspectives still further. In addition, I sought to help students become sensitive to national and international human rights concerns as I led in the development of an Amnesty International Chapter on campus and helped to plan trips to university campuses for Model UN sessions. I served as the faculty sponsor for the EMC AI Chapter during my remaining years of teaching as successive student committees carried it on. I also served on the Public Occasions Committee and as its chairperson. Among our visiting speakers were Alex Haley, John Howard Griffin, Max Lerner and Joseph Washington.

While teaching, I was asked to chair a three-person writing project with the late Robert Ulle and Richard MacMaster. All three of us did research and writing with MacMaster, who had a freer schedule to finalize the writing. This resulted in the 1979 publication of *Conscience in Crisis: Mennonites and Other Peace Churches in America, 1739–1789*, which became No. 20 in the *Studies in Anabaptist and Mennonite History*. As for my PhD dissertation, I declined reworking it for publication because of the pressure of my teaching load at EMC. Other scholars meanwhile published on the general subject; and when a publisher eagerly sought to have it published, I consented. Thus *Education for Manhood: The Education of Blacks in Virginia during the Civil War* was belatedly published after other works appeared. Richard MacMaster's review of this work in the *Mennonite Quarterly Review* (July 1989, 312–313) provides an insightful assessment of it.

It was also in 1979 that I was awarded two National Endowment for the Humanities Summer Grants for College Teachers. One was to join Bell Irvin Wiley, who called me personally to invite me into his seminar on "The American South, 1800–1865: Slavery, Secession and Civil War" at Emory University in Georgia. This was a tempting offer for me because of my interest in and work on those years. A day or two later I was called from Bloomington, Indiana, and informed that I had been accepted into Walter Nugent's seminar on "Social Change in the United States, 1865–1915." Now I faced a hard choice. Since Nugent's seminar concentrated on the shift from the frontier-rural to industrial-urban society between the Civil War and World War I, I was especially interested in his seminar because of its relevance to the Mennonite experience of transition from agrarian to urban situations, and I also chose Professor Nugent's seminar for several additional reasons. One was because of its more liberal financial considerations and another because I was already discovering the sources behind the Jacob Eschbach Yoder story. I had discovered Yoder while I was working on my dissertation and plowing through the Freedmen's Bureau records in the National Archives; I was trying to keep him on the back burner until I had time to pursue him.

During the late 1970s and early 1980s, when I learned that Yoder was from a Mennonite family at Gilbertsville in Montgomery County, Pennsylvania, I was hooked. How had he ever become a Freedmen teacher in Lynchburg, Virginia? Tracing his correspondence in the Freedmen's Bureau records, then learning from one of his granddaughters that he had left a diary, and still later visiting a grandson who had a trove of varied materials left by Yoder and his family, I plowed ahead in my research and writing. After I had worked through his diary and the other rich materials, I found out that the publication branch of the Virginia State Library was planning to publish the diary. When I informed them of what I had already done, they directed me to continue my work as the editor and said that they would publish it. Serious state budget cuts by successive governors delayed its publication until 1996.

Creative Retirement

I retired at age sixty-five in 1984, and after a year of part-time teaching I decided that I would be more satisfied freeing myself to engage in other pursuits. I still had several research interests especially pertaining to the Shenandoah Valley of Virginia and the Cumberland Valley of Maryland and Pennsylvania. After I began scratching around in the latter on my Horst family background, I was asked to research the Mennonite history of the area more broadly, which I agreed to do. Meanwhile, in 1988 Elizabeth and I were invited to join an MCC group, one of the four sponsored by the National Council of Churches, that traveled to Soviet Russia in commemoration of the millennium of the coming of Christianity to tenth century Russia. In these waning years of the Soviet Union, we visited, presented our cordial greetings and worshipped with Orthodox Churches in Moscow, Kiev, Odessa and Leningrad (presently St. Petersburg) and on St. Sergius Day the fourteenth-century St. Sergius monastery, a place of pilgrimage.

As I pursued the history of Mennonites in Washington County, Maryland, and Franklin County, Pennsylvania, I soon realized the significance of the well-kept records of Washington County's strong bishop and leader, Moses Horst. However, I was strongly warned by Franklin County churchmen that these records in the custody of his grandson, Oliver Martin, would not be available. My persistent efforts proved otherwise, thanks to the wise advice of a Washington County layman and careful and cordial contacts with custodian Martin. He eventually offered me the opportunity to research his grandfather's church records in a side room in his home under the condition that they not be photocopied. Ada, his wife, invited me to eat lunch with them and also supper, since I worked into the evenings over many extended weeks of painstaking notetaking. Oliver was highly respectful of his grandfather and was careful not to brainwash me as we ate our meals together.

Although the photocopy restriction was violated and copies were passed on to others, the committee sponsoring our project never faced up to this action. When our completed volume, *Building on the Gospel Foundation: The Mennonites of Franklin County, Pennsylvania, and Washington County, Maryland, 1730–1970,* was released in 2004, it was fitting that the Oliver Martin family and many other Washington and Franklin County Mennonites were present. It was one of my desires to have this happen. The new volume became No. 42 of the *Studies in Anabaptist and Mennonite History* and has already entered a second printing.

During this time my loving wife was diagnosed with malignant cancer that chemotherapy and radiation treatments were unable to eradicate. Only our God understood our trauma of this time and the consequent death of Elizabeth on August 9, 1991. After forty-three years of our life together, I lost a loving and faithful spouse and a wise and devoted mother to our son and five daughters. We had brought much into each other's lives. I have a strong sense of empathy for persons who lose their spouses after a good marriage. Fortunately, time does not erase deep memories. It does go on and bring healing. In 1995 Mary Ellen Stutzman came into my life and I into hers. God has been good to us. As for me, writing publishable books is hardly a continuing prospect. I still read, reflect, do some research, muse on history, and find these activities rewarding, especially as I continue to marvel at the love and mercy of God.

November 2005
Revised July 2007

HAROLD D. LEHMAN

From Park View to Wider Horizons

I agreed to join this autobiographical train because I thought this might be the time for a generalist to speak in the midst of distinguished scholars.

Ancestral Backgrounds

Originally from Switzerland, my Lehman ancestors and my Neff ancestors on my mother's side came to America by way of the Palatinate in the years 1716 and 1717. These pioneer families received land grants southwest of the present city of Lancaster towards the Susquehanna River. They were generations of farmers. On the Lehman side my grandfather, Bishop Daniel N. Lehman, gave his children the opportunity to enroll in post-secondary schooling a hundred years ago. My father and most of his siblings attended Millersville State Normal School and became teachers. His sisters, however, needed to drop out of formal teaching after marriage.

I pick up the story on my mother's side with a vignette dated 1531. In the Battle of Kappel, Switzerland, the conflict raged between the five Catholic Forest Cantons and the forces of Zurich led by the reformer Zwingli. On Wednesday October 11, 1531, as the Foresters were pushing back the Zürichers, the standard bearer for the Zwingli reformers accidentally fell into a mill stream and drowned because his heavy armor pulled him under the water. In the confusion that followed, a Forester began to seize the banner. The cry went out, "Is there no honorable Züricher here to save the army's banner?"

At that moment an Adam Neff heard the cry. He advanced on the Forester holding the banner. Swinging his broadsword, Neff severed his opponent's head. The banner was saved. On that day Zwingli was mortally wounded.

Subsequently Neff was honored for his distinguished service in battle. "He was bestowed the citizenship of Zurich, which shall also be extended to his descendants" *(The Neff-Naf Family,* Neff and Associates, 1991, 8–9). Today the broadsword of Adam Neff, his armor and the banner that he rescued are on display in the Swiss National Museum in central Zurich across from the main rail station.

Thus, having established my blue-blood heritage and my stature as a free citizen of Zurich, I proceed with a far less fascinating story.

I was born in Lancaster County, Pennsylvania, but when I was eight months old, my parents moved to Harrisonburg, Virginia. My father, a former high school principal in Adams County, Pennsylvania, had been recruited by President J. B. Smith to join the faculty of this young school in Virginia. Thus I grew up in Park View in a faculty member's home surrounded by other faculty families on College Avenue—Chester Lehmans, Ernest Gehmans, Henry Weavers, John Kurtzes (John was the builder of the campus buildings), and farther out the street, John Mumaws.

EMU's Influence on my Early Years

As I reflect on my childhood, the school was not only the focal point of my life; it was indeed my life. As boys we explored the Administration Building from basement to attic. We had free access to the old gym and the clay tennis courts. EMS was our United States post office, designated by postmaster Henry Weaver's official stamp, "Mennonite Station." As a young man I was frequently employed on the campus during vacation and summer breaks for maintenance jobs—washing windows, painting, moving furniture, or manual labor connected with building projects.

The school also provided our church and Sunday-school life in its services Sunday mornings and evenings. Here I responded to a revival invitation by evangelist J. D. Mininger, and here our class of converts was instructed and baptized by Bishop S. H. Rhodes. (For a description of the religious life of the school and Mennonite community of that era, I refer you to Chapter 1 of my history of the Park View Congregation, *Through These Doors, A Journal of Faithfulness,* 2003).

In addition the school was the scene of our social life. The monthly public literary was a community event. Other school sponsored opportunities for social interaction were Massanutten Peak climbs, ice-skating on Myers Pond, junior/senior outings, School Day Out, commencement activities, Young Peoples Institutes in the summers, and the traditional walk around the campus with an invited one.

Not the least, EMS was our educational life. At Park School, the nearby elementary school, we had student teachers from EMS. Standing out in my memory are Sanford Shetler, Elizabeth Showalter, and Paul Roth from Masontown, Pennsylvania.

I move now to my educational career as student and teacher. When I began high school in 1932, EMS was just fifteen years old. In some ways it was still a first-generational school. There was something of the first blush of pioneering endeavor about the place, and some of its early teachers were still around: President A.D. Wenger (Old and New Testament history and geography), J. L. Stauffer (Bible doctrine), D. Ralph Hostetter (biology), M. T. Brackbill (physics), and Dorothy Kemrer (Latin). Early EMS graduates had come back to teach: Harry Brunk (American history and problems of American democracy), Sadie Hartzler (English), and John Mumaw (Bible introduction). Most of these teachers also taught college classes, a fact that spoke well of the high quality of this high-school teaching corps. Among them the teacher who influenced me the most was Miss Hartzler, who in four years of high school English instilled in me an interest in literature, books, words, and writing.

After high school, following advice from my father, I pursued the two-year Normal Course. Those two years at EMS added teachers M. J. Brunk, C. K. Lehman, D. W. Lehman, Ruth Stoltzfus Stauffer and Ernest Gehman to my experience.

Teaching Experience Begins

Then, armed with a Normal Teaching Certificate (which marked a common entry point for elementary teachers at that time), I applied to Superintendent John C. Myers for a teaching job in Rockingham County Public Schools. The first year, 1939–1940, I taught the upper grades, four through seven, at Caplinger School, Criders, Virginia, in the northwest corner of this county. As head teacher in a two-room school, I found my starting salary to be $75 per month for nine months. Other prices, of course, were comparable. I boarded during the week with Joe and Dare Turner Stultz, who ran the country store and post office at Criders. When I asked Dare about lodging and food, she quoted the same price she had charged Frank Moyers, the teacher of the preceding year, $13 per month or, if I milked the cow in the morning, $12. I settled for the higher figure.

Of course the children at Caplinger tried out this new eighteen-year old teacher. However, most of the children came from Brethren, Lutheran or Mennonite homes that instilled respect for teachers. My success there I attribute to two factors: the support and advice of my co-teacher in grades one to three, Miss Edna Wampler, a Church of the Brethren woman with years of experience and a wealth of wisdom. Secondly, I was on the playground with the children regularly at noon and in recess times—mostly playing touch football with the boys. Associating with these rural folk in the foothills and hollows of the Shenandoah Mountain gave this Park View novice a cross-cultural experience.

As was the custom, the longer one taught in the county, the closer the next placement would be to Harrisonburg. My second year of teaching, with a $5 raise per month, was at the former school at Fulks Run—also with the upper grades in a two-room school. That year I drove back and forth from home each day, dropping off several other teachers along the way and picking them up on the return.

Sixty-five years ago for a Mennonite young person in this community, wanting to pursue college work beyond the two years at EMS, attendance at Goshen College was not an acceptable option. The local choices were either Bridgewater College or Madison College. In my case I received my liberal arts college training through three summers at Madison and one academic year at Bridgewater.

Civilian Public Service Interlude

I want to include here my Civilian Public Service, which I count as the most formative experience of my life, even surpassing graduate school experience. I was drafted in October 1942 along with five other Mennonite young men from this community to help open a new camp, CPS #39, at Galax, Virginia—a former CCC camp located on the top of the Blue Ridge Mountains along the Parkway, just north of the North Carolina state line. Living in barracks—eventually along with 150 other men—I worked in manual labor along the newly constructed Blue Ridge Parkway, doing forestry work and also fire fighting. While it was a Mennonite-administered camp, the CPSers represented a variety of religious groups. An important part of this experience was the learning and acceptance among the Mennonite groups: Old Mennonites, Old Order Mennonites, Amish, General Conference Mennonites, Mennonite Brethren, and Brethren in Christ, plus a variety of other religious groups.

I also had a short experience with mental hospital service at Greystone Park State Hospital in northern New Jersey, where I was an orderly on the medical-surgical ward. The use of physical restraint and electric shock therapy are vivid memories from that time.

Another opportunity to transfer came up shortly. President Franklin D. Roosevelt had approved a private school in southern New Jersey, the Vineland Training School for the Mentally Retarded, for a CPS Unit. This approval came about through the lobbying efforts of Pearl Buck, whose only birth child was a severely retarded adult in the school; national columnist Dorothy Canfield Fisher; and Eleanor Roosevelt. A unit of twelve men was set up with the requirement that each participant be a college graduate with at least two years teaching experience. I just qualified. Needless to say, this was a very stimulating unit to be a part of. Here I spent the next three years as a teacher and served as unit leader, or camp director, for the last half of that experience.

There was one other detour in my CPS experience. A Mennonite relief-training unit opened to college graduates was set up in the summer of 1943 at Goshen College. The majority of the 70 men, plus a few women, were graduates of Goshen, Bethel, Bluffton, and Tabor colleges. I was the only one with a connection to Eastern Mennonite School.

Now here I was at Goshen College, a place so anathema to my previous upbringing that it took some mutual adjustment to accept and to be accepted in that setting. Actually it turned out to be a rich experience of assimilation for me and an exposure to a wide range of teachers and lecturers across the Mennonite spectrum of that era: H. S. Bender, P. C. Hiebert, C. N. Hostetter, Henry A. Fast, Robert Friedman, Ed Kauffman, S. F. Pannabecker, and M. C. Lehman.

By the end of the ten-week summer term at Goshen, the word came through that the United States Congress had added a rider to the Appropriations Bill, stipulating that federal funds could not be used to send conscientious objectors overseas during the war. Thus ended that immediate program for overseas relief work. We were permitted to return to our previous camp or unit; and I returned to Vineland, New Jersey, for three school-terms of teaching as noted previously.

Before I get too far with my story, I want to pick up on the young woman whom my father recruited as a high school junior in 1937. While we had soon become acquainted, we did not date until after graduation—she from high school and I from junior college. Before I left for CPS, Ruth, having worked at the Akron MCC office for more than two years, returned for college at EMS. Eventually we pledged our lives together but planned not to marry until the war was over. However, the war dragged on too long! By the fall of 1944 we had decided to get married and planned for her to join me and my unit at the Vineland Training School. (Next month, on December 30th, we will celebrate our 60th wedding anniversary.) In January 1945 we began our married life with the unit at Vineland. She secured a job as secretary to one of the department heads, and she likes to remember this experience since she was earning a salary considerably higher than my $15 a month. I have been eternally grateful that we could share together the experience of CPS life during the first year-and-a-half of our marriage.

Back to EMS/C as Teacher-Administrator

Before my release from CPS, I had an invitation from Dean C. K. Lehman to come to EMS as a physical education teacher. However, even before returning home from CPS, Ruth and I went directly to Penn State University: I to start a master's program in physical education, health and recreation; and she to work in the university typing pool.

For the next ten years, 1946–56, I taught physical education classes at EMS and EMC, plus two sections of either high school English or American History. Along with the women's teacher, Miss Margaret Martin, we provided a full-blown intramural sports program in a variety of activities for high school and college students.

In the summer of 1955 President John R. Mumaw invited me to be Director of the High School. I was inclined immediately to accept because I realized the coming of pressures to provide some sort of interschool athletic activities at EMC. Not that I was opposed, but one thing I was certain of, I was not interested in coaching athletic teams.

Thus I accepted John Mumaw's invitation and used a sabbatical year to enroll in a doctoral program at the University of Virginia in Secondary Education and School Administration. For the next five years I held this administrative position with the high school. During this period, it became increasingly apparent to me and to others that the high school and college needed to be separated in program, faculty, and facilities.

Perhaps the biggest challenge was to lead the faculty in preparing application for high school accreditation by the Southern Association of Colleges and Secondary Schools. Because the high school and college were organically connected at that time, the SACS officials decreed that the high school needed to be accredited before the college could be considered. I had the opportunity of leading the self-study process and hosting the visiting committee on campus. The High School of Eastern Mennonite College received Southern Association accreditation in 1957. Two years later, in 1959, EMC received its accreditation.

Another part of the experience of being Director of the High School was to serve five years on the Administration Committee with President Mumaw and Dean Ira Miller. With a weekly meeting I soon learned the thought patterns and reactions of both men, as I am sure they did of mine.

In 1962 President Mumaw came with another invitation for me to become College Registrar. I do not think he was dissatisfied with my leadership in the high school, but he was resisting the push for separation of the high school program and facilities from the college. At any rate I accepted the position of Registrar, along with the assignment to supervise and teach secondary-level education students.

Meanwhile, by the mid-1960s I was beginning to feel a bit restive at EMC and questioned whether I wanted to finish my career in the institution that had been my lifetime shelter and occupation. President Augsburger, I think, was aware of this and suggested options both within and without the institution.

Transfer to Madison College (JMU)

But then came another one of those events that signaled a change of course. In the spring semester of 1967 I taught a course at Madison College in Secondary School Curriculum for a teacher on leave. At the close of the semester in conversation with the dean, I suggested that he might contact me if there was ever an opening in the department. A week later he called me about a teaching position in the Secondary Education Department.

How should I respond? It was no light thing to leave the institution that had nurtured me and at which I had served for 21 years in a variety of capacities. I chose deliberately to counsel with three persons: my father, my pastor Harold Eshleman, and a friend, Grant Stoltzfus. Without reservation, all three encouraged the move. Thus for the next nineteen years I taught at James Madison University—Philosophy of Education with undergraduates; and Comparative Education, Research Methods and Secondary School Curriculum with graduate students.

I was part of a department of eight professors. I liked the support of colleagues who were specialists in areas in which I was less versed, i.e., School Law, School Finance and School Plant. I myself was recognized as a specialist in Comparative Education. I appreciated the collegial atmosphere within the department. The nineteen years I taught at JMU were good years.

One bonus and responsibility was to be recognized as a religious leader on the campus. In the early years I served on the YWCA committee. Later I was faculty advisor to the Intervarsity Christian Fellowship chapter on the campus. With a student committee we sponsored a regular Sunday evening service with an attendance ranging from 100–150. We had occasional Bible study groups, plus a yearly rally. Another service type of committee work was the Foreign Students Committee with responsibilities for helping new international students with orientation, finding local sponsors, and arranging vacation housing.

I would yet like to comment on spin-off activities in three areas: physical education, Mennonite Church assignments, and voluntary service.

Physical Education

For five summers, 1951–1955, I served as the first director of the summer program at Tel Hai Mennonite Camp, Honey Brook, Pennsylvania. The sponsors, Atglen and Morgantown Mennonite congregations, had a vision for serving city children with a camp program and were willing to entrust the actual camp direction to Ruth and me. We enrolled children from Mennonite city missions in Philadelphia, Marietta, Wilmington and New York City, plus Fresh Air children from the Bronx.

We've had a long connection with Laurelville Mennonite Church Center, where I have served on the board, on committees, as director of Youth Camps and as author of their 50-year history, *Where There is a Vision, the Laurelville Story, 1943–1993*.

Sponsored by the Mennonite Board of Education, I had the opportunity to write the 1973 Conrad Grebel lecture, *In Praise of Leisure*. Giving the book a leader's guide resulted in its wide use across the church. As stipulated, the lecture was to be given at the three colleges: Goshen, Hesston, and Eastern Mennonite; and I was to be open to invitations from congregations and other groups. Over the next few years I spoke on the topic at some fifty settings from Pennsylvania to Oregon, plus on several occasions later while we were in England.

Mennonite Church Assignments

Like Irvin Horst, I went through the ministerial lot myself in the 1950s, twice for preacher and once for deacon. Del Glick mentioned at the Park View Mennonite Church the other Sunday that this method of choosing ministers was high drama, an emotion-packed experience, to say the least. There was no slip in the Bibles I chose. My testimony is "that God was gracious to me and to the Middle District of Virginia Mennonite Conference."

Most of my involvement in the wider church has been in the field of Christian or congregational education. I will simply list these items:
- Mennonite Teachers Association president

- Mennonite Commission for Christian Education
- Chair, Committee on Congregational Education and Literature
- Editorial Council of the Foundation Series, in which connection I wrote two booklets on teacher training, entitled *Called To Teach Adults*, published by Faith and Life Press)
- Mennonite Board of Education philosophy study
- Writer of adult Builder materials
- Reviewer for Provident Books
- Member of Mennonite Board of Education

A Vignette on Social Change

Everyone hopes that he or she may be able to do something in life that makes a difference. I want to tell you what that was in my life. You be the judge as to how worthy or unworthy the act was. In the rather turbulent period of the 1960s at EMC the dress restrictions for both men and women, plus other issues, such as interschool athletics, musical instruments, and drama, made for much discussion, often fraught with emotional turmoil for students, faculty and board.

By the early 1960s the plain coat requirement for faculty men, i.e., laypersons, became an issue. Several of us made adaptation to jacket and tie when off-campus for professional meetings. A few dared to appear thus at college social functions.

In the summer of 1964 Virginia Mennonite Conference considered pressures against the coat requirement. They could not come to agreement and deferred the matter to a special session to be held in the fall. For all practical purposes the requirement was not binding in the interim. Realizing some sort of opening here, I used the occasion of the church-wide Christian Education Convention meeting on the EMC campus in August. I was to appear on the platform the first evening to welcome the audience in the name of Virginia Conference and the College. Telling only my father beforehand, I came on the platform along with the evening speakers, dressed in coat and tie. My audacity shocked some people, and my popularity quotient took a precipitous decline. But by the opening of the 1964–1965 school year, other faculty laymen had followed suit. The board and conference never reinstated the plain coat requirement at EMC.

Looking back, I was not surprised at how quickly the change came in our community and across the eastern part of the Mennonite Church. I was surprised, however, that the change was eventually adopted by most of the clergy in our church. I say this because a Religious Welfare member had told us that we should wear the plain coat at EMC because men faculty had the same status and responsibility as did ordained preachers.

While I do not want to take undue credit or blame for the change, I had a part in it, and I know it made a difference.

Voluntary Service Experience

Following our respective retirements in 1986, Ruth and I had a two-and-a-half year voluntary service assignment with co-appointment by Mennonite Board of Missions and Mennonite Central Committee. We were seconded to the Centre for the Study of New Religious Movements located on the campus of the Selly Oak Colleges, Birmingham, England. This consortium of eight small denominational colleges provides programs of adult education for an international student body. The colleges are dedicated to the preparation of overseas missionaries and civil servants. During our time there, we lived on the campuses of colleges representing three denominations: Quaker, Methodist and Presbyterian.

Our main task was to assist four other staff members in collecting and disseminating information on New Religious Movements (worldwide) with particular emphasis on African Independent Churches, more recently termed African Initiated Churches. It was a rich experience to work closely with a world-class scholar in the field—Dr. Harold Turner, the founder and director of the Centre.

Specifically my job was to peruse the variety of journals missions, anthropology, sociology, etc.—and the breadth of sources in the library of Birmingham University for articles, letters, or documents on new religious movements. Ruth worked primarily in the Centre's library, maintaining the collection, binding, cataloging and shelving the materials. Following the choices made by Turner, we prepared over 8000 items for microfiche photography. These microfiche sets then were made available for sale to seminaries and missionary training centres around the world. Our last task was to prepare a bibliography of the 8037 entries, categorized by country and author, with notes prepared by Turner describing the new religious movements within each country. (Since our time at the Centre they have upgraded the technology to the Internet.) A bonus of this experience was to meet missionaries who stopped by the Centre for study and research, particularly from West African and Southern African countries. Mission scholars and/or executives also visited us periodically–just to mention the Mennonites you may know: James and Janette Krabill, Calvin Shenk, Wilbert and Juanita Shenk, Willard and Alice Roth, and Jonathan Larson.

In conclusion, in this reflection on my life it seems that the various shifts in my experience were often triggered by chance happenings, circumstances, or by conversations with others. On occasion I dared to step out in a new direction. I am quite willing to term these various twists and turns as the Lord's leading in my life. However, I seem to be better able to acknowledge this by hindsight. I am reminded of Jacob in the Old Testament who had a bad night with a strange dream, no doubt because he slept with his head on a stone for his pillow. In the morning, as his senses cleared, he remarked: "Surely, the Lord was in this place and I knew it not."

November 2004

GERALD R. BRUNK

From Rocking Horse to Rocking Chair

I am both humbled and honored to be asked to share my life story with you. As I reflect on my life, I see it as a story with four chapters.

I

The first chapter begins with my birth as the oldest of five children in Denbigh, Virginia, to George R., II, and Margaret Suter Brunk. Since I was born on St. Patrick's Day, my great aunt thought I should be named Patrick; but my parents thought otherwise. Actually, my birth certificate has the name "George" with a line drawn through it and "Gerald" written in. My parents had changed their minds about naming me after my father, but two years later they named my brother "George" because my grandfather, George R., I, had died the year before. I have never regretted their change of mind.

Since my father's ministerial duties frequently took him away from home, we children were raised mainly by my mother on our 30-acre fruit farm, where we could enjoy all the peaches, apples, pecans, figs, and cherries we wanted. In addition, our family grew several fields of daffodils, which persons from the community helped to pick and box to be sold to florists in Newport News, then twelve miles from Denbigh. Our farm also included a pond where we children spent many hours fishing, swimming, and canoeing. I do not think that I appreciated at that time what kind of a paradise that was.

My earliest memory as a child was my first lesson on what it means to sacrifice in order to obtain something. One day as I was looking through the Montgomery Ward catalog, I spied a beautiful rocking horse and immediately began begging my father for it. Now for some time my parents had been trying to persuade me to give up my bottle, but to no avail. So when I insisted on having that horse, my father wisely saw the opportunity to inform me that anyone who needed a bottle was not old enough to have a rocking horse. The only way I could hope to get it, he told me, was to give up my bottle. I marched forthrightly to the kitchen with my bottle and surrendered it to my mother. I shall never forget the day that big box arrived; and today that rocking horse sits in my home, having been ridden by me, my four siblings, my four sons, and now my four grandchildren.

Now no longer a Mennonite colony, Denbigh is the hub of Newport News; and during World War II, we were in the center of military activities. Nearby were the Norfolk and Langley Air Force bases, and warplanes were constantly roaring overhead. From Mulberry Island across the Warwick River came the thunder of artillery practice during the day. There was much talk of Hitler, and in my childish imagination he was a giant like Goliath. When the war was nearly over, I heard that President Roosevelt had died and that the next president of the United States would be Truman. My immediate reaction was one of elation because I assumed that if my Uncle Truman Brunk owned the Warwick River Mennonite Church, it was only natural for him to be the next president of the United States! Obviously my political knowledge needed much more development.

Our family was living here in Harrisonburg when I began first grade at Park School, where the physical plant now stands. My experience as a first grader was horrible since my teacher, Mrs. Hartman, would hit first graders' hands with the edge of a ruler if they did not give the right answer and because I was bullied by the older students. More than once my father found me crying along the road on the way to school. Shortly before the Park School building was torn down, I went into the first grade classroom; but I had to get out because I smelled the same odor that was there when I was a student. It is a wonder that I continued my education later. Nevertheless, from the time I began attending school in 1943 to my retirement in 2001, I was either a student or a teacher every year, including my sabbaticals and year leave of absence. Of those 58 years, 41, excluding graduate school and sabbaticals, were on the campus of EMU if Park School is included, for I also went there for the seventh grade. I spent the other seven years at the Warwick River Christian School, founded by my father in 1942.

At the age of nine, I responded to an invitation given by William Jennings in a series of revival meetings held at Warwick River Mennonite Church and was baptized by Uncle Truman, who was the bishop. I remember that Brother Jennings gave me a bookmark ribbon with John 3: 16, but he had replaced "For God so loved the world" with "For God so loved Gerald Brunk." Since our home was two doors from the church, we children knew that our parents expected to see us there twice on Sunday, as well as on Wednesday nights. The Sunday evening services were often young peoples' Bible meetings where youth and young adults gave prepared talks.

In 1951 when I was fourteen, my father became involved in the first of thirty years of tent evangelism. I remember when he phoned to tell my mother to come with us children to Lancaster, Pennsylvania, to attend the tent meetings, which eventually continued for seven weeks. I shall never forget seeing that overflow crowd of 15,000 people on the last Sunday night of those meetings. I had never seen so many people at one place at the same time. I shall never forget, either, the spirited singing led by my Uncle Lawrence Brunk. It was also during that time that I met Janet High, the girl whom I would marry nine years later.

From then on, our family accompanied the tent meetings every summer. The campaigns, as they were called, took us from Pennsylvania to Oregon with states in between, and from Ontario to British Columbia in Canada. Contacts with the Russian Mennonites in the western provinces gave me my first introduction to the heart-rending stories of the Mennonite experience in the former Soviet Union.

All seven of us lived in a small 32 x 8 foot house trailer, and we dressed up to go to the revival meeting every night. My brothers and I did odd jobs such as picking up trash and straightening chairs in the tent(s); and when we were old enough to drive, we took the wheel of the tractor-trailer trucks. After the two secretaries were no longer with us, I did the secretarial and accounting work. Included among my courses here at EMU was Choral Conducting, taught by J. Mark Stauffer; so after song leader I. Mark Ross left, my father asked me to lead the singing, which I did in the summers while attending college and graduate school. For part of my second sabbatical I returned to the communities where the tent campaigns had been held and interviewed persons and groups with my tape recorder about their memories of the tent meetings. These tapes are now in the EMU archives for any historian who may someday write a history of the Brunk Revivals.

During my four years of college here at EMU, I majored in pre-theological studies and social science. Upon graduating, I decided to apply for graduate study in history at the University of Virginia, since I had more hours in that discipline than in any of the other social sciences, and was accepted. For the first time I was thrust into an academic environment far different from any I had been accustomed to. I will not forget the shock I felt when my blatantly racist professor, who taught Human Growth and Development, wrote the word "faith" on the blackboard and then proceeded to draw an X through it, declaring that there was no such thing. When a couple of us dared to challenge his assertion, he declared that we had been brainwashed by our misguided Sunday Schools.

II

After living in the dormitory during my first year of graduate school, I married my childhood sweetheart, thus beginning the second chapter of my life. Janet was the daughter of Ben and Catherine High of Lancaster, Pennsylvania, and had attended Goshen College, earning her degree there in nursing. During our remaining years in Charlottesville, she worked at Martha Jefferson Hospital, where she also gave birth to our first two sons.

I shall never forget what happened the day I was preparing to take my doctoral orals in Alderman Library. The chair of the history department telephoned, asking me to come immediately to his office. As I made my way to Cabell Hall, I worried about what I might have failed to do in my doctoral program. I was even more terrified when Dr. Younger's first words to me were "Mr. Brunk, you're in trouble, deep trouble." Then he proceeded to tell me that I was needed to teach a Western Civilization class to undergraduates that was to begin in just a couple of days. Despite the fact that my orals were already scheduled, he told me that they could be postponed and that the teaching experience would be to my benefit.

After much discussion and prayer with my wife, I decided to take the class, even though it meant delaying my orals, and immediately began preparing lectures for the course. In retrospect, I am glad I did, for it gave me an opportunity to teach university students prior to being hired, and it convinced me that teaching would be my profession.

After taking my doctoral orals, I joined my peers in exploring possible teaching positions. Responding to an invitation to visit Virginia Tech, I was quite pleased with its location and the potential salary. However, while I was contemplating that possibility, I received a telephone call from John R. Mumaw, who told me that I was needed for the history department at EMC and urged me to return to my alma mater. He did not say a word about my salary; and when I asked, he told me that it could be negotiated after I came. He assured me that having two children would bring an additional benefit to my salary.

After much prayer and heart searching, Janet and I decided to accept Mumaw's invitation, especially after we learned that our good friends, Al and Leanna Keim, had also been invited to come to EMU. Al was also in graduate studies at the UVA, and we would both be joining the history department with John A. Lapp and Samuel Horst under the incoming president, Myron Augsburger in the fall of 1965. I came to EMU with a Master of Arts in Teaching and completed my doctoral dissertation while teaching, earning a PhD in history in 1968.

I have never regretted my decision to come to EMU rather than go to Virginia Tech. Not only did EMU give me the opportunity to help prepare students for Christian service, but also it shaped my own thought and development as a teacher.

Perhaps one of my most significant experiences came in 1975 when the administration approved my first sabbatical and a year's leave of absence to go to the Middle East. With my wife and four sons, aged two to twelve, I served as the first resident country director for Egypt under Mennonite Central Committee. My responsibility was to supervise the English teachers, nurses, and agriculturalist under the auspices of the Coptic Evangelical Church and to cultivate relations with the leaders of the Coptic Orthodox Church, providing them financial assistance for their social services. I taught fifth-grade English at Ramses College for Girls in Cairo the first thing in the morning to fulfill my work visa and went about my MCC duties the rest of the day. The leaders of the Coptic Orthodox Church were willing to accept material aid from MCC but were reluctant to have MCC teachers in their educational institutions. However, I became very good friends with Bishop Samuel, who was later killed at the same time that President Anwar Sadat was assassinated, and my efforts eventually paid off: the Copts later welcomed MCC teachers into their schools. I was pleased that my son Steve and his wife, Beth, later returned to serve three years with MCC in Egypt.

This assignment gave me the opportunity to visit Jordan, Israel, and the West Bank, introducing me to the realities and complexities of that region. In 1987, my second wife, Shirley, and I led 35 EMU students for a semester of study in the Middle East. Later, during my third sabbatical, we spent a semester of study in Jerusalem. These experiences had such an impact on me that I introduced a course on the history of the Middle East to prepare students for their cross-cultural experience there.

They also influenced my views on the Middle East. When I read the promises to God's chosen people of land in the Old Testament, I see that those promises are always given on the condition that Israel will pursue righteousness and be obedient to God's commands. I also observe that Israel is to welcome rather than oppress the alien. When I read the New Testament, I see very little about land, but much about the poor and oppressed. I therefore find it difficult to believe that the current secular and godless government of the state of Israel is the recipient of the Old Testament promises. I cannot agree with those Christian Zionists who give their whole-hearted support to the Israeli government, which oppresses the Palestinian people. Furthermore, I find it difficult to comprehend why certain Christians who proclaim the death and resurrection of Christ desire to see the temple rebuilt, animal sacrifices reinstituted, and the veil restored, thus again preventing direct access for us to the throne of God. Many of those same Christians support the development of nuclear weapons in order to hasten the possibility of an Armageddon. Such thinking seems to me to be contrary to God's plan for peace on earth, good will to humanity. It disturbs me greatly when these Christian Zionists ignore their fellow Palestinian brothers and sisters in Christ as well as the many other Arab Christians throughout the Middle East.

III

The death of my first wife, Janet, in 1980, opened the third chapter in my life. Little did I know then that both of my colleagues in the history department would experience similar losses of their spouses to cancer. Fourteen months earlier she had been diagnosed with lung cancer, and during that time it spread to her brain. I learned through this experience that you have to deal with more than just the disease. It was discovered that whoever had read her x-ray the year before the malignancy was detected had missed seeing the tumor, which had grown rapidly over that year. She underwent lung surgery and then radiation and chemotherapy. Further, because of the unprofessional behavior of her doctor, it became necessary for her to change to another physician.

I also learned that Christian brothers and sisters say some of the most hurtful things during a time like this. More than one asked me what the Lord was trying to tell me through all this or what I had done that would have caused this to happen. I was also told that if we had enough faith, she would be healed. At least two persons in separate states assured me that they had received a revelation from the Lord that she would be healed. After her death I was told that our faith had not been sufficient.

I shall never forget that during Janet's last days in the hospital, one day while driving to the hospital I was listening to WEMC when I heard the song, "Nothing is Impossible When You Put Your Trust in God." While I was grasping at that truth, the song was immediately followed by a number of songs in succession on heaven. It was as if God was saying, "Yes, I have the power to physically heal her, but I am allowing her to be eternally healed."

I must also say that I have never felt the support of Christian brothers and sisters as I did during her illness and at her death. In fact, during the late stage of her illness and at the time of her passing, a film was being produced called "606" that reflected that incredible outpouring of community support.

I also learned that it is unwise to try to be strong at a time like that. I was left with four sons, aged seven to seventeen, and I tried to be strong for them by internalizing my emotions and grief. The persons who applauded my apparent strength reinforced this choice. However, I paid the consequent price of being hospitalized for depression and later having a hemorrhaging stomach ulcer, one of the three times I nearly lost my life had it not been for the assistance this time of Daryl, my oldest son. He had wisely kept his hearing aid on when he went to bed because he knew I was sick, and he heard me cry for help when I collapsed on the bathroom floor. He phoned my father, who immediately called the rescue squad when he could not feel my pulse. In the hospital my stomach was pumped, and I received four units of blood. Another close call had occurred years earlier when I was driving a tractor and the rear tire ran over a large rock that was hidden in tall grass. The tractor went over on its side but did not completely overturn on me. Then when the tent meetings were near Kitchener, Ontario, Canada, my father took us boys to a water-filled quarry to swim. I was just learning how to swim and got into trouble in the deep water. My father jumped into the water fully clothed to rescue me from drowning. After surviving these near-death experiences, I was convinced the Lord wanted me here for some reason.

From 1980 to 1984 I tried to be father and mother to my sons, while at the same time teaching a full load at the university. Then on a snowy evening in February of 1983, I met Shirley Nafziger, daughter of Villas and Erma Nafziger of Hopewell, Illinois, on a blind date set up by mutual friends, and the following year we were married. This past summer we celebrated our 20 years of marriage, the same number I had with my first wife.

As I stated earlier, I did not opt for seminary after graduation because I never felt called to the ministry. Despite being twice invited to pastor congregations by Virginia Conference overseers, the second just last month, I have always felt that my gifts lie in the teaching rather than the preaching ministry, and I have often been affirmed in that.

I have tried to make the teaching of history interesting by using different methods in my classes. One of these opportunities came to me in January of 1986 when I received a phone call one day in my office from the late President Richard Detweiler, telling me that because he was sick, he would not be able to speak in chapel as scheduled. Since it was the 450th anniversary of Menno Simons' departure from the Roman

Catholic Church, he asked whether I could give something on Menno for chapel. I agreed and decided to give it as if Menno were speaking. Without costume or props, I gave the monologue and was amazed at the attentiveness of and the positive comments from students. Since that time I have given "My Road to Decision" with costume and props over fifty times in nine different states from Florida in the south to Colorado in the West. My most interesting reception was at Southwestern Baptist Theological Seminary in Fort Worth, Texas, at the invitation of my good friend and colleague in church history, the late William R. Estep, who was on the faculty there. The Baptist seminarians of course had no problem with believer's baptism, but Menno's teaching concerning the sword generated considerable discussion and debate.

Because of their effectiveness, I did impersonations of other historical personages in my classes, including such men as Rousseau and St. Augustine. Just recently I have given several impersonations of my great-grandfather, Henry G. Brunk, on his experiences as a conscientious objector who found it necessary to leave his wife and child and travel by foot from Harrisonburg to Hagerstown, Maryland, during the Civil War.

Another sabbatical included a semester in northern Wales at an Anglican residential library. During that time, Shirley and I had the privilege of traveling all over the United Kingdom, visiting historic sites about which I had taught for years. It was exciting to visit such places as Hadrian's Wall, Whitby, Wearmouth and Jarrow, Lindisfarne, Canterbury and Hastings. My readings at the library and the travels, including a trip to the island of Iona, greatly enriched my teaching of early England.

IV

My retirement three years ago from 36 years on the faculty of EMU opened the fourth chapter of my life. Prior to my retirement I had numerous things in mind to do when that time came, but I have yet to get to most of them. I tell people that I am so busy I don't know how I ever had time to teach, and one of the most frequent statements made by my wife is, "Are you busy or what?"

I find that I have much more time to spend with my grandchildren than I had with my own children, and we are privileged to have all four of them close by. Two days a week Shirley and I help with babysitting.

My love of music has involved me in numerous musical groups. I enjoy singing in the Eversole Road Men's Quartet, so named because all four of us live within a half mile of each other on Eversole Road. We practice once a week at 7:30 in the morning. I also sing with the Valley Table Singers, the Harrisonburg Mennonite Church sanctuary and men's choirs, and the Shenandoah Valley Men's Chorus.

Both Shirley and I love to travel, and retirement has given us the opportunity to visit such places as Arizona, Florida, and Alaska, New Brunswick, Prince Edward Island, and Nova Scotia. Next we plan to drive to Texas to visit our son and other friends we know there.

I am also privileged to have hobbies as recreational activities. This year marks my 50th year in amateur radio, and I serve as president of the Amateur Radio Missionary Service organization, which has members all over the world. Since I live only a mile from the Heritage Oaks Golf Course, I enjoy getting my exercise on the golf course and having father-son time there with three of my sons who also play. I enjoy fishing, too, in the nearby ponds, lakes, and streams; a highlight of our visit to Alaska was catching thirty-five pounds of red salmon in the Kenai River.

Finally, one of the projects of which I have just scratched the surface, is going through my father's voluminous papers, preparing them for the EMU archives. That major task still lies ahead for me; and with her organizational ability, Shirley will be of great help.

Thus ends my attempt to recap the four chapters of my life. In doing so, I am impressed with the way the Lord's blessings have been so abundant, even through the dark valleys He has allowed me to travel. It is apparent that the "rocking chair" terminus in the title of my presentation is more of a symbol than a reality in my retirement; and as long as I am able, it will continue to be so.

December 2004
Revised July 2007

JAMES R. BOMBERGER

An Ordinary Boy with Extraordinary Experiences

Part I: Childhood

Mother wanted a girl. She was so sure her first baby would be a girl that she had Elam open an account at the bank for Lois Bomberger. When Lois turned out to be a boy, he became Luke. Three and a half years later she was ready for a boy and named him Elton. She considered him her pretty baby, confirmed by those early photographs of a dark eyed porcelain doll. When it was my turn, two years later, she looked at her mother and aunt (fraternal twins) and decided she was carrying twin girls, something to do with size and the way she carried the pregnancy. The twins were pre-named Mary and Martha.

Now our father was a banker, and President Roosevelt, facing the worst depression the nation had ever seen, closed the banks. As you know, some never reopened. But The First National Bank and Trust Company of Mt. Joy, Pennsylvania, did open again, March 15, 1933. Our father stayed home for an extra day; James (not Mary and Martha) arrived. Mother often reminded me of what she said, "There better be something in that big head." Five years later David arrived with a head of blond curls, everyone's favorite. I was reported to have said about the new baby, "Can't touch him, can't play with him, Lord take him back." Soon enough, of course, we all learned to care for him and to play with him. What a happy noisy bunch. Mother used to say, "I have a quartet of boys and an octet of noise." We certainly did not disappoint as we raced through the house chasing each other and shouting up and down the stairs. "Pipe down, pipe down; I can't hear myself think," she called to us, laughing at the happiness of her four boys. Who needs girls?

If this was the depression, we did not know it. Perhaps being too small, we were not aware of what was going on around us. I do remember years later when my mother said, "We never knew where our next meal was coming from." But Daddy replied, "Violet, I always had a job (I am sure he knew many who didn't) and a regular pay check." Surely it was a scary thing for her to have the banks closed. But for us four boys life was normal.

We all were born and lived at 26 Donegal Springs Road, a new development at the edge of Mt. Joy in the mid-twenties. We had a big yard to play in as well as a small barn (before the advent of the suburban two car garage). But we were town enough to have three cars in the barn, space rented by two neighbors who had neither barn nor garage. At one stage when my older brothers were teens, we actually raised chickens in the second story, a real mess when the litter got soaked from a hose hooked up to water the fryers. But neither of my parents were farmers at heart; even their gardens produced less than the neighbors'.

We lived two doors from the Mt. Joy Mennonite Church, and we were never late. At least fifteen minutes before services, we gathered on the front porch and walked together to church; the littlest children with their mother sat on the "ladies'" side and the older ones with Daddy on the "men's" side. Church was important to our family. We always attended Sunday school as well. As a small child I remember summer Bible school, the preschoolers meeting on our front porch, the rest scattered around the church. And I remember the singing led by Miller Hess. We shouted at the top of our lungs.

Daddy was a song leader at church, frequently raising the tune from the place where he was sitting near the front, sometimes getting up and leading with his hand. He had a good tenor voice. We sang around the house as well. Daddy and Mama also played the piano. We children each took lessons, some of which took better than others. I remember one day complaining about having to practice; so Mama, knowing what was coming, said that I didn't need to play if I didn't want to. That afternoon a big truck arrived and delivered a baby grand piano. What a fix I was in, holding back, but so much wanting a turn to play. Music, an important part of our lives, included visits to concerts at Lancaster, dress up occasions with Mama and Daddy. Once shortly after we started piano and horn lessons, the new teacher gathered Luke, Elton, and me for a performance of her own singing. When she launched into something operatic, I started giggling. Luke, six years older than I, hissed at me, "Quiet, this is supposed to be good." Perhaps today I should have a little sympathy for those who detest operatic singing, which I now enjoy.

Everyone in our family read: the newspapers (early in the morning we would shout "paper first" to have first chance at the comics), novels, magazines, children's books, the Sunday school quarterly, *The Gospel Herald*, *The Words of Cheer* and *The Youth's Christian Companion* (never better than when Christmas Carol Kauffman was being serialized). Daddy recited poetry at the dinner table from his one-room school days: "The Village Blacksmith," "Leetle Yakob Straus," and "In School-Days." He always regretted that when he was in school he had raced through the poems instead of reading them with expression. Finally he had a chance to redeem himself when we all gathered at Airey Hill schoolhouse with his former classmates to celebrate another era, his recitation the high light of the day for me.

Reading and reading, I would go from one book to another. One day Daddy said, "James, why don't you put down your book and go out and play with the other boys?" And I remember saying, "I just want to read to the end of the chapter." Now I hear our son saying to his son as Daddy said to me, "And how many pages is that?" It wasn't always only one or two.

This is taking too much time with childhood, but I want to point out two other important parts of my development. Our family always valued family and friends. My mother visited her mother every Tuesday to go shopping or go visiting with other relatives. Grandma and Grandpa Rohrer lived at 1010 North Duke Street, one block from the Lancaster train station. "The Depot" we called it. As a five year-old I once traveled on the train alone from Mt. Joy to Lancaster. Of course, Mama put me on the train and told the conductor when to set me down. Surely Grandma came to the station platform, or did I march up the steps to that grand marble station and then down the steps and up the sidewalk to Grandma's house? We children would go to Grandpa's office on King Street to be joined by our cousins. Grandpa said, "When I have one boy

I have a boy, when I have two boys I have half a boy, when I have three boys I don't have any boys." He knew how to keep us busy, though, straightening bent nails and breaking up stones in the driveway! That was Lancaster city.

The Bomberger relatives lived in and near bucolic Elm in Penn Township just north of Manheim and Lititz. Grandma Bomberger, Aunt Katie, Aunt Lizzie, Uncle John and Aunt Elizabeth, the cousins Arlene, Henry and Roy. We enjoyed the country store started by our grandfather. We enjoyed the animals and the big barn. We enjoyed those grand Sunday dinners, what we would now call a sinful spread of meats and vegetables with at least seven sweets and seven sours. Mama never cooked like that at home. Once on a snowy December day Daddy hired a horse and sleigh to go to Elm, a nostalgic trip for him and a novelty for us. Unfortunately for the horse, the sun melted some of the snow on the plowed roads.

In addition to family we had a wide circle of friends, some from my parents' younger days, some from church circles, some from our neighborhood. Suffice it to say that relationships with family and friends were part of the hospitality that made up family life. Those who moved on (Fannie Heisey, the baby nurse, and Ruth Funk, Mama's helper when David was born) were remembered with stories and visits.

One other thing, a story that has followed me. When I was not more than four, perhaps three, my mother and I sat at the edge of a meadow on canvas chairs. When a cow came by and swished her tail, I reportedly said, "Oh, Mama, look at the cow's tail blooming." This descriptive but not accurate view of what I saw came to be coupled with another phrase, "Mama, I'm for pretty." Art, in one form or another, was an important part of our lives. Our living room walls had paintings and prints, including *The Return from Calvary* and *Christ at Gethsemane*. Being visually oriented, I often took art courses in school and noted carefully art in homes and public places, paying attention to form in architecture.

Part II: Education

I eagerly awaited the first day of school. I did not know when I first became eager for my chance to trot off to the big brick school house at the center of town, but it must have been sometime shortly after Elton started, almost a two year wait. No kindergarten or preschool got me out of the house early. With a birthday in March I was one of the oldest in my class when I skipped down the sidewalk with my two older brothers and started on the great adventure at age six. I still have that early reading/writing workbook, a precious possession given out by Miss Charles, a warm and understanding young teacher. We did learn to read, the magic key to all learning. It was harder to learn to sit still and listen. Miss Heim in second grade gave us a unique way to subtract, a math fad of the thirties. Miss Taylor taught me a new word by marking thirteen on my third grade report card. I turned the card over to find "13, incessant whispering." And so it went up through the grades. The learning was fun. The teachers often enhanced learning. Somewhere along the way I declared that I wanted to be a teacher the students would enjoy, a teacher who made learning fun. As a senior I admired Miss Zeller and decided on English as my college major. She was working on a master's at the time at Breadloaf and had Robert Frost as a teacher. "What would you be if you had two masters," he asked her. He, of course, answered the question, "A mama." In those days, the early fifties, she did not mind the sexism implicit in his answer even though she was feminist long before the word was used.

Our parents were happy to have us decide to go to college even though they had not. Our father, who became a bank cashier, went to business "college" after elementary school. Mother had finished high school. I was the first in our family to go to college. Elton and David followed. Luke had taken the EMC short term Bible course. At EMC I found an environment where I could join in all activities, no family forbidden dances. But I arrived as the typical freshman, holding my umbilical cord in hand and looking for a place to plug it in. My freshman year biology class under D. Ralph Hostetter helped make the transition from high school student to college student. Mrs. Brackbill's "Intro to Lit" gave me the key elements of literary appreciation and interpretation, skills I still use today. Finally Brother Pellman (who at 32 seemed so old and learned to me) became a mentor and eventually a dear friend as we taught together.

Later when I taught at Lancaster Mennonite School, Jesse Byler introduced me to the Temple University Ford Foundation experimental master's program for teachers being given at Franklin and Marshall College in Lancaster. With Calvin Shenk and others I joined in a fascinating humanities program that emphasized literature, social studies and science. Unknown to me at the time, it became the best preparation for helping to teach the EMC interdisciplinary course, Global Civilization. As I graduated in 1960 with a Master of Science in Education, I was well on the way to becoming a generalist instead of a specialist.

Having moved on to college teaching at my alma mater, I determined to earn a doctorate before getting too old (whatever that might have meant). After two years of teaching I explored various programs and settled on Teachers College at Columbia University, perhaps the most prestigious teachers college in the nation at the time. It offered a doctorate in education in the college teaching of English. That program included literature (Lennox Grey with literature and the literary audience), communication (Louis Forsdale introducing us to Marshall McLuhan's "the medium is the message"), and linguistics (Robert Allen with structural grammar and the idea that usage determines correctness). These were exhilarating times for me, rubbing shoulders with nationally known professors and with fellow students, many graduates of major universities. Again my horizons were broadened rather than narrowed. Over the years I have pondered the road less traveled by that I chose. Would I now opt for the MA in literature or the PhD in linguistics? Would I choose to be narrow and focused in my studies? But I always realized that I could not do without the broad education, which was such a good preparation for the varied teaching I did at EMU, in Africa, in China and in Japan.

After graduation I continued to take courses at JMU, UVA, Virginia Tech and North Carolina A & T. I still read, especially fiction. There is always so much new to learn. We can no longer be Renaissance persons who found it possible to read all the books of their time. I also discovered that it is not necessary to have read everything in someone else's field. I am content with all the learning and the joy in continued learning. And always I am aware of how much I do not know.

Of course education includes learning outside the classroom. My first visit to a great art museum occurred on a family trip to

Washington, DC, when I was seven or eight. Our family entered the east wing of the National Gallery of Art. I'll never forget the four of us boys giggling at the Greek statues of naked boys. My memory says our parents said, "Don't laugh; they can't help it." Go figure. I still remember from that visit that the Mellon Gallery is made of limestone that turns pink when it gets wet. After that we went to visit the National Cathedral, marching across the tarpaper roof of what would later become the foundation of the nave. We gazed up at the crossing and imagined the finished building stretching out to the west. (I got to see the latter stages of the building when our humanities teams took students to DC.)

When Doris and I dated, we went to museums, trudging up those steps at the Philadelphia Museum of Art, the Chicago Art Museum, and the various DC museums. A common experience for both of us was to realize suddenly how hungry we were. Looking at our watches, we realized that we had missed the lunch hour because we were so engrossed in the art. On my graduation trip to Europe the Rijks Museum in Amsterdam was not the least impressive art gallery I saw. Later, when we lived in New York City, we visited the Metropolitan Museum of Art, the Guggenheim, the Huntington Hartford, and others.

We increased our art education by buying early on from Paul Friesen and Irvin Horst (a Rouault) and putting aside our prints for originals. Our collection of art represents joint decisions about what we wanted and how much money we wished to spend. We each have favorites, of course. In Africa we collected West African masks from Charleys (usually Muslim tradesmen) who came to our door. When we returned to the States, we visited galleries to see African collections and bought books on art. Doris developed a separate collection of cloth. Her studies in textiles at Penn State helped her to analyze fabrics wherever we lived. In China and Japan we again broadened our horizons. Personally, I'm still waiting to find an original Russian icon. Doris has encouraged me in this. In the meantime I have a decoupaged print.

I still play the piano, as Allie Lapp said, for my own amazement. I enjoy singing in church. I enjoy singing with our VMRC Tet. (We never know if it will be an octet or a nanet.) But I have not pursued music far. I enjoy performances and listening to my CD's, including a goodly share of opera singers.

Part III: Family and Friends

Remember *South Pacific?* The young guy is told he will discover his special someone across a crowded room. "And somehow you'll know, you'll know even then, that somehow you'll see her again and again." And I do, across the breakfast table in the morning and from one Lazyboy to the other as we sit knitting, reading or watching TV. She is always there. I begin with this most important of relationships, because it has been the most meaningful relationship of my life. To rob this first meeting of some of its sentimentality, I must admit it was in broad daylight. Ira Miller's secondary education class was not crowded. Oh, yes, I had seen her when I was fifteen, and she seventeen, sitting with her sisters at North End Mennonite Church when my parents and I visited my grandmother Rohrer. But that was too soon. At that time I saw all three sisters. In college I saw her with the awareness that here was someone so special she could not be ignored. Lucky for me, she accepted my overtures, and the rest is history. Our relationship remains the most important of my life. It brought us, of course, our two children, for whom she laid aside her career to make use of her graduate school minor, child development. She did not go back to teaching and furthering her graduate work until the children were well established in school.

The children with this solid foundation went on to excel in academics. Doris gets the credit for helping them with their homework, learning new math with them, and helping them become independent learners. Doug is Professor of Music and Chairman of the Department of Fine and Performing Arts at Elizabethtown (PA) College. Cathy is Associate Professor of Emergency Medicine at the University of Virginia. Each has published both books and articles. At twelve and ten they traveled with us three-quarters of the way around the world to spend two years in West Africa. Eventually Doris and I were proud to see them grow up and leave for Goshen College.

Everywhere we went we found new friends, friends we still keep in contact with. Back home we rejoiced each time at the friendships that continued to grow deeper. Our invitation from the Kralls to join their K-Group has provided a stability and security here in Park View, where we have so few relatives. In these later years Doris also rejoices to have her two sisters nearby. We have found departmental friendships that are unusually strong and include the spouses on many occasions.

Part IV: Faith and Service

Somehow, faith and service go together in my mind, in my earliest choices, in my life's work, and finally in my retirement. I was raised in a Christian family with parents of deep faith more often felt than expressed. I went willingly to church each Sunday, to Sunday school, and to summer Bible school. I say willingly, meaning without question and, yes, with joy. I went the same way I went to school when I turned six. It was what you did as a family, no questions asked. No one wanted to stay home.

And so I absorbed Christianity as a way of life. It was the revival meetings that presented me with the need for a conscious choice. I squirmed at the invitation as a preteen. I knew I loved Jesus and that I was somehow in the kingdom. Yet I knew that I must make a choice and "stand" at the invitation. Looking back, I wonder why I resisted and how long it was before I finally went forward at a campfire invitation at Laurelville Mennonite Camp. I was twelve, the age when my fellow classmates also stood to declare their intentions. For me surely faith came earlier. It was a natural transition with growing understanding, a growth that has continued through life. Looking back at the Laurelville experience, I remember the strong emotional response and the felt need to confess. But what sins could I confess, a good little boy who tried too hard to please? So I declared my unworthiness. Looking back, I perceive a preteen often displaying the exuberance of a child as well as the intense emotional stress of a teenager.

I remember that as a teenager I went happily off to our youth group's Lord's acre project. I am not sure it was the hoeing of weeds so much as it was the fun of our all being together. We also handed out *The Way*, but that put us in the position of more actively witnessing. I found it easier to join a group singing at the Welsh Mountains or the Wernersville Hospital. In college I began to struggle with intellectual doubts about faith, but I lived by choice the totally committed life. The YPCA, gospel teams, street meetings and more were all a regular part of college life, where service and faith walked hand in hand.

The summer between my junior and senior years I worked in a student-in-industry program in New York City. By day I was a courier for a major Wall Street bank. In the evenings and on weekends I sang tenor in a quartet for street meetings. New York was exhilarating, but street preaching was not to my liking. Merit Robinson screamed at the top of his lungs, his powerful voice reverberating off the brick walls of the tenement houses. "Repent and be saved." Surely earnestness counted for something. The beautiful four-part harmony of our quartet must have sounded tame to those used to listening to Frank Sinatra.

After graduation I was all set to go to a mental hospital in Philadelphia for my I-W service when I received an invitation from the Relief and Service Office of MBM (Mennonite Board of Missions) to serve as Relief and Service Editor for two years. I accepted. Those two years changed my whole perspective. I discovered the larger Mennonite Church. Lancaster, Virginia, and EMBM (Eastern Mennonite Board of Missions and Charities) were not nearly the whole. From then on, my perspective would grow: later in Liberia Doris and I met, lived and worked with Episcopalians, Lutherans, Methodists and others; in China we learned to fellowship and enjoy the indigenous Three-Self Patriotic Church; and in Japan the Mennonite Church at different locations with meaningful small fellowships challenged us to be faithful disciples.

Halfway through my I-W service, Doris and I were married. As the two years drew toward a close, we considered service in West Africa with MBM. Then Doris' father, Noah G. Good, wrote with an invitation for both of us to teach at Lancaster Mennonite School. That first year at LMS I learned Doris' capacity for work. While carrying our first child, she spent half time teaching, half time helping to remodel an old house in Mt. Joy, and half time completing her thesis and thus graduating with an MS in Clothing and Textiles at Pennsylvania State University. I spent four years teaching at LMS, good years, getting a feel for teaching, learning to communicate with young people to help them achieve as they were able and interested. I also served in my home church, Mt. Joy Mennonite, as Sunday school superintendent and song leader. Doris was always at my side, supporting me in my master's program and raising the children while keeping house.

Those were busy, good years. The last year I served as editor of *The Missionary Messenger*, the official organ of EMBM. As you can see, there is little that is directly evangelistic, yet all these provided opportunities for service, service that strengthened my faith and helped me as much as it helped others. This has always been the case. I gained more than I gave.

Teaching at EMC followed teaching at LMS. At the time, John R. Mumaw stated that all the teachers had felt a call to serve at EMU. I was not sure what or how that call could be known, but I did know that I wanted to go back to my alma mater. President Mumaw also mentioned that Doris might some day come back to teach again. She had taught in the home economics and art departments in the mid-fifties. We returned to EMC in 1961.

By 1966 I had completed my doctorate and was back at EMC, ready to be part of the major curriculum revision taking place under the administration of Myron S. Augsburger and Ira E. Miller. We sat around discussing the radical revision of the school calendar, the class schedule, and the course credits. We designed humanities courses that included the history of civilization and of the church, the growth of the arts, and the wonders of great literature. Psychology and the sciences were included. When I retired in 1998, I received a certificate of commendation for 32 years of service. But I always like to think of them as 37 years, 1961 to 1998. The year at Columbia University, one of two years in Liberia, two in China, and one in Japan were leaves-of-absence. While those five did not count as service to EMU, I see them as Eastern Mennonite's contribution to each of those places, part of the mission of EMC, now U. I also know how much I gained from those experiences and in turn brought back to enhance my teaching.

When we decided to accept the Fulbright to Liberia, a friend wrote, "We would be scared to go." But we were not scared; we were eager and in a way called. Doris was invited to teach as well, and our service there was clearly appreciated and reflected our ties to EMU. We happily accepted the invitation to stay a second year. We went to the People's Republic of China for Doris' sabbatical. In preparation, Doris took work in teaching ESL; and she taught composition to one hundred students, assigning an essay each week. Again we accepted an invitation to stay a second year.

In China (1981–83) we were among the first foreign teachers allowed into the country after the Cultural Revolution. We got to visit and fellowship in the church in China as it came back from thirty years of being silenced. I remember one of our Chinese leaders' question to a British teacher: "Why must these people worship God? They are good teachers and very effective. Their religion is their only flaw." As you can imagine, our witness in China was a witness of presence. Occasionally we found how clearly it spoke.

It was not easy to live in a country that was avowedly atheistic. During those two years, I often repeated the closing verses in Jude, "Now unto Him...." They served as a mantra, a reminder of my commitment. I had and have a hard time reconciling the idea of a loving God and of over a billion people who do not know and do not have a chance of knowing his plan of redemption.

When asked what Christianity has to offer that is unique, I thought for some time. I finally said, "I think it is the possibility of forgiveness." Forgiveness is not easy in general, and it is almost impossible when the individual has not received forgiveness. One of my final experiences in China was to have a frustrated administrator take my hand to get my attention and then spit on my shoes. I forgave him, but not by my own power. This was a man for whom we worked, sacrificed, and gave our all. We were later to learn that he had always hated Americans. The whole experience left me with a sad and tired feeling.

In Japan we were needed to satisfy the National Board of Education requirement that a new junior college be adequately staffed by qualified English teachers. Doris had to give up her seminary job so that we could go together for this assignment. Our year and a half there was blessed by the many friendships we developed with both faculty and students, especially with two Christian couples who accepted us for who we were. We are delighted with the success of some of the students who came to EMU and are now living and working in the U.S. One has taught at EMU. Again, we gained more than we gave. In both China and Japan we served as mission associates with MBM.

Both China and Japan provided us with insights into Asian culture. I have to smile, though, when I remember (during World War II) my fifth grade teacher's saying that we would skip studying Japan since we were at war with Japan and China and Japan were basically the same. Nothing could be further from the truth. Aside from chopsticks and beautiful calligraphy, the cultures of China and Japan have little in common.

Two things in closing. I remember Richard Detweiler's saying, "God is a choice." While I do not know exactly what he meant, I have taken it as an answer to the intellectual doubts that come. I have also found strength in the response of the VMRC community to death. Thirty of our friends have died since we moved into Park Gables five years ago. The Christians of varying faiths have come together to take comfort in their belief that their friends are with God.

Recently I read in *Mennonite Weekly Review* an editorial by Bradley Siebert. He said that he keeps looking for an epiphany. "Do I expect a revelation, a clear doubt-dispelling bolt from the blue? Or accept what God reveals?" Remember the Misfit in O'Connor's "A Good Man is Hard to Find." In talking about Jesus' raising the dead, he says, "I wasn't there so I can't say....I wish I had of been there…because if I had been there I would of known." He can't take the leap of faith that would redeem him. Too often I want to substitute proof for faith. But faith is a choice. Siebert wrote, "I believe I have a brand of personal relation—amazed gratitude for the providence displayed in creation and an accompanying devotion to the call to love its creatures and Creator." I am struck by the phrase "amazed gratitude." This is what I feel, daily. Seibert went on to say, "I pray…for the grace to offer my witness to others in an humble spirit, as one sharing stories of the road with my fellow travelers."

Looking back on the college freshman trying to find a place to plug in, I recognize a pattern in life. I committed myself (plugged in) at each of the places I served. I felt that I was serving more than I felt that I was working or earning money. At the mission boards, the schools, and in the foreign assignments, I felt I belonged. I have carried that loyalty with me to this day. It was good to hear Diana Enedy say as a number of us retired, "It will be difficult to find staff with the commitment you guys have brought to your teaching." She sees the next generation as more career oriented and less institutionally committed. But also I have unplugged. I do not worry about the changes going on at EMU. I invested a lot of time and energy in participating in the growth of EMC to EMU. Now it is someone else's turn.

So I've plugged in at VMRC. I have a service oriented part-time job as resident services assistant. While not forgetting my former friends and colleagues, I appreciate our church and its fellowship more and more. I find in the singing that truly our hymnody is a book of common prayer for me. Both the words and music express and reinforce the faith I have chosen.

Part V: Conclusion

This then is the life of an ordinary boy who was privileged to have extraordinary experiences. I have had my set of frustrations and disappointments and grief, especially the early death of my father and the umbilical cord accident of our unborn granddaughter, Lauren Elizabeth Custalow. But I have arrived at retirement with a great sense of contentment. My father kept a motto on his desk, "Godliness with contentment is great gain." Contentment is a feeling that, for me, comes with joy. Daily I give thanks that "my lines have fallen in pleasant places." Church, family and friends make life meaningful. I continually find new things to learn, new experiences to enjoy. Not least is the promise found in each of the grandchildren: Nick, Joe and Matthew. There is always Doris, the love of my life, who walked and walks with me. I still see myself as that ordinary boy, a boy who has arrived at retirement filled with contentment. I, too, call it *amazed gratitude*.

December 2005

PART IV

…and Globally

PAUL PEACHEY

A Hippocratic Mid-life Course Change

This telling of my story I will organize around two restaging moments in my life: the first in early adulthood; the second, rather more drawn out, a "Hippocratic" (first, do no harm) mid-life career change.

Somerset County, southwest Pennsylvania's "roof garden" bordering on the Mason Dixon line, was my native farm home. There, in space, I was born and raised between two mountains, and in time, between two wars: born a month and a day before the end of World War I (1918) and coming of age (21) a month and a week after the outbreak of World War II (1939). That region in Pennsylvania had been opened legally for settlement in 1769. Mennonites and Amish filtered into the area soon afterward, though a few may have come earlier. This area also became a stepping-stone for early settlers moving west, perhaps wearied after climbing the Allegheny Mountain range directly to the East.

My father came to Somerset County from Mifflin County in Central Pennsylvania—where he had been born in 1889 into an Amish family—to work briefly during the maple sugar season, presumably in early spring, 1914. He left no record as to why and how he came. Two or more years earlier (1911?) he had spent a summer in the West, working his way from Kansas north into the Dakotas during the wheat harvest. According to his younger relatives, his home Amish congregation was in turmoil during those years. While in the West he heard of Hesston College and might well have sought enrollment there. However, his older sister was to be married that fall, and for this purpose he had to return.

Whatever the reason for the Somerset jaunt in 1914, he there met a progressive young Amish, zither-playing blond named Saloma Bender, and "the rest is history." They were married on January 2, 1916. Her grandfather, Wilhelm Bender, had been sent to America by his parents from Langendorf, a village in west central Germany in 1830, when he was merely 15 years old. Why? Otherwise he would have been drafted into the Prussian Kaiser's army a year or two later. He landed in Baltimore where, to pay for the ocean voyage that had brought him there, he became an indentured servant. An Amish minister in Somerset County—on the Pennsylvania side of the Mason Dixon line—on learning about his situation, rode to Baltimore by horseback to fetch him. The minister paid the remainder of Wilhelm's debt to obtain his release. Some ten years later Wilhelm was able to purchase a nearby tract of land on the Pennsylvania side of the Mason-Dixon, which was later subdivided into several smaller holdings. The farm on which I spent most of my childhood was one of these.

As I grew up in that community in the 1920s and 30s, five varieties of Anabaptists were scattered on both sides of the Mason-Dixon (in Garrett County, Maryland, and Somerset County, Pennsylvania) along the conservative-to-liberal continuum: Old Order Amish, Beachy Amish, Conservative Amish Mennonite, (Old) Mennonite, and the fledgling General Conference Mennonite (that never quite made it). My family was in the middle group, with carefully calibrated relations to the two groups on each of the opposite sides. Curiously (as a product of history too tortuous to be traced here) we were a congregation with two church buildings and alternated between them, Sunday by Sunday. One, called Maple Glen, was three miles away to the south in Maryland; the other, called Oak Dale, was about six miles to the north in Pennsylvania. We lived on a farm a mile from the village of (formerly Chestnut) Springs, the site of an "old" Mennonite church that we visited on special occasions, usually when well-known Mennonite church leaders came to speak.

I belonged to a devout family and when about eleven years old (in 1929), experienced a personal conversion, which turned out to be quite an emotional experience. What triggered this event, I do not recall. However, one summer evening after the milking, while hand cranking the cream separator, I found myself in tears. Someone was present, presumably my older brother, Mark, though here memory fails me—but I have no doubt about the authenticity of that moment. My sense of guilt was overcome, and I was truly "born again." Though baptism came three years later, I have known myself as Christian ever since that cream separator moment.

On a summer Sunday about two years later—in 1931—in our conservative congregation, my family reached an important milestone. I will never forget watching my father, Shem Peachey, being chosen by lot (with six other men being in the pool) and ordained as a minister. Self-educated, he had been increasingly concerned about church renewal. Whether he anticipated ordination, I do not know. As I look back, with that ordination he faced two competing challenges: his new ministerial calling on the one hand; and on the other, the Great Depression, unfolding even as his young family grew. However, these became the teen years for his two oldest sons, Mark and me; and soon we were able to carry the brunt of the farm work. At the same time, our father's other role assumed mentoring importance to us.

Widening Horizons

We children, at least the older cohort, attended the two-room, two-floor public school, which offered grades one through eight in the village of Springs a mile away. We walked to and from school, nearly half of the way through woods and slightly more than half along unpaved country roads. High schools stood in each of the two nearest towns: Grantsville, three miles to our south in Maryland, and Salisbury, five miles to our north in Pennsylvania. However, attending high school was not an option for us, partly because teenagers in those days were needed on farms. Moreover, for us there was a more fundamental problem: higher education loomed as too "worldly."

Meanwhile, that "world" was coming closer as farming itself became more enmeshed with the world beyond. By the mid-1930s we were in conversation with the County Agent, a consulting service to farmers provided by the state. Also, long after graduating from primary school, I took a couple of the farming correspondence courses offered by Pennsylvania State College. Though journals and books in our home were limited, I read voraciously and was delighted when, at a sale, our father acquired a used set of the 1896 edition (my mother's birth year!) of the *Encyclopedia Britannica*. Still, I loved farming and assumed that this was my destiny, albeit dreaming of better lands than our hilly plateau afforded. Thus when I turned twenty-one, I remained at home but now as a "hired man," receiving $25 monthly salary plus room and board.

In the late 1930s my brother Mark married a young woman from a sister congregation a bit farther south in Maryland. They decided to make the annual January-February, six-week Bible course at Eastern Mennonite School (EMS) in Harrisonburg their honeymoon. Their plans, however, were "nixed" by four of the five ordained men in the congregation in an action that vexed me though I was as yet little aware of what was at stake.

Yet in the summer of 1940, a year or two later, I was surprised to find myself in a car heading to EMS, where I would attend the annual three-day Young People's Institute. Though EMS was in an early stage of development, that experience provided me a taste of larger possibilities, and I decided to try the six-week Bible school offered the following year (January–February, 1941). That experience really turned me on, especially when I learned that entry to the two-year junior college Bible course was available for older applicants without high school credentials. By the following September, I was there.

World War II and My Early Adult Years

Meanwhile, already two years earlier (September 2, 1939) what became World War suddenly loomed. My father and I were in a hayfield, harvesting a late second cutting of clover, when John B. Meyer, our livestock dealer from Meyersdale (about ten miles away), came driving his small truck into our field. My father had inquired about the availability of some shoats (young pigs) to supplement a shortfall in that season's baby pig "crop" on our farm. Now Meyer exited from his truckload of fourteen sleek shoats with this announcement: "You can't go wrong on them; there's a war on this morning." Nazi forces had invaded Poland! Without radios and daily papers we had been blissfully unaware of what had taken place the previous day.

Today, more than sixty years later, this scene remains seared in my memory. Why? While I had no direct World War I memories, this announcement triggered a recall of early post-war (WWI) echoes: occasionally seeing someone in uniform; elementary school classmates carrying souvenirs from the war brought home by their fathers; and once in a while passing the home of a World War I veteran, whose sleep was reportedly disrupted by front-line memory-triggered nightmares. Above all, there were stories of the difficulties that conscientious objectors had experienced. Now, a few weeks short of my turning twenty-one, the announcement, "There's a war on this morning!" struck home. This time I was one of those about to be summoned by the military. The wider world was for the first time breaking directly into my experience. For the moment, though, the shoats were what we needed, and the deal was quickly closed. I am sure that the livestock dealer's sales pitch, "There's a war on this morning," had no influence on the transaction.

In time the call did come for me to register for the military draft, and I registered as a CO at the local Elk Lick Township office in West Salisbury a few miles away. My CO status was later confirmed at an office in Somerset, the county seat some twenty-five miles to the north. Nonetheless, I began the two-year college Bible program at EMS in early September 1941.

About two months later came the first lottery-based call up for draftees to be inducted. I happened to be in that initial group. As was known, a variety of circumstances, listed numerically and alphabetically, exempted draftees from actual induction into the military. They included occupations (other than the military) considered of vital interest to the nation, such as the ministry. Thus seminarians and pastors falling in the draftee category were classified as 4-D and deferred from actual service. However, Mennonites had no seminaries and hence no seminary student deferments.

Newly lodged at EMS, I phoned Dean Chester Lehman, who turned out to have surprising news: he had just been notified that Selective Service had classified the four-or-five-year college Bible programs in Mennonite colleges as seminary-equivalent. Though enrolled only in the two-year program, I had learned that Pennsylvania offered pre-professional examinations which, when passed, were accepted as high school-equivalent. Aware of my situation and confident that I could thus qualify for the four-year program, the Dean offered that option to me as an alternative to induction into the Civilian Public Service (CPS).

At this point I was merely two days from induction; and while by then I had a growing sense of a Christian calling, I did not view the professional ministry as an option for me. Still undecided, I phoned the Dean at the last minute. When he answered, what tumbled from my lips was the phrase, "I guess I'll stay."

Barely a month later came Pearl Harbor (in December, 1941). With some discomfort I spent the next four war years at EMS while most of my age peers were in the military or (CO) alternative service. Indeed, the end of the war in Europe and my graduation at EMS both came in May 1945; and the end in the Pacific came that August. I never regretted my decision to stay at EMS, instead of accepting induction into CPS, though unanswered questions remain, principally the following. For a few of my Mennonite age peers who had completed college earlier, the draft steered them into MCC service; for most others, college came afterward. Which would have been better for me? I will never know.

Earlier, by the summer's end in 1944, another problem had arisen. Aware of the "liberal-conservative" dissonance between our denomination's two higher educational institutions—EMS and Goshen—several us EMS students had gone to summer school at Goshen. We wanted to see for ourselves. There I had taken my first sociology course. On returning to EMS for my senior year as a Bible major, I commented to several colleagues, "Theology may reach heaven, but I'm pretty sure it doesn't reach the earth. I'll have to study sociology as well—*as well*, not *instead of*." But whatever the validity of that observation, I surely had little awareness of what it would entail!

From "I" to "We"

The end of World War II in May 1945 in Europe and in mid-August in the Pacific was an important benchmark in modern history. Between these two events came the first of two touchstone moments that changed my personal life during that season as well. A few weeks after my May graduation from EMS came my June 10th wedding to Ellen Elizabeth Shenk. She had come to EMS from nearby Newport News, Virginia, for her high school senior year in 1942–43 and begun junior college there a year later. Not only, as in marriages generally, did my "I" in fundamental ways become a "we," but she became my most important confidant, associate, and partner for the rest of our days together. After a brief honeymoon, we moved to a Philadelphia suburb for me to begin graduate school in sociology at the University of Pennsylvania. "To put her hubby through school," Ellen found employment in a men's pants factory.

My admission to the University of Pennsylvania, however, was provisional. I still needed a credentialed BA; the ThB degree was not enough. Moreover, although the war had ended, the draft was still in effect. EMS and Virginia Conference officialdom quickly reminded me that I had been deferred from military service to train for church work. While for me some sociological training was part of my sense of vocation, externally that was not evident and I had been offered two full-time church options upon graduation. I had declined them. At best, this summer at Penn would be transitional.

Finally, the Touchstone Moment

By summer's end, when we returned to Harrisonburg, two part-time assignments had been improvised for the next year. I would teach a high school Bible course at EMS and assist the pastor at the Chicago Avenue Mennonite Church in preparation for a new outpost assignment across town. Longer-term solutions meanwhile lay dormant. Then by late September (1945) Ellen and I made our first post-wedding weekend visit to her parental home near Newport News. Not yet able to afford a car of our own, we drove a vanload of chicks for her uncle Jacob's Shenk Hatchery to a local poultry man in the Newport News area. We expected to return to Harrisonburg the next Sunday afternoon.

Midway through the Sunday morning service in Ellen's home church, I was gripped by a sudden epiphany unrelated to the sermon. Suddenly "I knew": *I am going to Europe under the Mennonite Central Committee (MCC).* MCC preparations for postwar relief had evolved as the war progressed. At the time most U.S. Mennonites were farmers, effectively providing a base for food supply donations for shipment overseas. Informally related to this was the mid-century comprehensive publication of sixteenth-century Anabaptist sources then underway—legal records as well as writings. American Mennonite scholars and agencies were becoming involved in the project. Until then, historians had relied chiefly on official church and state condemnatory records of that movement. But by mid-century Anabaptist and Mennonite history had begun to undergo radical revision.

While Ellen and I were vaguely aware of these two developments, until that moment the possibility of MCC service had not been part of our calculations. Back in Harrisonburg, I listed at the top of my Monday morning agenda a visit to the Dean's office. There, simply on the basis of that Sunday morning epiphany, I knocked on his door and asked to be released.

He returned a puzzled look. "Didn't Brother Mumaw see you on Saturday? He was sent to ask you to go to Belgium for MCC."

"No," I replied. "I was away for the weekend."

Suddenly, clarity. Here, too, "the rest is history," eight years of personal history. Logistics and red tape took several months; but at last on February 13, 1946, Wilson Hunsberger, a Canadian MCC volunteer likewise assigned to Belgium, and I set sail for Southampton, England, on the SS Washington for its first post-war civilian voyage. Going via London and then Amsterdam, we were to join Cleo Mann, already in Brussels, to become a three-man postwar MCC relief team in Belgium.

Nonetheless it was not all that simple. Although Ellen and I had been married less than four months, I was being asked to go alone. The immediate postwar turmoil in Europe was such that MCC was not sending married couples. Moreover, twenty-four was the minimum age for appointed workers. While by then I was almost twenty-seven, Ellen was twenty-two. We needed time to reflect and share, but our common faith enabled us to resolve the matter amicably. After all, married draftees were not exempt from military assignment abroad. Happily, a year later, though only twenty-three, she was permitted to join me. Married couples had proved to be a stabilizing presence in the MCC teams of largely unattached young workers!

That dual Sunday-Monday call, at once personal and communal, yet with each aspect emerging independently, was unique. Though not a blueprint or a literal precedent, it became a touchstone that has prevailed for me to this day. It was an experience resonating with that of Jacob, the Genesis patriarch, recorded in Genesis 28. Setting out on foot for his ancestral land to find a spouse, he slept in the desert with a stone for a pillow. Following a deep sleep with a nighttime vision, he awoke frightened: "Surely the LORD is in this place…and I did not know it." No, the LORD is not a handyman with a quick fix for our run-of-the-mill daily inconveniences. But we are instructed repeatedly to wait for his larger direction, not determined by our own self-improvised calendar.

Our European Sojourn

From here on, this story must be compressed. Antwerp had quickly become the major port of entry of supplies for the immediate postwar American military, thus indirectly resulting in an early postwar boost to the Belgian economic recovery. We provided mostly small-scale food and clothing distributions for those left behind in the margins. Meanwhile, MCC plans were underway to bring a housing reconstruction team to the eastern tip of Belgium, where towns and villages had been devastated by the "von Rundstedt offensive," Hitler's final lurch to the West near the end of the war. Also, MCC traffic through our Brussels center increased, where Ellen served as matron after her arrival in early 1947.

Soon afterward, I began my final Brussels assignment—with the help of a Belgian Protestant chaplain's assistant—delivering MCC clothing packages to families of Belgian political prisoners scattered over almost the whole country. Great numbers, perhaps a tenth of the population, had been arrested at war's end and accused of collaboration with the Germans during their occupation of the country. Only a tenth of that original tenth were found guilty and sentenced. While most were given brief sentences, in early 1947 many were still detained in varied camps. Naturally, the country's public welfare system did not provide family assistance; thus without their usual breadwinner, many prisoners' families found themselves in dire straits.

By the summer of 1947 our transfer to the MCC team in the French occupation zone of West Germany beckoned. Given the impoverishing impact of the German occupation prior to the war and then of the war itself, the French zone was the poorest of the three western zones (the American, British, and French). Large-scale MCC food and clothing distributions peaked there during the 1947–48 academic year. We arrived early that fall to join the MCC team of about a dozen workers headquartered in Neustadt/Haardt in the Palatinate, some ten miles west of the Rhine River and opposite Heidelberg.

MCC assigned teams, mostly couples, to towns and cities in the surrounding region. Ellen and I were sent to Pirmasens, a small city near the French border with a population of 37,000, the shoe-manufacturing metropolis of the country. We returned to the Neustadt headquarters each weekend, but during the week we stayed in a hotel occupied by officers of the French military occupation forces. MCC was not yet permitted to operate within the German economy. That winter in Pirmasens, through the work of a local coordinating committee and some forty volunteers, we did the following: organized a twice-a-week feeding of all the elementary and middle school pupils; distributed bread weekly to all the city's elderly; set up clothing distributions; and provided programs for special groups such as infants and returning prisoners of war. With these activities well underway and with Ellen continuing to oversee them, I went north a hundred miles to the newly founded University of Mainz. There with assistance I set up a weekly soup feeding for six thousand students and a Christmas party with goodies for half of the faculty.

By the spring of 1948 a new political stage was emerging in postwar Europe. Relations between the war-time allies of the Soviet Union and the West had deteriorated to the point where the three Western allies and their zones of occupation agreed to the formation of the German Federal Republic and hence the formal ending of the Allied occupation. Money reform was included, and the new German mark quickly became a stable currency. With the economy now recovering, the MCC program was rapidly altered. All the while the eastern zone, which remained under Soviet control, was eventually declared the German Democratic Republic and part of the Soviet Bloc.

Another Change of Course

Meanwhile, it was assumed that Ellen and my terms of service would total 48 months, the equivalent of two, two-year terms. In April 1948, after having already extended my two-year stay by three months, I ended my service to enroll in the University of Basel. Professor Fritz Blanke, church historian at the University of Zurich and a leader in the publication of the sixteenth Anabaptist records, had already agreed to my doing a sociological dissertation on Swiss Anabaptist origins. A semester at Basel would be a preliminary step. I would attend lecture courses with scholars that semester like the theologian Karl Barth, philosopher Karl Jaspers, and church historian Oscar Cullmann.

While Ellen remained part of the Neustadt team, I took up residence at the MCC-Europe headquarters in Basel and volunteered part-time activity in the MCC office there. Midway through the semester came a moment somewhat akin to the memorable September Sunday-Monday moments in the Warwick River church and EMS nearly three years earlier. On this occasion it was a deep awareness that, with the West German recovery now launched, this was not the time for MCC to leave. Real recovery would now become possible.

After raising the possibility of a new project with the MCC administrators both in Europe and at home, we saw a vision quickly emerge for a center based in Frankfurt/Main that would contribute to the social rehabilitation about to begin. Ellen and I would return stateside for a two-month furlough and then come back to begin a new five-year term in Frankfurt. During that term, I would also continue my graduate work and finish it with my dissertation at Zurich.

(A special institute of sociology was flourishing at the University of Frankfurt, appropriate to my sociological interest. In the winter of 1949 I attended a colloquium offered by the key figures there: Theodor Adorno and Max Horkheimer. Having just returned from their wartime sojourn in the USA, they had yet to begin their formal programs).

Logistics for that furlough included our accompanying the ocean voyage of the European delegation—a group of thirteen from France, West Germany, Holland and Switzerland—to the 1948 Mennonite World Conference at Goshen and Newton. We set sail from Rotterdam for New York on July 22, 1948, on the Veendam, a vessel from the Holland-America Line. That voyage with the delegation was a ringside seat to the bitterness between the Dutch and the Germans, the legacy of the war just past.

At summer's end Ellen and I returned to Germany. For initial explorations we commuted from Neustadt to Frankfurt by MCC jeep. Finding the German economy still dependent on the US military economy, we rented an apartment in an American officer compound (Karl von Weinbergstrasse 9) and remained there for a full year. We faced two tasks: finding a suitable setting for an MCC center geared to German reconstruction; and beginning projected activities, the most immediate and concrete of which were international volunteer student work camps, mostly summer programs that had recently begun. One year-round program was already in progress: building homes for Russian Mennonite refugees in Germany at Espelkamp, a new North German town growing from the remaining buildings of a previous poison gas manufacturing compound.

By late 1949 Vogtstrasse 44 emerged as MCC headquarters for international activities and exchanges. In lieu of paying rent, MCC restored a war-damaged three-story plus basement and attic mansion, which afforded space for staff housing, offices and guests. The largest first-floor room contained both a meeting room and chapel that served the small Mennonite congregation in Frankfurt for several years. For me personally two problems quickly began to emerge. As indicated, completing my graduate education was part of the five-year package. In the fall of 1949, as noted, I enrolled at the University of Frankfurt for part-time study. However, the challenge of the new MCC project in Frankfurt took priority in my time and energy, and I had to miss classes repeatedly. Part time study was clearly not an option.

The second problem emerged a bit later as an anecdote will illustrate. As I began explorations with Protestant churchmen and scholars, speaking opportunities emerged. Once I was invited to address a meeting of German clergy at the Evangelical Academy in the Ruhr area on early Christian pacifism. Yes, I had taken a course in church history, and the topic was part of the agenda in peace discussions during the recent war. But as we got deeper into discussion, it became evident that these well-educated German clergy knew early Christian history better than I did. It took only a few such experiences for me to get the message: The challenge before us lay beyond my competence.

With part-time study already ruled out, all I could do was to bow out in order to continue my training. This meant, following due deliberations with MCC administrators, terminating the five-year agreement at the end of three years. By the summer's end of 1951, Ellen and I, with our first child, a daughter born in Frankfurt the previous year, moved to

Zurich. Enrolling at the University there, I would soon begin work on my dissertation. In 1946, not long after getting started in MCC-Brussels, I had chauffeured Harold S. Bender from there to Zurich for his conversation with Professor Fritz Blanke, active there in the publication of the sixteenth-century court and other records of original Anabaptism. When at the end of the visit I indicated an interest in the sociological analysis of Anabaptist origins as a possible dissertation topic, Professor Blanke pulled out a listing of references from a desk drawer exactly on that topic. We agreed that in a few years I would pursue that area.

Finally, after my first semester there in 1951, the several departments and schools—church history, sociology and general history—approved that topic, each appointing a professor to my dissertation guidance committee: Rene Koenig from sociology, Fritz Blanke from church history, and Leonard von Muralt from general history. Meanwhile I took courses from all three, as well as from many others. By the summer of 1953 I had concluded my dissertation and was admitted to the two-week long doctoral examinations. Only in 1954, after publication of the dissertation, did I officially receive my Doctor of Philosophy diploma. Written and then published in German, it is entitled: *Die soziale Herkunft der Schweizer Taeufer in der Reformationszeit: Eine religionssoziolgishe Untersuchung*, Karlsruhe: Buchdruckerei und Verlag Heinrich Schneider, 1954 *(The Social Origin of Swiss Anabaptists during the Reformation: a Study in the Sociology of Religion)*.

Finally, One More Event in Europe

In the spring of 1952 seven young American men on various assignments in Europe, all at varied stages of graduate study, had conferred for ten days at the MCC center in Amsterdam, The Netherlands. Ours was the generation directly impacted by the war, either to participate in or to act in alternately as COs. We in the Amsterdam meeting all fell into the latter category. Additionally, we were impacted indirectly, if not directly, by the fresh perspectives emerging from the publication of sixteenth century Anabaptist materials then underway. New challenges were emerging, not only about Christendom generally, but also about current Anabaptist and Mennonite practices.

We devoted our first week in Amsterdam to Dutch Anabaptist

history lectures by several Dutch Mennonite scholars. After the weekend in Menno Simons' historical country to the North in Friesland, during the second week we wrestled with our own ideas, though without aiming at agreements. A year later we met again for a few days, this time in Zurich. While working mostly with our own concerns, we had a fruitful session with Emil Brunner, one of my professors there. He had just been immersed in his own small book entitled in English translation, *The Misunderstanding of the Church*. Soon he would be off to a two-year scholarly sojourn in Japan, where he was further stimulated by encounters with the *mukyokai* (non-church) movement. In the Zurich meeting we reached agreement about further such occasions and also the publication of a continuing series of occasional papers as a journal entitled *Concern*. From 1954 to 1971 a total of 18 collections of *Concern* papers appeared, authored by a widening circle of conversational participants.

More Forks in the Road

Now this account must shrink to a mere outline. After the completion of my studies and dissertation at Zurich in the summer of 1953, Ellen and I with our two young daughters returned to the U.S. in time for the fall semester of the new academic year. EMS had become an accredited four-year liberal arts college known as EMC, and the high school had become independent. I was to begin sociology in the college curriculum and also to teach Anabaptist studies as part of church history.

Here I need to interject an aftermath from my European sojourn. In 1951 the Continuation Committee of the Historic Peace Churches (HPC) in Europe, child of its elder stateside committee, began a conversation with the executive of the newly formed (1948) World Council of Churches, Dr. Willem A. Visser t' Hooft, located in Geneva, Switzerland. In the fall of 1952, while at the Sorbonne in Paris on a trimester assignment from Rene Koenig, my Zurich sociology professor, I had been asked by the European HPC Committee to draft an introductory paper on the pacifist-just war problem as the basis for a discussion with WCC circles. That paper was finally submitted—after several editorial sessions—to the WCC, triggering, during the 1950s and early 60s, a series of European conferences named for the Swiss village, Puidoux, near Geneva.

While en route back to the U.S. I stopped for the final editing of that paper with the committee in a Paris hotel, and after that I was not directly involved in the Puidoux events that followed. However, that brief involvement in the ecumenical peace and war discourse brought me in touch with the Church Peace Mission (CPM) in the U.S. on our return. That independent ecumenical initiative in this country had sprung from a Detroit conference convened in 1950 with HPC participation. After attending its second gathering in that city in the fall of 1953, I was put on a committee charged with long range planning.

My plate meanwhile was already overflowing. After my mostly European public and academic experiences, getting settled and integrated into the relatively new EMC setting was at once challenging and exciting. At the same time, we needed to find various places to live until the spring of 1957, when we could finally move into our own still unfinished house on College Avenue. Also, the previous autumn we had been confronted by a totally unexpected challenge: Orie O. Miller, the MCC executive with whom I had become well acquainted during our years in Europe, came in effect knocking at our door. Given my growing involvement in the peace-war discourse, he asked us to take a two-year leave of absence to serve in a peace witness consultancy to missions and churches in Japan by the fall of 1957. That program had been initiated by Goshen College historian, Melvin Gingerich, whose two-year assignment was now ending. Our initial response was understandably "no way." Not surprisingly, however, Orie persisted and eventually won. On August 22, 1957, with our three young children, we set sail on the SS President Wilson from San Francisco on the thirteen-day voyage to Yokohama with an overnight stop in Hawaii.

Just weeks before our departure another request had come. Ferment was building in our Mennonite churches in the U.S. over the above noted *Concern* discussion begun in Amsterdam in 1952. Four of the Amsterdam seven had meanwhile returned stateside. In the summer of 1957 church leaders from Goshen College, the Mennonite Publishing House in Scottdale, and EMC called a daylong meeting with these four in Cumberland, Maryland. The hope was to calm the waters of this ferment; and this meeting, conducted in that spirit, succeeded in some measure. Since I was then removed from the general scene in the U.S. by our leave of absence in Japan, I was not fully in touch with the immediate heartbeat thereafter. What I gained from the events, however, was a better understanding of the predicament of the leadership generation at the time and, thereby, of the rather different level of experience and thought crystallizing in Amsterdam.

Suddenly our forthcoming leave of absence for the Tokyo assignment took on a new dimension—minimally, it offered a breathing spell! What if this leave of absence ended by taking us elsewhere? For now we were headed into another plunge into a radically different world, this time an Asian country about which we had virtually had no direct education! As "what if?" simmered, a wonderful experience lay ahead. Then all too soon came the request to extend the two-year term to five, and once again we yielded. However, before the first year in that extension ended, illness in the family brought us back to Harrisonburg and then soon for treatment to Washington, DC, where we lived nearly three decades for other reasons.

Mid-life Career Change

With our departure for Japan, a decade-long life career change, 1957–67, had effectively begun. This change profoundly underscored for us the mystery that as Christians "we walk by faith, not by sight" (2 Corinthians 5:7). Each of us in the Amsterdam group coped with Concern-related issues in our own particularities and in our own settings, whether wisely or unwisely. Accommodations are almost always possible and "go with the territory" of our human life together. Particularly in my instance was my dissertation's engagements with the pioneering founders of believers churches in the bosom of late medieval Christendom, in court records left by some seven hundred of them, arrested for that forbidden action. That investigation came on top of our prolonged MCC service in postwar Europe and now more recently in Asia.

The above noted Cumberland meeting raised for me this acute question: Should I simply "knuckle under," which at EMC would have indeed been possible, or was further probing in other settings, given my background, more appropriate for me? And if the latter, what would it be and how would it come about? Whatever the answer, as heretofore, it would have to be *by faith, not by sight*. Here the Hippocratic oath became an important aid: *First, do no harm*. By the time of our return from Japan in the summer of 1960, we had reached the first part of our conclusion: we would not return to EMC or to any other position in the *institutional* Mennonite framework. After all, there were other Mennonite options.

This adjective, *institutional,* was critically important—we were not leaving Anabaptism, but rather responding to the more deeply grounded dimensions in the Anabaptist legacy than such institution building was expressing. In thus leaving, we hoped we would *do no harm;* and if thereby some good were to emerge, it would become evident in due time. Meanwhile an invitation had come for me to serve a year as research fellow at the Institute of Mennonite Studies at Elkhart, Indiana. I would devote seven months to study and produce a publishable essay on the church and the city, and in the remaining five months, a pamphlet on Christians and social welfare. Full-time residence at Elkhart, however, was not mandatory.

Though not a solution, the Elkhart appointment served well as an interim activity—reminiscent perhaps of God's word to Moses, when the latter faced a far more awesome challenge: "What is that in your hand?" (Exodus 4). Retrospectively, it is now clear: The call to draft the HPC statement, to be offered to the World Council of Churches, became the opening wedge to an eventual change in my life course. I was brought into the peace-war discussion, first in Europe, then in my homeland, and next in Asia. Several months after beginning the year-long IMS assignment, I received a request from the CPM (Church Peace Mission) to serve as organizer for another national conference. An arrangement was quickly worked out whereby the IMS assignment would be extended by way of half-time employment with CPM providing the other half during that interval. This, of course, was not a lasting career alternative.

When it soon became clear that the time was hardly ripe for another national conference—not much activity had followed the previous conference—my assignment was redefined. I was to become the CPM executive and to function primarily as study secretary. We were to focus on a discourse in American seminary contexts similar to what had been underway in the Puidoux series in Europe. Soon thereafter a theological advisory committee to me was formed with both Protestant and Catholic members. Study conferences were to be organized in varied settings along with occasional pamphlets and press releases. When in 1967 CPM was discontinued, that advisory group nevertheless met annually for the next 20 years. Using the title of the CPM quarterly newssheet, that group with a somewhat fluid membership became the off-the-record War-Nation-Church Study Group. Only as we disbanded in 1987, did we publish a celebrative volume of papers entitled *Peace, Politics, and the People of God* (Philadelphia: Fortress Press).

Meanwhile, back in the CPM years in the 1960s, I had collaborated with John Heidbrink, a Presyterian minister, then church secretary at the Fellowship of Reconciliation (FOR) in Nyack, New York. In the summer of 1964 he had invited me to co-lead a church-persons traveling seminar, Protestant and Catholic, to Europe, West and East. The pivot of the tour was the five-day Second All-Christian Peace Assembly held in Prague, Czechoslovakia, that summer. A movement had emerged in central Europe in the late 1950s, then part of the Soviet Bloc, to support Soviet leader Nikita Khrushchev's peaceful co-existence foreign policy. They hoped thereby to overcome the restricted access of the churches in the Soviet bloc to the then new ecumenical movement. After stops in Paris, Rome, and Zurich in the West, we flew to Prague, entering the Soviet world. After Prague we were hosted by the Reformed Church in Hungary and then guided by Intourist, along with a young Russian Baptist minister, through visits in Russia proper to Kiev, Moscow, and Leningrad (today, once more, St. Petersburg). Then came Scandinavia, with a final contemplative pause at the historic Iona Community on the island with that name off the west coast of Scotland.

At Last, a Resolution

The richness of this tour cannot be traced here. Yet totally "out of the blue" from this tour emerged the two pivotal dimensions of my second career—a twenty-year long appointment to the sociology faculty at the Catholic University of America and a thirty-year long involvement in organized participation in bridge building between the U.S. and the Soviet Bloc. Daniel Berrigan, S. J., soon afterwards to come into the limelight of protest to the war in Vietnam, was a member of our 1964 traveling group. He and I, having met previously, became friends in the course of this five-week tour. Learning that in a year or two I would be job-hunting, he, without my knowledge, recommended me to the chair of the sociology faculty at Catholic University of America in Washington (CUA) soon after our return to the U.S. While I had eyed several other area universities in the region as possibilities, for obvious reasons CUA had not been part of that pool.

A few weeks after our late summer return, I received a phone call from the sociology chair to come in for a job interview. During this time, the Vatican II Council was well underway, in the course of which this directly pontifical university was largely secularized. That process both facilitated and slowed my admission. Though I taught there in the summer of 1965, my regular appointment did not begin until the fall semester of 1967. Tenured after two years, I remained at that university until my retirement in 1987. For me these were fulfilling years; and Ellen completed her BA there, as did three of our five children.

Back again to 1964, a few weeks after my first telephone call from CUA came another ring. Among the thousand participants at the Second All-Christian Peace Assembly in Prague, there had been a motley group of about seventy Americans students and professors, tourists, sent church observers and yes, a few fellow travelers. One afternoon in this five-day event we Americans caucused, soon reaching a consensus that while this conference was too tightly Soviet controlled for formal American church participation, an orderly process of communication with the church in the U.S. was needed. John Heidbrink, already earlier acquainted with the Assembly leadership and now nominated to its executive board, was asked by the caucus to implement that process. Then, having become seriously ill, he phoned me to take over the organizing task.

With my long-delayed sociology career about to begin, an extra-curricular task of such magnitude hardly seemed well advised. At the same time, after a decade of peace studies conversations, efforts at bridge-building during the Cold War appeared a challenge to be met. I yielded. The following spring, the U.S. Committee for the Christian Peace Conference met for the first time in a Washington suburb. A few turbulent years following the "Prague spring" of 1967, the Christian Peace Conference was reconstituted. Our U.S. Committee became in due time Christians Associated for Relationships with Eastern Europe (CAREE). A decade later we formed also an Institute of Peace and Understanding to facilitate Christian-Marxist dialogues with scientists and scholars in the state Institutes of Philosophy throughout Soviet lands. Eventually I also became active in a globally involved Council for Research in Values and Philosophy, independently based at CUA and active also in Eastern Europe.

During our Washington, DC decades, we were active members of the Hyattsville Mennonite Church, named for that Maryland suburb, and participated as well in informal conversations. From these emerged the vision of a mountain resort for study and retreat west of the nation's capital. Memories of a few experiences with the German Protestant "Evangelical Academies" many years earlier figured importantly in Ellen's and my background in those conversations. Suddenly in the early 1970s a 1400-acre, Quaker-inspired nature preserve on the west slope of the Blue Ridge south of Harpers Ferry, West Virginia, became available for a very small land-lease for a retreat center. A year before my retirement from CUA (1986) Ellen and I began our fifteen-year residence there as charter members of what became incorporated (501c3) as the Rolling Ridge Study Retreat Community.

Any Good from the Hippocratic Alternative?

Describing and assessing the results of my career change lie beyond the scope of this paper. That task is addressed in a book length autobiographical treatise entitled: *A Usuable Past? Living Vocationally at the Margins* now in press (Cascadia). That treatise is neither fully autobiographical, nor formally academic. Instead, though academically informed, it is more experience- than data-based. Here one brief example must suffice. After numerous and prolonged conversations about pacifism versus just war commitments, I became increasingly impressed that resolution of that problem lies deeper than the terms of that debate. Coming adequately and fully to terms with the symbiosis of God's agency as Creator and as Savior in the biblical story is a larger confusion in need of clarification.

I end with a tribute to my spouse and family, full partners in the costs and enrichments of the pilgrimage here described. I can only applaud Ellen's resilience and contribution after she entered my life. Two daughters and two sons arrived, each born in a different country, Germany, Switzerland, the U.S., and Japan, and afterward, a fifth, a son, in Washington, DC. Disrupting moves increased Ellen's challenges as wife and mother. Yet her resilience brought her personal growth as well—in her continuing education in Europe, Japan, and Washington, DC, particularly in literature and the arts, with eventual part-time careers in teaching English as a Second Language, editing, and Japanese flower arranging. Above all, she has been a steadfast, reliable, and indispensable Christian partner, whose presence and loyalty I have never had reason to doubt. In November 2001 came our privileged move to the Virginia Mennonite Retirement Community. Thus ends this abbreviated story.

March 2003
Revised February 2006

ESTHER K. AUGSBURGER

From India to Virginia

Growing up in India

"It's *just* a girl!"

This is how the villagers in our small India village announced my birth! Girls did not count in India in those days! But my parents told me that they had wanted a girl and that my brothers prayed every day especially for a baby sister, and I have felt their joy in me ever since. My parents had chosen another name, but my brothers wanted to name me Queen Esther as my mother had been reading that biblical story at the time. They all compromised by leaving out the Queen—to my gratitude—but my brothers have treated me like one ever since. My brother Paul was a baby when my parents went to India; Mark and I were born there; and David was born when we were home on furlough.

I was born in the Dhamtari hospital, the center for the Mennonite Church at that time. Our family lived in Mohadi, a tiny jungle village forty-five miles though the jungles from Dhamtri. We made many trips over the oxcart-rutted road through the jungle, where we often saw a variety of wild animals and even tigers. Our beds, covered with mosquito nets, were carried out to our long bungalow veranda every night for our health and for safety from possible robbers who would kill anyone they found in a room they had entered. Outside then, after checking for snakes or scorpions when my mother pulled back the covers to tuck us in at night, we slept healthily, sometimes hearing the tigers roaring or bears fighting—and of course the jackals all around us every night, all night. We did have a night watchman—*sleeping* at the other end of the veranda! A leopard took our dog from her kennel close to my father's bed one night. After that, Papa slept with a gun at the head of his bed.

We loved our life. The three months of vacation at home from boarding school was quality family time. Most of that time we traveled together through the rice fields and jungles by ox cart—sometimes by car and bicycles—to jungle villages where persons had never heard the gospel of Christ. Packed in our ox carts were not only food but also tents, which would be set up in a semi-circle, two for our family and the rest for our cook, nanny, the Indian Bible women, and the evangelists from our church. After inquiring whether there might be an epidemic of small pox or any such disease, we prepared to stay for several weeks in each village. Indeed, sometimes we spent up to two months in these jungle villages and have such good memories of our living in tents, sleeping on camp cots with straw-filled mattress, listening to the staff singing by the fireside for the villagers who gathered, eating rice and curry every day cooked over a trench plastered with cow-dung (nice and smooth) and playing in the jungles! My brothers had left home with the bags of mud-balls they had made of clay to shoot doves in the jungles with their slingshots. Those meals were special!

My parents were criticized by some of our missionaries for letting us play with the village children, climb onto buffaloes with them and learn their homemade games. But this is what Pyarilall Malagar recently described to John Lapp as one of the many of my father's "model missionary attributes," as he put it. Papa was contextualizing before we used that word. My parents always made us feel as though we were a part of India and were so very privileged to be there. They helped us enjoy all the good things that India had to offer, such as my favorite pet deer.

When I was about three years old, my father came home with a tiny chetah faun that had been found abandoned in the jungle. I named her Betty, and she was my constant companion until we left for our first furlough. Indeed, she followed me everywhere; and when she was older, sometimes my mother would find the two of us in the yard asleep with my head on her belly. I was heartbroken when my father needed to take her out to the jungle before we left. We knew she would never survive.

Nurturing our spiritual growth was a priority in our family. Papa spent time teaching us Mennonite history, frequently reading from *The Martyrs Mirror*. I can still see him weeping as he read some of the stories. Evenings we often sang from the hymnal since our parents wanted us to know the traditional hymns from "back home," not just the Hindi songs we sang in church. Mama was once known as a soloist in her Johnstown, Pennsylvania, community, so her lovely contralto voice and Papa's bass led our little choir. Papa also read from the Bible, and we prayed together every evening. At age ten, I approached my father one afternoon in tears, saying I felt God calling me. We did not have revival meetings where I could follow friends down the aisle as people did in evangelistic meetings in the U.S. This was totally my personal, individual call by God. I was baptized between two adult Indians in our tiny church by the late J. D. Graber, our bishop.

Then there was the boarding school in Darjeeling high in the Himalaya Mountains, fifty miles from the foot of Mount Everest (by the way a crow flies). As did most of the Mennonite mission children then, we, too, beginning at the age of six, lived and studied for nine months each year at this school one thousand miles and a three-day train trip from home. Six months of the nine months we did not see our parents. However, the first three months of the nine, our missionary mothers stayed with us in Darjeeling, partly to escape the intense heat of the hot season in the plains and also to be with us children. We lived in cottages until their return to the plains. We could see the snow-covered Kanchenjunga range of mountains from our cottage most mornings. Papa, who could visit for a week or two each year, usually chose the end of the three months in order to accompany Mama home.

As I remember, our first day or two in the dorm after they left were difficult, but after a few tears we were okay the rest of the year. Sponsored by the Methodist Church, this international school had a solid British curriculum. Also, during my last two years there, my art teacher was Ezra Hershberger from Goshen, Indiana, who was sent by the Mennonite Board of Missions. Actually, we have so many good memories, the best of which, however, are of the days of the "going home" songs. The whole school sang many of these rousing songs for two weeks prior to our leaving.

One of the dads from our mission would then arrive to take our whole gang down home to the plains. Our trip began with a ride of several hours on the winding "toy train" down the hairpin curves to Silaguri to catch the regular train. One of my most vivid memories of these trips home occurred when J. D. Graber came up to take us down on the long three-day trip. On the second day we had a few hours layover in Calcutta, so he gave us each a couple rupees and took us shopping. My best friends, Laverne Vogt and Lois Hostetler (who were my age), and I each bought a small stuffed rabbit. When all of us were back on the train, "Uncle" Graber, as we "mish-kids" always addressed the adults, soon had all of us settled for the night. The seats ran the long way down the middle and on the sides of the car, all of which we occupied. Some of us slept on the seats and some above in the luggage racks. I was on a luggage rack in the middle of the car, and Ronald Graber in the rack across the isle. Uncle Graber was sound asleep on the floor between us. Ronald, always the tease of the bunch, reached over and grabbed my rabbit; and we each pulled hard until we pulled ourselves off our luggage rack beds and down onto our *sleeping* Uncle Graber! Needless to say, we were severely reprimanded and told in no uncertain terms to settle down.

We are often asked why none of my three brothers or I have negative feelings about our tri-cultural childhood—American, Indian and British. Many "mish-kids" carry strong resentments about the limitations and adjustments they felt. We can honestly say that we do not have these resentments toward our parents or our experience. I believe the answer is that Papa and Mama never complained about our so-called "deprived" life as some missionaries did in front of their children. They always made us feel it was special and included us in their joys of being there and experiencing the many good things that came with it. They made us feel that the Indians were a part of who we were. They also modeled for us faith and trust in a God of love and the certainty that it was a *privilege* to be in India serving Him. For this I have always been grateful.

A War-time Voyage

One evening in 1942, when I was 12, some of my friends and I were playing on the Darjeeling school playground when one of my brothers came and said we must go home at once. We were being evacuated from India by the British government because of the threat of World War II. Mama and we kids were living in the log cabin at the school that year together with Auntie Graber and their two children, Eleanor and Ronald. Mrs. Graber and my mother stayed up all night making pajamas and fulfilling the other requirements that had come with the notice about the trip aboard ship to prepare for our possibly needing to hurry to the lifeboats in the middle of the night. The next morning we left for the plains. There we packed the one trunk allowed for the whole family, gave other things away, and left for Bombay to board the S.S. Brazil.

The voyage was a difficult one, to say the least. We had not been told where we would be taken, just ordered to board this ship. Our ship had been built for 300 passengers, but crammed into it now were 1500 missionaries, government personnel and 600 Chinese soldiers. We had to wear life jackets and carry survival kits with us at all times, and we had frequent lifeboat drills. My father prepared us children for the possibility of being separated or dropped off in some strange country or even of dying from an enemy attack. He spoke in such a reassuring way that we lost our fear and placed our trust in God.

Adding to the difficulties of this trip, a missionary doctor came on board with his five children, who had whooping cough and measles. Thus around fifty children were soon sick from one of those diseases. Mrs. Graber, Ronald, Eleanor, my mother, my brother David and I were all together in a cabin meant for two passengers, and the men and older boys had to bunk in the barracks in the bottom of the ship with the Chinese soldiers. The six of us in our tiny cabin could barely walk around the bunks, and all four of us kids came down with the measles at the same time! To make the situation worse, the portholes were sealed before dark each evening, leaving only a blue light in the hall too dim to read the time on a man's watch. Since no light was allowed in the rooms or on deck, caring for us was extremely difficult. And during the two times that we crossed the equator, to knock the pursuing German enemy off any calculations, the heat was intense. Our moms and dads took turns staying with us at night while the others tried to sleep on the deck where it was a bit cooler.

Many more stories could be told about that six-week voyage. The ship zigzagged the whole way to avoid the German enemy's torpedoes. At one point we came frighteningly close to being attacked. We felt a loud bump, and the sirens sounded for us to rush to the lifeboats. Our ship threw out four depth charges against the enemy submarine and hurried on. After a couple weeks we docked at Cape Town, South Africa, for a week to knock off the enemy's calculations of our location. From there on a battleship accompanied us on each side and two fighter planes overhead. The Germans were determined to get us, perhaps because we were bringing the 600 soldiers to train for the air force.

My relationship with one particular group became my one good memory of that trip. The day we left India I had made friends with several Chinese soldiers on the deck. Before I came down with the measles and then after my recovery, several of them asked me to sit in the bar a while each day to listen to them take turns reading from the *Reader's Digest*. In exchange for my correcting their English pronunciation, they would buy me a dish of ice cream. What a treat that ice cream was! As our group waited out on deck the day we disembarked, a couple Chinese soldiers lifted me to their shoulders for all six hundred to cheer in thanks for my help with their English and for our friendship.

When we were notified our last evening to be on deck with all our belongings by ten o'clock the next morning ready to disembark, no one would tell us where we were landing. Thus the next, very foggy, morning we all waited anxiously on deck for several hours to see where our ship would dock. Suddenly, rising out of the fog, was the Statue of Liberty. Through many tears of joy, the group broke into singing, "Praise God from Whom All Blessings Flow" and "God bless America, Land that I Love!" What joy we felt!

When we disembarked, Red Cross personnel served us children milk. I had never drunk anything so delicious! Our milk in India had been delivered in smoky earthen pots and always needed to be boiled!

Remembering this trip, I have often wondered why no one ever wrote about this memorable event, at least as far as I know.

A Strange New World

The two years following our arrival in the U.S. were not easy years of adjustment for me. Living in Johnstown, Pennsylvania, where my parents were from, was actually a very difficult experience. The culturally rural and parochial community, which then had very little understanding of people from other countries, made my life painful. I was teased mercilessly at school as a "high hat" because I had a bit of British accent.

The first time I had to write on the blackboard, my sixth grade teacher ridiculed me in front of the class because of my British penmanship. I worked hard to change and almost "de-cultured" myself to try to fit into a culture so different from the two surrounding me, as I had grown up—British and Indian. Life in the church community there was also difficult. I felt keenly the negative antagonistic atmosphere.

Then Papa was asked to go to Elida, Ohio, to start a Christian day school. This was a good move for us all. There we met young people in the church who were so very kind and thus made our adjustment much easier. However, that church was much more conservative than I was used to in India or Johnstown. I needed to leave my ankle socks at home, put on black stockings and a cape dress, and wear my covering all the time. But at that age and stage of adjustment, when peer acceptance was important, I found that none of these changes really mattered. This way of dressing meant just another cultural identity to me.

As I noted, these young people were loving and kind. And this is where I met Myron. We began dating when I was sixteen and for the next two years kept our dates according to my parents' rules of only once a month. But we sat together on the school bus every day!

A year later my parents expected to return to India. At that time the Mission Board no longer supported missionary children after they turned eighteen; instead, we were to remain in the U.S. Thus my parents sent me to Eastern Mennonite High School for my second year of high school because they wanted me to adjust to the lifestyle of "winging it without us" in a good environment; summers I would spend with grandparents. (Actually, due to several different circumstances, my parents never went back to India, except once some years later to teach a couple months.)

I came to EMHS reluctantly, but my year here was the best thing that could have happened; and I wanted to return for my junior and senior years. My parents could not afford to send me again, but Dwight and Ellen Hartman came to the rescue and invited me to live with them my junior year and room with Ellen's sister, Fern Pellman, who had become a good friend. Dwight and Ellen were wonderful mentors in their quiet and loving way. In my senior year I lived with my brother Paul and his wife Esther, who were again great models for me.

Though my years at EMHS were very good ones, they were not

without difficulties. I was still making adjustments, both in terms of cultural aspects and the curriculum, in which I had to study American, not British, history. However, with my background in strict British education, I found English easy and those classes a pleasure, especially the ones taught by Harold Lehman and A. Grace Wenger. In fact I thought of majoring in English in college. I also really enjoyed the semester of art, my favorite subject, under Margaret Gehman. EMHS was a good chapter in my life.

Myron, at the Elida, Ohio, high school, and I corresponded that first year, but broke our relationship a few months near the end of the year until my return home to Ohio for the summer. Myron had prayed fervently that if it was God's will for us to go back together, at the next youth meeting (which we called a "literary'") I would address him *by name* and speak to him *directly!* Well, I did not until just as my brother Mark and I were about to leave in our old Model A Ford, which suddenly would not start. Mark got out and cranked and cranked, but it simply would not start.

Myron, waiting in the shadows to give me every chance to speak, came over and quietly made one crank. The motor started right up!

I leaned out the window and called, "Myron, you must have had Wheaties for breakfast!" We've liked Wheaties ever since!

We were both at EMS the following year, where the other college students gave him some grief about dating a high schooler! Myron stayed home the next year, and we were engaged by the end of my senior year. The next year I worked as head cashier in a supermarket, living at home in Dayton, Ohio, while Myron came to EMS for his second year of college.

From Florida to EMC

Fifty-six years ago, after having postponed our wedding two days due to a thirty-six inch snowstorm, we were married in Ohio.

We planned to return to EMC for college the following year; and while here to arrange for an apartment during Homecoming weekend, we were asked by Bishop Truman Brunk to go to Sarasota, Florida, to pastor the new Tuttle Avenue church. After prayer and counsel, we left some weeks later for Florida in our little rumble seat Pontiac coupe with all our possessions (some on top of the car) and a hundred dollars in our pockets.

We were young. The first Sunday in church I overheard two women behind me, "Is that his wife? Why, she is but a child!" I guess I was!

We loved the church, the place and the people. Our sons, John and Michael, born there, were welcome additions to our little family.

We had five wonderful years of pastoring in Florida with a rapidly growing congregation. Then, in response to the strong urging of President Mumaw for Myron to come to EMC to be the campus pastor, Myron agreed to serve on a part time basis so that he could finish his college and two years of seminary.

I was content with mothering and homemaking in which I could be creative in my own untrained way. I made paintings and drawings for the bare walls of our home, did art with the children, sewed all our clothes (including Myron's plain coats), and generally enjoyed those years. They were also extremely difficult ones financially since our salary was only ninety-five dollars a month. Myron cut the hair of Ray Himes and his sons in exchange for milk and eggs from their farm out by Mole Hill. Thus we made it okay.

Beginning in the spring of 1955 and for the six years that followed, we traveled each summer in Evangelistic Crusades with Mark and Eva Stauffer, the Witmers, the Neuenschwanders and later the Mastermans, Loren and Pat Swartzendruber, and others. Our third child, Marcia, was born in the year we lived in Goshen to complete Myron's Bachelor of Divinity studies. We were all thrilled to have a girl join our family! She was so beautiful and loved by all of us.

In our earlier school years at EMC I had begun taking one college class each semester. It was not until later, after all the children were in school, that I took more than one class at a time, most of which were after Myron had been called to the college presidency.

A College President's Wife

Being a president's wife in those days was so very *different* from what it is today. I was told in the beginning of the first year that I should not have close friends—I must be a friend with everyone alike. I was young and took this directive very seriously with the consequence of living through some very lonely years. Another not such a good event happened the morning I arrived at the chapel for Myron's inauguration. When I asked the usher where they had arranged for me to sit, he replied that I could sit anywhere I pleased. Thus I sat in the audience like a good girl. Myron had thought that a place had been arranged for me. Quite embarrassed, he made sure to change the arrangements for the next president's wife. It must be added that when we left the college fifteen years later, the board and faculty more than made up for that kind of oversight at our farewell exercises.

As the president's wife I wanted to carry on the tradition of inviting the seniors and parents to our house for tea at graduation time, so I would begin preparing tiny sandwiches, cookies and petit fours two months ahead for the freezer. My first year I remember being called the day before the tea by one faculty wife, asking if she could help. By then all had been prepared and students engaged to help serve. The word went out that I did not want help, but really I was too timid to ask. The college budget was also too limited to cover this expense. However, this tradition went on until the year the numbers reached 400, after which I insisted that the board approve engaging the school kitchen to provide most of the food. I prepared a few things, directed the servers, etc.

In general, my years as the president's wife were very good. I enjoyed the entertaining end of it, and we had many groups of faculty and students in our home. Our children suffered though, which we regret, and we tried to compensate for Myron's position and schedule. Actually, I believe we did more with our children than the average parents in terms of travel and special projects.

Sometimes Myron would come home on Friday evening and say, "Pack your bags everyone; we're going to Natural Bridge." We loved going there for a time of eating good food, swimming in the indoor heated pool, and hiking. These numerous times of hanging out together where no one knew us or would call were so special.

At other times when Myron was away preaching in order to bring in more students and funds, I would occasionally rent a camper and head for Todd Lake with the kids. We would swim, fish, play games at night, and sleep in the camper.

We took parenting seriously. Quite recently, a man from another state came to me in anger. He still strongly resented what had happened years earlier when he had come to EMC for graduation. When the ceremonies were over, he had come up to our house to talk with Myron, who was then sitting on the couch reading to the children, as he had promised them he would after commencement was over. I had told the gentleman that Myron was busy.

Now, years later, with anger still in his eyes he said to me, "Your husband was not busy. I saw him through the picture window reading to the children."

I calmly replied, "Myron *was* busy." I wanted to say that we were a happy family. We have always had a wonderful relationship with our children in spite of some personal difficulties.

Called to be an Artist

As my college credits accumulated, I took classes more seriously, majoring in music even though visual art was my first love. I thought that the church would have no use for, and even frown on, an art major. After taking all the voice EMC offered, I was sent to JMU for additional training and earned a total of twenty credit hours in voice. During these years I very much enjoyed singing solos for a variety of oratorios and cantatas on the campus and being a part of the Mennonite Hour Choir.

However, my lifelong gratitude goes to Myron for his sense of who I am and his continual nudging for me to reconsider my direction and switch to art. Thus one day I brought this subject up to my voice teacher, Miss Edith Schneider, who was about to retire from teaching at JMU, expressing my strong interest in art.

She looked up at me from her seat at the piano and said, "Esther, when you reach my age you will lose your [vocal] instrument." Showing me her hands, she added, "In art, you will have them forever."

Thus began my never-to-be regretted career in art. I took all my art courses at JMU and was the first and only art major to graduate from EMC in 1971. When I crossed the platform for my BA degree, the president kissed me! (Myron!) I will always be grateful for all his support in my work, whether in art or in the other related ministries in which I have had opportunities.

After my graduation from EMC, Sam Weaver, then the principal of EMHS, asked me to begin an art program there. Even though I was the president's wife, I was required to meet with the Religious Welfare Committee of the Virginia Conference before Sam could hire me. Moreover, since EMHS was still an arm of EMC, Myron was accused of nepotism by some faculty, but it was Sam Weaver who had hired me!

My first year I taught in the old Park School building, where the only source of water was a child's drinking fountain in the hall. At that time EMHS was planning to build a fine arts wing onto the high school building—with no art room in the plans, only music and English rooms. When I asked Sam why, he replied he had not thought about that and would I serve on the building committee and plan an art room? The next year we had a fine new large art room with a walk-in closet.

Sam was a generous and encouraging principal, and my eight years of teaching at EMHS were truly enjoyable ones as I watched many of my students become active artists.

After teaching five years, I took a leave in order to enter graduate school at James Madison University, where in two summers and a year I completed my Master's degree. I then returned to teach at EMHS until 1980.

The day after Myron terminated his fifteen years as president of the college in 1980, we left for Oxford, England, where we each took month-long courses and scouted out the art. In the fall we went to Princeton, where Myron had been invited by the seminary to be a Scholar-in-Residence. That year I began producing significantly more art and worked part time at the famous Johnson Atilier Sculpture School and Foundry, where I learned much about casting sculpture. The Presbyterian Ministers' Life Insurance Company gave me several major sculpture commissions that year. Subsequently, they sent a recommendation to Grove City College in Pennsylvania to award me an honorary Doctor of Fine Arts—a true surprise to me! However, this means no more than an honor, which I gratefully acknowledge.

Ways for an Artist to serve in Washington, DC

In 1981, as requested by several mission boards, we went to Washington to plant a church. Our fourteen years there were the best! Myron and I worked *together* in ways we never had before! We walked the streets together, making new friends whom we invited to our home and thereby building the church community.

As time went on, I saw the tremendous needs of the poor and abused. Knowing I could not do it all, I focused mainly on one family: a mother and four children who were living in a terrible situation and abuse. Their home was one room of a prostitute motel, and the father was a pimp. I put in many hours and days finding jobs for this mother, teaching her how to open a bank account and how to ride the Metro, and getting the children into proper schools. I worked on decent housing, even with police protection standing on each side as I confronted discriminatory landlords—both white and black. One of my rewards came when I was awakened at one o'clock one morning by the phone. It was little Evette. In her small child's voice she said, "Esta, my cat just had a kitten!" I told her to watch since there might be more and to call me in the morning. I was her friend!

I challenged EMHS to find the funds for the oldest daughter to attend that high school so that her father would not use her. Les Helmuth graciously found a woman in Ohio who sponsored each of the children, one at a time. I am thankful that today two are college graduates and the oldest one became the director of the church's after school learning center for inner-city children. The youngest one works there now, also. They are active in the church. The other two finished high school and now have families of their own.

In the early years of the church and until the church needed more space, I had a studio in a room in the beautiful old Lutheran Church building that we had purchased for our new congregation. It was an inspirational place to work. After a couple years of entering exhibitions and meeting artists, I began getting calls from artists to meet for coffee and talk. Their anxious question was, "How can you be an artist and a Christian?" They had had training, had been practicing art, had then became Christians, and their church then urged them to give up their art. This is a question I have since been asked by artists all over the world. Actually my major professor in my Master's program tried to convince me that my religion would be a hindrance to my creativity.

Thus I began a Christian artists' group, which met weekly to talk, study and pray. It was not long until their concern for studio space to resume using their God-given gift as artists precipitated my applying for a grant for studio spaces and a room for the art classes for inner-city children that I wanted to start. Given the grant, I rented a third floor flat on Maryland Avenue and 8th Street that was large enough for rooms for each of the six of us artists and also a large room for the kids' classes. The occupant artists were required to help with the kids' classes and to keep their studio doors open for the children to come in and chat when they wished, thereby building relationships. As time passed, the elders of the church thought I should be commissioned for ministry in art. Thus on a Sunday morning the elders and Myron laid hands on me for this ministry. I will always be grateful to God and to the Washington Community Fellowship elders for this affirmation.

Sculpture Commissions

In 1981 I was elected to the Mennonite Board of Missions, where I served for eight years. That same year I was asked to be on the Eastern Baptist College and Seminary board, where I served for fourteen years, including the year the college and seminary divided. I was persuaded to stay on both boards. During this time, I taught a short-term course called "Art and Faith" in the seminary. I was also commissioned to provide a major sculpture for inside the main building of the seminary. After I resigned from the board, they awarded me another honorary doctor's degree.

In 1985 we took a sabbatical from the church in Washington and went to Pune, India, to fulfill a promise we had made before being asked to go to Washington. There I was asked to teach a course on art and worship. I struggled with this. How could I teach a course on art and worship in a land where people worship the visual object? Myron kept encouraging me, saying that I should take a day at a time and it would be okay. However, at breakfast the first morning there, I met the campus architect, who asked me to consider making a large outdoor sculpture for the center of their beautiful new campus. The campus building committee, of which Anil Solanki was the chairman, enthusiastically concurred. I told them I could not both teach and make the sculpture in two months' time. They opted for the sculpture. It is the first of similar sculptures I have designed and built in places like Eastern Mennonite Seminary. I was commissioned by ServiceMaster's to make one to be placed in front of their headquarters in Chicago and by Warner Southern College in Lake Wales, Florida, for another on that campus.

The process of creating the Pune sculpture is a story in itself. After I made several models, bathing each in prayer that it would not be taken for an idol, the committee chose the one to be made of white concrete. However, the Muslim contractor of buildings, who had been instructed to *help* me, would not let me work, nor would he take orders from me. He insisted he would do it. One day he came with a large plywood board with a fat, seated Buddha figure cut out—big belly and all!

I told him as kindly as I could that this was not what this project was about, nor was it the process for construction. I would build the sculpture. He should get the materials I needed.

Finally, the oxcart brought the materials, the footer was dug, and reinforcement rods were in place.

Catching on that neither he nor his mason would take orders from a woman, Myron came after his class and told me to give him orders and he would help me begin the process while they stood by and watched. After that the mason still would not give me a cement trowel, so I simply went down the hill to the hardware store and bought one. As I reached into his hand-mixed cement and began to work, they caught on that I really meant business and knew what I was doing. By then, they needed to set up lights so that I could work on into the night in order to complete it before our time came to leave. Then with the help of the mason, I literally built the forms in eleven days! I had so much joy in this project. I could use my limited Hindi language, dialog with students and leave a monument like this in the country of my birth.

I must also say that in those two months of working on the sculpture, I was able to teach art and worship more effectively than I would have in a classroom. The students congregated around me in every break time, watching and asking many questions. The whole experience was a wonderful highlight in my career!

A New Venture: Conferences for Artists

The path on which I believe God has led me has been a "way leads on to way" journey. It was during this time in Pune that I became acquainted with Kathleen Nicholls, a missionary from New Zealand who taught drama at the seminary. Kathleen asked me to help her begin art conferences for Christian professional artists in Asia. (Christian artists in these countries are a minority, and the church gives them no encouragement or guidance. Consequently, they separate their gift of art from their faith.) I agreed and in 1985 began a new ministry for me, which continues today. We have convened conferences in numerous Asian countries and one in Africa, sponsored by the International Christian Media Commission (of which Mennonite Media was a member a while). In 1991 I was asked to organize an exhibition of international Christians' art for the ICMC conference, held on the campus of Sheffield University in England. We had artists' works from twenty-one countries. There I was urged by Eastern European artists to come to their countries for conferences. After I had worked with Kathleen in Asia for seven years, this group spun me off to begin organizing conferences in Eastern Europe.

I began with an all Europe conference in Mittersill, Austria, after which I was invited by InterChurch, Inc., Myron's accountability board, to work under their guidance and financial accountability. Since ICMC was having mega financial difficulties at the time, this arrangement turned out to be much better since it has been more efficient for my purposes and it brought Myron's work and mine together once more.

I asked Timothy Bentch, a wonderful Mennonite opera singer, to lead the evening worship in this first all European conference. It was there that I asked Tim, who later moved to Budapest in mission, to partner with me; and we have enjoyed working together to include musicians in the conferences. We have had an attendance ranging from fifty to eighty participants in these conferences, convened about every two or three years. We have held "gatherings," as we call them, in Austria, Hungary twice, Russia, Lithuania, Bulgaria and Romania. The last one was held in Hungary in 2005 for visual artists.

Both Tim's growing ministry among musicians in Hungary, called *A Song for the Nations,* under Eastern Mennonite Missions, and also the increase in the number of participating artists then led us to separate the visual arts and music. I have continued however, to help with each Asian art conference under the leadership of Steve Scott of California. The last one was held in Bali, Indonesia, in 2006. Steve and I are planning a conference to be held in 2008 in Bulgaria for Asian and European visual artists together. At this time I wish to turn the leadership of this ministry over to Steve Scott and Hari and Penka Atanosov from Bulgaria, who have been regular participants in the Eastern European conferences. I believe it is time for me to retire from this work.

In especially recent years Myron and I have enjoyed much dialog concerning art and Christian faith, and now we are working together on a possible book on art and theology in conversation. We have both also enjoyed teaching missions and lectures here as well as abroad, such as in India, Japan (with Bob and Nancy Lee), Croatia, Russia, and Ethiopia and others places, where I teach classes on art and faith.

Back to Sculptures

Over the years I have truly enjoyed and been challenged by numerous sculpture commissions, some large and some smaller. My sculptures can be found in nine countries. My most notable sculpture project so far was commissioned by the Chief of Police in Washington, DC, in which I used the turned-in guns from off the streets. Our son Michael, also an artist, and I built the "Guns Into Plowshares" with 3,000 guns welded onto the sixteen-foot huge steel sculpturally shaped plowshare. Weighing four tons, it sits in Judiciary Square in Washington. It was a special joy to do this with my son.

Most recently I was invited by the governor of the northern part of South Korea to spend ten days there to talk about making a very large (likely 60 or 70 feet high) sculpture for a Peace Park they are placing close to the border of North Korea. He offered to pay for Myron to accompany me so that I would not need to travel alone and would have an even more enjoyable time. This trip was most challenging! The governor wants me to create the sculpture with tanks and missiles. I am not sure how it will all work out, but I am truly challenged. The invitation came after the Governor had seen the "Guns into Plowshares" sculpture in the news and on the Internet. If God wants me to do it, all the apparent present "kinks" will be solved.

I have often been asked, "When did you begin working in sculpture?" My answer goes right back to my childhood in India. We children did not have many toys, so I would go out in the yard and pick up the green fruit blown off the trees and carve it into toys or make them of clay. I would collect sticks and scraps from my mother's ragbag and make them into toys for my village friends and myself. Also, I loved sitting in the trees and watching with fascination the flexing muscles of the loin-clothed coolies carrying their heavy yokes across their shoulders as they paced in a rhythmic trot. This, I believe, was preparing me for sculpting the human form. The human body with strong muscles is in my mental computer. I never need to use models. Also, my father, an artist, was encouraging, as I spent evenings at home drawing and asking him to critique my pictures. However, those experiences were only the seeds for all that has grown through family, study, maturity and service.

I believe that my childhood experiences also prepared me for the cross-cultural ministries I have enjoyed. I feel comfortable with any culture or dialog with any religion in my own simplistic way.

My life has been full of unexpected surprises. This simple little "mish-kid" may not be a dynamic person, but I have done what I could; and I leave it to God to use. My husband has been my coach, my encourager, my cheerleader and my best friend. God has led me in pleasant places, and I want to continue to be all that God intends for me until I can no longer use my "instruments!"

To God be the glory!

January 2006
Revised April 2007

CALVIN E. SHENK

My Pilgrimage: Missional Education

1936–1960

Born in 1936 in Lancaster, Pennsylvania, I was the first of four children in my family. Not all of my experiences in the one-room county schoolhouse, where I studied from grades one to eight, were positive: my first-grade teacher said she was going to get tape to "tape my ears back!" Ever since that comment I have known that my ears protrude more than some people's ears! My second teacher was also a female, but for most of my elementary education my teacher was "Mr. Shank."

I attended Lancaster Mennonite School for my secondary education, graduating in 1954. After high school I worked as a carpenter for one year before enrolling at Eastern Mennonite College in 1955. (Sam Strong and Lester Shank recruited me). At EMC I majored in Bible, graduating in 1959. Paul Peachy, Hubert Pellman, and Irvin Horst were important teachers in my life.

Marie and I met in Lancaster in the summer of 1956. She later attended EMC, and we were married in 1958.

While at EMC I participated in YPCA ministries. I served as treasurer and commissioner for extension and taught in rural congregations of Virginia Mennonite Conference at Mountain Top in West Virginia and at Crossroads near Broadway.

Following graduation from EMC, Marie and I were both employed at Lancaster Mennonite School, she as the secretary to Dean Noah Good and I as a teacher of Bible. We felt called to overseas service but needed to pay off some college debt, and I was glad to get some teaching experience. During those two years at LMS, I took several undergraduate history courses at Millersville University and completed a Master's degree from Temple University, with some credits from the Lancaster Theological Seminary.

Our first year in Lancaster, Marie and I attended Andrew's Bridge Mennonite Church, a rural mission where Marie's father was one of the pastors. I taught Sunday school and Bible school there. The following year I was ordained to the Christian ministry by David Thomas for overseas service and served as an apprentice in the New Danville district of Lancaster Mennonite Conference, which included my home congregation where my father was pastor. While David Thomas was conservative in practice, he was open in manner, affirming of my gifts and education; and I value the experience he made possible for me as a recent college graduate. Later he commissioned us for ministry in Ethiopia and maintained contact with us while we were there.

Ethiopia 1961–1975

In 1961, bound for Ethiopia, we sailed from New York on a freighter across the Atlantic and into the Mediterranean, stopping at Tripoli, Alexandria, Beirut, Port Said, and continuing through the Suez Canal, down the Red Sea to Port Sudan, and on to Djibouti. From there we traveled by train to Ethiopia. The month of travel provided us with an informal orientation to the world outside the provincial confines of our earlier years. A shipmate, observing our ignorance of a lot of modern culture, quipped, "Where have you been all your life—in a cave?"

In Ethiopia we spent our first year in language study (a Semitic language, Amharic). For this year Marie and I were assigned to live with four single women, and we still joke with these women about my "five wives!" That year was a time for learning about Ethiopia and the Meserete Kristos Church (Mennonite) within the Addis Ababa context and beyond. The name Mennonite had no meaning for Ethiopians; Meserete Kristos means "Foundation on Christ."

Following language study, we moved from Addis Ababa to Nazareth to teach at Nazareth Bible Academy, founded by Chester Wenger. This was a Christian secondary school that provided not only basic academic training but also theological studies for persons in Christian lay ministries. Many of the students were older than the usual age of secondary students. During our seven years there, I served as teacher, business manager, and later principal. The courses I taught included Bible, history, church history, Ethiopian history, Ethiopian religion, and African history.

I developed an interest in Ethiopian history and religion, not only as preparation for teaching but also as a way of understanding Ethiopian culture. The students were happy to contribute to my exploration and writing, considering them an affirmation of the importance of their history and culture; and I researched and wrote materials on Ethiopian religions for use in class, which were collected into a booklet. Students continued to request copies even after we left Ethiopia.

During our furlough in 1965–1966, I began a PhD program at New York University and in a later furlough both in Ethiopia and in the States, I completed my degree in 1972. New York University had a cooperative program with The Biblical Seminary in New York. Kenneth Scott Latourette at the Yale Divinity School commuted down to the Seminary from New Haven to offer a course in Church History in which I was enrolled. With his missiological perspective on church history, Latourette was a great inspiration to me; and I wrote a paper for him on the Ethiopian Orthodox Church as a test to see whether or not this could be a possible dissertation topic. To my delight he encouraged me to pursue it, which I did.

The title of the dissertation became "The Development of the Ethiopian Orthodox Church and Its Relationship with the Ethiopian Government from 1930 to 1970" (the Haile Selassie period). I explored whether change in the church was initiated from within the church or was a part of Haile Selassie's modernization program. I think it was both. Since the Ethiopian Orthodox Church was a state church, it changed as the state changed; but it was also in contact with other Oriental Orthodox Churches, which stimulated change.

Between 1972 and 1975 I taught at Haile Selassie I University (a government university) and at Mekane Yesus (Lutheran) Seminary, both in Addis Ababa. At the University I taught Eastern and Western Philosophy: A Comparative View. Claude Sumner, a Canadian Jesuit from Manitoba arranged for me to teach in the Faculty of Arts Department. The Jesuits had started the university and turned it over to Ethiopians as trained administrators became available. (Sumner informed me that his grandfather, a judge in Manitoba, granted Mennonites permission to "affirm" in court rather than "swear." We developed such a close friendship that he agreed to be a resource person for Mennonite Retreat.) Since my dissertation was on the Ethiopian Orthodox Church, I tried to get a job at The Ethiopian Orthodox Theological College, which was part of the university system, but they replied that they were trying to Ethiopianize.

At Mekane Yesus Seminary, founded by Lutherans from Germany, Norway, Sweden, Denmark and the United States, I taught Ethiopian History, Comparative Religion, and African Traditional Religion. (Note that I did not teach theology!) I also wrote African Traditional Religion materials for Theological Education by Extension (TEE) for use by the Seminary for non-resident students in the extension program.

Because of my teaching at this seminary, I hoped that the Meserete Kristos (Mennonite) Church would send some students there, but only a few Mennonites enrolled. For me, my experience at this Lutheran seminary was a highlight in my Ethiopian experience, and I felt respected by the Lutherans. When Marxism threatened the church, a professor from Germany, referring to the church under persecution said, "We need your kind of theology (Anabaptist) for this time."

Actually, Norman Kraus nearly jeopardized my position in the Lutheran Seminary! When Kraus visited Ethiopia, he was invited to give a lecture at the seminary on "Luther and Menno." Kraus deliberately changed the topic of his presentation to "Menno and Luther!"

Indeed, the Lutherans were very gracious to Mennonites. During the Marxist period when Mennonite churches were closed, the members met in house churches. Five of their leaders were imprisoned for more than four years, several of whom had been my students at the Bible Academy. Some Christians buried their Bibles. While most Protestant churches were closed, Mennonites secretly convened seminars at the Lutheran Seminary. I remember that we shut the windows to sing; for when Mennonites met in house fellowships, they could not sing for fear of having their neighbors report them to the Marxist officials. Participants in the seminar would arrive at different times in order not to raise suspicion. While I was riding with one of the seminar participants on the way to the seminary, he described the situation this way: "The Devil took out his calculator to press the minus button, but instead he pressed the multiplication button, and the church increased in membership!" It was his commentary on how persecution was causing the church to grow.

The seminary remained open during the Marxist period because a Lutheran faculty member from Norway resisted the government official who had come to close the Seminary. Instead of trying to preserve their own privileges, the seminary administrators tried to accommodate Christians whose churches were closed, including Mennonites.

Back in Ethiopia for a visit after the Marxist period, I expressed my deep appreciation for the Seminary's willingness to "put their neck on the line" by giving Mennonites a place to meet occasionally. My Lutheran friend replied, "We owe it to you: we put your necks on the line during the Reformation." I was glad he remembered! That was a wonderful moment!

The Marxist period was frightening. Haile Selassie was executed. The Patriarch of the Ethiopian Orthodox Church was executed as was the President of the Lutheran Church. Fifty-nine government officials were shot dead without trial about three miles from our house.

Before the churches were closed, I was asked by the Meserete Kristos Church to teach a Sunday school class on a "Christian perspective on Marxism" to senior high school and university students who were being sent out by the Marxist government in a national work campaign to work at literacy and development. They were to live in camps with other students, including Marxist students. About 200 persons showed up for the class.

Ethiopia was very formative in our lives. Our three children were born there. We consider Ethiopians our teachers in many areas. While teaching later at EMU, I learned that my middle initial "E" was understood by EMU students to stand for Ethiopia!

Although our family left Ethiopia in 1975, we have returned to Ethiopia many times for visits and for teaching—in 1984, 1987, 1988, 1989, 1993, 1994, 1995, 1996, 1997, 1998, 1999, 2000, 2002, and 2005. My teaching was in the context of church leadership seminars, Meserete Kristos College, and the Ethiopian Graduate School of Theology. I taught topics such as History and Theology of the Old Testament, Relationship of Old and New Testament, History of Christian Theology, Biblical

Interpretation, New Religious Movements, Christian Faith and Other Religions, Understanding Islam, Christian Witness to Islam, Christology, African Church History, and African Theology.

Eastern Mennonite University 1976–2005

When we returned to the U.S. from Ethiopia in 1975, I taught part time at Messiah College for one year in addition to pastoring part time again in my home congregation, River Corner Mennonite Church in Lancaster County. My father, who had pastored there, had died suddenly several weeks before we left Ethiopia. (We were not able to attend his funeral.) Since my home congregation had supported me while we were in Ethiopia, I agreed to fill in as pastor during this time of transition.

After one year in Lancaster and at Messiah College, I joined the faculty of the Bible and Religion Department at EMU; and Marie was employed as Administrative Assistant in the Dean's Office. At EMU I have taught Old Testament, World Religions, New Religious Movements, Missiology, Anthropology and Mission, Marxism, Contemporary Issues in Africa, and Interdisciplinary Studies. I served on the General Education Committee and was very active in the development of the required cross-cultural program. In fact, I wrote a major paper promoting the benefits of cross-cultural education. Marie and I also led EMU cross-cultural semesters to the Middle East (Egypt, Jordan, Israel, Palestine, Greece and Rome) in 1978, 1986, 1990 and 1992.

In the fall of 1987 I spent a sabbatical as Research Scholar at Tantur Ecumenical Institute in Jerusalem, focusing on contemporary Judaism. In the spring of 1988 we were guest lecturers at Union Biblical Seminary in Pune, India.

I have taken numerous study trips abroad to become better acquainted with issues in religion and mission. From December 1981 to January 1982 I went to India and Sri Lanka to explore Hinduism and Therevada Buddhism. I did this alone, and I had no hotel reservations in advance. I will never do this again! I realized I needed someone with whom to discuss what I was experiencing. However, a highlight of my trip was a visit with Mother Theresa. When I asked her what motivated her in her work, she replied, "It's Jesus. I have had two hours of fellowship this morning with Jesus, and now I am ready for my work." Later when I met with Ron and Shirley Yoder in Delhi, I found they understood my "exposure overload." What a blessing!

I was a member of the International Association of Mission Studies and on its Executive Committee for some time. With the Association I traveled to these places: Bangalore, India; Harere, Zimbabwe; Rome; and Hawaii. As a result, I became more aware of the missiological issues of each region.

In 1983 Marie and I traveled to Japan, Taiwan, Hong Kong and Thailand to get exposure to the practices of Shinto, Chinese religion and Mahayana Buddhism. We visited with the Krauses and explored Japanese religions together.

Our Jerusalem/Ethiopia Assignment 1994–2001

Since 1950 Mennonites have worked in the Middle East in relief, development and justice ministries and with Messianic Judaism. In 1988 Mennonite Central Committee (MCC), Mennonite Board of Missions (MBM) and Eastern Mennonnite Missions (EMM) executives, wondering what more they might consider in the region, decided that the religions of the Middle East must be taken more seriously. They identified Eastern Orthodox Christians, Islam and Judaism. We were asked to consider one of these assignments. On the basis of having taken students to the Middle East and having done a sabbatical in Jerusalem, we decided we would be most interested in exploring Judaism and the Jewish-Christian relationship. Since it is difficult to get a resident visa in Israel for anything that would "smell" like mission, it was agreed that I would retain my EMU academic credentials and spend one semester each year at EMU and one semester in Jerusalem. In this way we were able to enter the country on tourist visas.

We lived at the Tantur Ecumenical Institute, half way between Jerusalem and Bethlehem. Tantur is a safe place for Israelis and Palestinians to meet together and for Jews, Muslims and Christians to engage in conversation. As a Research Scholar at Tantur I was able to participate in interfaith conversations that were scheduled in the Jerusalem area—at the Ecumenical Research Fraternity, Rainbow Dialogue Group, and Shalom Hartman Institute. Our being from a university in the States was an advantage for the Christian-Jewish dialogue, and I was accepted into the major dialogue groupings. While in Jerusalem I also taught part time at the Israel College of the Bible. Though our primary assignment was the study of contemporary Judaism and the Jewish-Christian dialogue, this did not exclude relationships with Middle Eastern Christians and Muslims.

At the same time we were asked to go to Jerusalem, Ethiopia requested us to return. The church was gaining more freedom after the Marxist period. It was agreed with our sponsoring committee that we would spend a month each year in Ethiopia at the conclusion of our semester in Jerusalem. We did this for eight years. I taught in church leadership seminars and more recently in the Meserete Kristos College.

In the fall semester of 2005 we returned for several months to Ethiopia to teach in the inter-denominational Ethiopian Graduate School of Theology, which was established by the Lutheran Church and the Evangelical Church that grew out of the Sudan Interior Mission. These are the two largest Protestant churches in Ethiopia, but the students come from a variety of theological and denominational traditions. I taught Christianity and Islam and African Theology.

Reflections

I believe in holistic mission—evangelism and justice—and I have great appreciation for Anabaptist theology, which incorporates the two. From my experience in Ethiopia I also believe in the attractiveness of the gospel. The Meserete Kristos Church has grown from several thousand when we left Ethiopia in 1975 to 125,000 baptized church members today.

From my experience in Jerusalem I believe in biblical justice as an essential part of the gospel. The Christian faith provides a fresh perspective on justice between Jews and Palestinians.

Also, from my experience in Ethiopia I believe in personal evil and structural evil. One of my seminar students (now a medical doctor) reported on his childhood experience. When he was ill, his mother in desperation took him to a Muslim witch doctor who said, "This one can only be healed by Jesus." The gospel must address personal issues (e.g. witchcraft) and social issues (Marxist exploitation).

Also from my experience in Jerusalem I am convinced that Jesus offers hope for peoples' personal lives and addresses issues of social injustice. I believe that interfaith dialogue is an important part of witness.

I celebrate the Jewish reclamation of Jesus; Jesus is on the Jewish agenda. I work for a biblical interpretation that embraces Isaac (Jews) and Ishmael (Arabs). Many Western Christians identify with the Jews because the first covenant continued through the line of Abraham and Isaac, but in so doing have neglected or discriminated against Ishmael's people—the Arabs, whether Christian or Muslim. The covenant choice of Isaac and his descendants is not a rejection of Ishmael any more than it is a rejection of Gentiles. I believe Western Christians must embrace Arabs and Jews, and we must also make place for Ishmael's people in our theology. The record of Abraham's sending Hagar and Ishmael away was a description of what happened, not a prescription for a permanent pattern of relationship. Western Christians should emphasize reconciliation between Jews and Arabs, particularly in the Israeli-Palestinian context. God is not pleased when we discriminate against Arab Palestinians, whether Christian or Muslim. We should not abandon the children of Ishmael to a second-class or under-class position. Ishmael will have dignity when he can live in peace and security with Isaac, when he is no longer harassed and humiliated, and when he is liberated from fear and hatred.

My more recent writing and speaking tend to focus on Middle East religions, justice and peace in the Middle East, and the Christian encounter with other religions. Since September 11, 2001, I have had many invitations to speak about Islam and teach courses on Islam. I consider this an opportunity to provide a broader perspective on Islam and the Christian-Muslim relationship.

My theological passion centers on the Christian relationship with other religions. I believe it is possible to have dialogue with other religions and to witness respectfully to Christ.

January 2005

Publications

After a consultation on Christian presence by the Council of International Ministries (1982), I was asked to write a pamphlet on "A Relevant Theology of Presence." In 1988 I published a book entitled *When Kingdoms Clash: The Christian and Ideologies* (Herald Press). This was published also in Spanish and Dutch.

Because of my interest in world religions and Christian witness to other religions I researched and wrote *Who Do You Say That I Am: Christians Encounter Other Religions* (Herald Press, 1987). The International Bulletin of Missionary Research selected this book as one of fifteen outstanding books on mission studies for 1997. My book argues that we can be respectful of other faith traditions and still retain the integrity of Christian faith. One can believe in the finality of Christ as well as value positive aspects of other religions. Witness should be a positive statement about the gospel rather than a negative statement about religions. I have friends of other faiths and have taught students of other faiths. I am open to the presence of God in other religions but believe that the gospel of Jesus Christ should be shared with people of other religions. While respecting other religions, we can still view Christ as normative for all.

Most recently I wrote "Understanding Islam: A Christian Reflection on the Faith of Our Muslim Neighbors," *Missio Dei*, No. 1 (Mennonite Mission Network, 2002).

Among the articles I've written related to Ethiopia are the following:
"Renewal in the Ethiopian Church"
    Gospel Herald, July 2, 1968
"The Italian Attempt to Reconcile the Ethiopian Orthodox Church: The use of religious celebrations and assistance to churches and monasteries"
    Journal of Ethiopian Studies, Vol. X, No. 1, January 1972
"Ethiopian Socialism and the Church"
    Gospel Herald, Sept. 23, 1975
"The Ethiopian Orthodox Church's Understanding of Mission"
    Mission Studies, Vol. IV, No. 1, May 1987
"The Ethiopian Orthodox Church: A Study in Indigenization"
    Missiology, Vol. XVI, No. 3, July 1988

"The Demise of the Church in North Africa and Nubia and Its Survival in Egypt and Ethiopia: A Question of Contextualization?"
Missiology, Vol. XXI, No. 2, April 1993
"Church and State in Ethiopia: From Monarchy to Marxism"
Mission Studies, Vol. XI, No. 2, 1994

Articles related to the Middle East include:
"A Theological Response to Christian Anti-Semitism"
MCC Peace Office Newsletter, Vol. 23, No. 2, March-April 1993
"Religion and the State: If Judaism is to be Saved from Israel"
Mennonite Weekly Review, Jan. 2, 1997 (reprinted in *Mennonite Reporter*, Jan. 6, 1997, and *Gospel Herald*, May 13, 1997)
"Who Do We Blame for Jesus' Death?"
Gospel Herald, March 25, 1997
"The Middle East and the Year 2000"
Gospel Herald, Aug. 26, 1997
"No Room in Bethlehem for Arrogance or Argument"
Gospel Herald, Dec. 16, 1997
"Jerusalem as Jesus Views It"
Christianity Today, Oct. 5, 1998
"Oneness in Christ for Palestinian Christians and Messianic Jews"
Missionary Messenger, Aug. 1999
"Embrace Ishmael and Isaac"
The Mennonite, Dec. 5, 2000
"The Middle Eastern Jesus: Messianic Jewish and Palestinian Christian Understandings"
Missiology, Vol. XXIX, No. 4, Oct. 2001

My thinking, teaching, writing and practice have been profoundly impacted by the interrelationship of scripture, history, religion and culture.

NANCY V. (BURKHOLDER) LEE

An Unexpected Life

A Key Question

In February 2004 I again enjoyed attending one of Pat Schneider's writers' workshops in her and her husband Peter's home in Amherst, Massachusetts. In view of Cal Redekop's guidelines for "ACRS' Personal Stories," which I found helpful in choosing what to include in this autobiographical piece, I would like to begin with one of the poems that I wrote at the workshop, a poem that asks a major historical/theological question in my life. It takes as its frame the end-of-the-term assignments in the Christian Tradition course at the seminary here—the creation of a historical, theological, and worship timeline stretching over given periods—and it includes some of the highlights in the span of my life.

Timelines

Where does the timeline of faith begin?
With the Torah, the prophets, the wisdom writings?
With Jesus, the tongues of fire, Paul on the road to Damascus?
With the monks and nuns in the desert?
Perhaps with Martin Luther, Calvin, or the Anabaptists?
Vatican II? Ghandi and Martin Luther King?
Mother Theresa in dusty Calcutta?

Where does my timeline of faith begin,
    and where do its epiphanies break through?
With the first measures of "The heavens are telling
    the glory of God" and the burst of thunder?

With Handel's Messiah? Bach's St. Matthew's Passion?
Marian Anderson's singing, "Nobody Knows the Trouble I've
 Seen" [and inexplicably] "Glory, hallelujah!"?
With Mary Eleanor Bender among the blazing windows
 of The Little Saints' Chapel in Paris?
Trailing the singing pilgrims behind the black Virgin Mary
 in the town of Chartres on Annunciation Day?
Sitting alone on a bench in the Canterbury Cathedral
 during Evensong?
Or drinking mint and lemon-grass tea with Bob above
 the blue Lake of Galilee, where, as Pat Schneider wrote,
 "Jesus walks on the water of the mind"?

Where does my timeline of faith begin? Where does it continue?
And where do its epiphanies break through?
On a frigid January night in Harbin, a far northern city in China,
 wandering through the neon lighted ice sculptures
 of laughing Buddhas and mythological beings and
 coming suddenly upon a towering basilica with crosses,
 gleaming in the darkness?
In Shenyang early one cool, smoggy Sunday morning
 outside an overflowing church?
Among a gathering of two or three
 under windows filled with ice ferns?
Or in a taxi dodging bicycles and other taxis?

Do my epiphanies also find me in America now?
Below wild geese honking over my head
 near great trees pointing their spires to the stars?
When a warm fuzzy little head is tucked under my chin
 or leaning with me over a book?

Actually, in going back through letters, journals, and diaries, I discovered again that my timeline of faith began with my father, John David Burkholder, Jr. One of the smallest but undoubtedly most powerful ways in which he gave me a faith that has sustained me was the Bible verse (of course from the King James Version) that he shared with me usually every evening. He did not explain the verse or give me even a mini-lecture about it. He just repeated the verse, word for word. These were always verses about how the Lord was personally involved in a person's life in a caring way, and they settled into my mind and heart and stayed with me through the years. They included such verses as these: Psalm 27:1, "The Lord is my light and my salvation; whom shall I fear? The Lord is the strength of my life; of whom shall I be afraid?"; Psalm 34: 7, "The angel of the Lord encampeth round about them that fear him, and delivereth them"; and Isaiah 26:3, "Thou wilt keep him in perfect peace, whose mind is stayed on thee: because he trusteth in thee."

You are perhaps wondering why I have been emphasizing my father's influence on my faith and not my mother's. Young women who were in her Sunday School classes have told me that she was quite helpful to them. Also, I still have and prize the stories she wrote before marriage and published in our church periodical, *The Youth's Christian Companion*, when she was teaching school in West Virginia. Yet because she dealt with health problems during most of her adult life, it was that aspect that I was most aware of for many years. To the surprise of those who knew her well, she outlived her two sisters and her brother; and when she died at almost 93, she had held and played with two of her grandsons, the oldest of whom, Gabriel, at almost four, volunteered at her memorial that she "was a very special lady."

Growing up in this home and within close range of the influence of EMC and the congregation that met there, I think that the Christian faith came to me in different degrees of illumination and commitment. To me as a child, the God in the Bible was like my trusted, loving earthly father, and "Jesus loved me, this I [knew]." What was there not to believe? Then, when I was eleven, I considered myself old enough to attend the last of a series of evangelistic services and stand during the invitation hymn.

Fortunately, it was Dean of Women Ada Zimmerman who was my counselor; she had won my heart as a little girl by calling me by name one day as she passed me on Smith Avenue. She gently placed me in the key Bible verses that made me sure, before I left the room, that I was indeed a Christian.

I have always regretted that baptism was less meaningful to me than that night of choice. I think that I was yet a little girl on that occasion. Also, joining the Mennonite church—actually something quite foreign to Anabaptism, not a gathered congregation but an impersonal area called the Middle District—held little significance for me, except as an organization to be loyal to as a Christian member. It was not until later in high school, listening to Stanley Shenk bring to life the beginning of Anabaptism in Zurich, Switzerland, that I began to value my Mennonite heritage.

High School and College Perceptions

Among the references in my "Timeline" poem, some belong to my years at EMC—four years of high school and four years of college. Having grown up with many Burkholder-related and Heatwole-related cousins, as well as childhood friends at Park School, who never allowed me to feel lonely even though I had no sisters or brothers, I was also fortunate to find close, accepting friends and wise, caring teachers at EMC. Indeed, one wonderful year, classmate and friend Margaret Jantzi (now Foth), accepted my invitation to live in my home. Moreover, with gifted teachers like Ruth M. Brackbill, Hubert R. Pellman, and A. Grace Wenger (who became a true mentor and rescued me on more than one occasion from the emotional roller coasters of the yearly "revival meetings"), it was inevitable that I would major in English.

In truth, very little during my years at EMU made me feel invisible or put in second place as a woman—in spite of my entering high school in black hose, a cape dress, and a covering. In my student world the recognition of abilities was seemingly not tied to one's gender. Thus I could become the chief editor of *The Weather Vane* and have as one of my associate editors someone well qualified to be the editor, the now well-known church historian, John Ruth. Also, the year of my graduation, 1952, I could serve, along with Irene Benner and Jay Landis, as a college associate editor under the chief editor, Daniel Hertzler, of *The Shenandoah*.

Moreover, while in my experience the male professors treated me and their other female students with respect, it was the women deans and professors who became challenging role models for me. Their focus was outward, not toward themselves; they loved their various fields of study, their students, and their God; and their happiness lit up their classrooms and the girls' dormitory floor. And on the desk in Ada Zimmerman's office sat a photo of a beautiful woman: her sister, a missionary nurse in far country that would enter my life many years later, China.

At the end of my junior year, after a summer of volunteering under MCC at the state hospital in Allentown, Pennsylvania, I came back to Virginia headed toward a drastic career change: I was going to become a nurse. In fact, I planned to enter the nursing program at Goshen College, which would give me credit for many of my EMC courses and allow me to register immediately for the nursing courses. I was so serious about entering this new profession that in the fall of my senior year at EMC I enrolled in and survived such subjects as chemistry, bacteriology and anatomy. Yet, when the next spring the invitation came to teach music and English in Canada at what is now known as Rockway Mennonite Collegiate, I thought I could delay entering nursing for at least a year. True to Robert Frost's poem, "The Road Not Taken," for me, way *did* lead on to way, and my choice at the divergence did make all the difference. I never returned to nursing.

Continued Illumination

During my four years of teaching at Rockway, I went south to George Peabody College (now part of Vanderbilt University) in Nashville, Tennessee, for three summers, where I happily earned an MA with a major in English and a minor in music. Once at Peabody I was asked to give a lecture, in what turned about to be a large crowded room, about what Mennonites believe. After having reviewed the resources available to me, I told my audience something of the history of the Anabaptists, named the values most Christians now hold regarding the separation of church and state and adults' right to choose their faith, and also attempted to explain how we are different—in our commitment to the "gathered church" of believers and to a nonresistant way of love based on the teaching and life of Jesus. It was another moment of illumination and commitment for me.

In the winters, living in Kitchener and attending First Mennonite, I found from John Hess' sermons that the Bible was more exciting and had more to teach me than I had thought. I was, also, not a little moved when he and his wife, acting on their convictions, left that wealthy congregation for a small mission church in Toronto. More illumination.

At Rockway, too, I learned a great deal—for instance, that I did not know anything about Canadian writers and that certain Canadian rivers do not fill up the Great Lakes! I learned that both keeping students busy in class and also letting students know that a teacher cares about them can result in happy, usually well-behaved teen-agers. I also learned, to my astonishment, that not all parents there thought a Rockway teacher should teach C.S. Lewis' *Screwtape Letters* or go to ice hockey games, even when one went with a deacon's daughter!

More significantly for my future, I learned that although conducting the high school choir was a joy, as was conducting the Wilmot Chorus in the country, I was more at home teaching English literature and writing than in teaching music courses. Thus, given the choice of moving completely to English when told that a music major from Goshen—Marie Moyer (to become Mrs. Harold Good)—was interested in coming to Rockway, I happily turned to English. That, also, was the major reason for my decision when the president of EMC, John Mumaw, dropped by to invite me back to Virginia to teach music at my alma mater. I declined. I am not sure what I would have said if he had asked me to teach English since by then the prospect of again putting on the cape dress would have been a real problem for me. In Cal Redekop's words, this had become "a major issue" for me.

It is quite possible, of course, for a woman—like a man—to choose to belong to a group that wears a uniform of some kind and feel perfectly comfortable and even proud of visibly belonging to this group. Also, I understood the appeal to dress modestly, but I found nothing in Scripture on which to base the cape dress. I thus had no compelling reason to choose to wear it.

Frankly, I doubt if even men who have worn the plain coat fully understand the psychological implications of women's having to wear the cape dress. Since the men wore their plain coats only to church or on other formal occasions, during the week when they went downtown, they looked like all the other men there. They fitted in with all society. However, since the women were expected to wear the cape dress wherever they went, they were always demonstrably different from other women, even other Christian women. They did not fit in anywhere except with similarly dressed women. For myself, I came to feel like an odd outsider. Eventually, the person I saw in the mirror did not look like the real me.

It was George Brunk, II, who came to my rescue. Earlier at EMC, when he had been asked to have an open discussion with the students about the issue of "plain" attire, I carefully wrote down and handed in all the reasons I could think of for wearing the cape dress, asking if each of these reasons was sufficient for wearing it. To his credit, he gave his honest opinions: not one of those reasons was sufficient. Later in Canada when he was in the Kitchener area, I asked to talk with him privately and shared with him my conflict about what I now believed and what my parents wanted me to do. He asked me simply if I had peace about my decision. When I said that I did, he replied that I should then do as I believed. His response was a great relief because in a real sense he represented for me the pastoral leadership of my home state, Virginia. Soon, in ordinary clothes, I felt that I had joined the rest of the human race.

After leaving Rockway, I moved to Scottdale the summer of 1956, where in a little office without windows, I wrote Sunday School materials for high school students and their teachers and also, in a room with a piano, had a lovely time composing the parts for the songs in the children's book, *Our Hymns of Praise*. During my year in Scottdale, though, I realized that I missed the classroom. Thus in the spring of 1957 when President Mininger of Goshen College visited me and asked if I would come to teach there to take Roy Umble's place for two years while he was away, I agreed.

Then in February 1958, during my first year at Goshen, I lost my father, who was only 52, to cancer. When I knew, late in the fall of 1957 that I needed to be at home with my mother and him, I offered to resign at the College. However, my colleagues there generously added my classes to theirs, and Dean Carl Kreider refused to accept my resignation. I will always be grateful, also, that some weeks later my father's oldest sister, Bertha Bender, came to stay with my mother and me. My father's funeral took place at Weavers Church on February 15, 1958, during a huge snowstorm, which made travel extremely difficult for the relatives coming from Ohio but which for me was strangely comforting.

New Truths in a New Home

At Goshen again, I found that I enjoyed teaching and interacting with college students; and during my second year there, because of what Dean Kreider said to me, I think I could have chosen to teach there longer. However, a certain seminary student named Robert Lee had other ideas. I had seen him in the spring of 1957 at Scottdale when he had stopped there with other seminary students and met with the church members in an informal gathering in the pastor's home. To my surprise, the pastor's wife later teased me about this man who could not have seen me in the crowd. However, after I began teaching at Goshen in the fall of 1957, he called me one day from the infirmary, where he was getting over a bad cold, and asked for a date. It was not until the Christmas vacation of 1958 that Bob and I were married, and we left under the Mennonite Board of Missions that next August in 1959 for Japan on a little ship called the *Hikawa Maru*.

This voyage was my introduction to several facts. The first one was that MBM missionaries traveled as inexpensively as possible—Bob's and my little cabin was down in the heart of the ship, next to the cooks' galley. Now I am very fond of Japanese food, but I was unprepared then for the constant aroma of cabbage, garlic, fish, soy sauce, and probably *sake*. It also became very clear that although in the past I had been quite at home *in* ocean waves, riding *on top of* them was an entirely different proposition. Fortunately, at some point in the voyage, when other people were also in various stages of being flat on their backs, the ship's doctor came around with appropriate shots—and additional shots for me for an infection related to my pregnancy.

It would have been a totally miserable trip for me had it not been for another fact: traveling on the same ship were Don and Barbara Reber and their daughters and Arletta Seltzer, who provided a warm introduction to the MBM (now MMN) missionary family in Japan. Over the years in that country, this family would also come to include Carl and Esther Beck, Mary Beyler, Eugene and Louella Blosser, Ralph and Genny Buckwalter, Kaz and Lois Enomoto, Lee and Adella Kanagy, Norman and Ruth Kraus, Grace. L. Martin, Marvin and Mary Cender Miller (MBM Associates), Gerald and Rie Neufeld, Ruth and Rhoda Ressler, Wesley and Sue Richard, Joe and Emma Richards, Charles and Ruth

Shenk, Mike and Theresa Sherrill, Angela Wenger Yamamoto (MMN Associate), and Marvin and Neta Faye Yoder and all the children in these families. We also appreciated the presence of James and Doris Bomberger in Wakani from EMU, MCCers Paul and Ellen Peachey and Ferd and Viola Ediger, General Conference missionaries Fritz and Ellen Sprunger, and Florence Roes from Canada, a senior citizen volunteer under the Mennonite Association for Retired People. Like the members of natural families, not everyone in this missionary family has agreed about everything. Yet our ties remain strong, as evidenced again in the warmth of our last Japan reunion. We were blessed, too, with such MBM directors as J.D. Graber, John Howard Yoder, Wilbert Shenk, Ron Yoder, and Sheldon Sawatzky.

For Bob and me, since that first trip to Japan our lives have been divided into four distinct periods: (1) the five years in Japan, from 1959 to 1964; (2) the twenty-two years in the U.S. from 1964 to 1986; (3) the seventeen years in Japan and China from 1986 to July 2003, with several months in the U.S. during the last number of years until my mother's death on August 31, 2000; and (4) now our retirement years.

Our Early Years in Japan: Surprises along the Way

Those first five years in Japan were mainly family years for me since our three children arrived then: Steven Paul in November 1959, Suelyn Virginia in May 1961, and Robert John (Bobby) in November 1963. I was thrilled at the birth of each child and immensely grateful for the life of each one, particularly because—the American doctor at the Seventh Day Adventist hospital in Tokyo discovered shortly after we arrived in Japan—I was Rh-. Every child is a miracle, but there must have been heavenly angels, along with the many human ones, watching over the life of especially our third child as in the first week of his life he had to undergo the surgical procedure of a blood exchange six times. Among his human angels and mine were Marvin Miller (then with Mary in language study in Tokyo), who had and gave the kind of blood Bobby needed, and Esther Beck, who served in the hospital as his nurse during crucial hours, as well as our missionaries who came to visit, Barbara and Don Reber and Ruth and Charles Shenk. Then six weeks after Bobby and I were home in Hokkaido, I had to rush him back to Tokyo, where he received two ordinary transfusions. Today, well over six feet tall, the husband of Elaine Meyer and the father of three little sons, he is teaching in the English department at Goshen College. His newly published book is *Poets and Power from Chaucer to Wyatt* (Cambridge University Press, 2007).

As many missionaries have discovered, we saw our children, also, open doors into people's hearts. Remembering, too, J.D. Graber's statement that a missionary wife's role was for her to be helpful to her husband, I tried to be supportive of Bob's efforts in the churches he was responsible for after we finished our two years of language study and moved to Hokkaido. Some of my efforts were less than successful, however.

Take, for example, certain episodes that occurred with my neighbor women, who had asked me to give them cooking lessons. Protesting that I had never taken any home economics or nutrition courses, I finally agreed to try if they would teach me how to prepare some Japanese dishes; and we also decided to study flower arranging with a teacher. Of course everything they prepared turned out beautifully, as did their flower arrangements; and working with the flowers, I learned how to see and place them in more than one dimension.

However, not all my cooking lessons turned out as I had planned. Perhaps my worst mistake occurred in relation to the large, luscious blue grapes that grow in the fall in Hokkaido. They would certainly make delicious grape juice, I thought, and what could be easier than washing the grapes and putting a handful of them into a sterilized jar, adding sugar and boiling water, and sealing the jar? And that's what we did.

A few weeks later, they asked me, "Did your grape juice run out and down the sides of your jars?"

I did not think so, but I did know that sometimes even the jars of food that I had put through my pressure canner had not sealed because the glass of the jars was somewhat thin, as was the rubber on the lids.

Nothing more was said. However, at the doll festival the following March, what they served to drink was this grape juice–only it was no longer grape juice.

I could see the headlines: "Mennonite Missionary Teaches Natives To Make Wine!"

"No," my cousin Fred Brunk said later, coming to my rescue after hearing this story, "Mennonite Missionary Turns Water into Wine!"

Not everything I was asked to do, however, led to such embarrassing results. Since no other church member could play the little church organ, it was my pleasure to provide this music in the services. We moved the instrument to the back of the little church where I could both keep our children quietly occupied and also play the organ. In addition, after we had been in Hokkaido for a while, I was asked to be a member of the executive committee of the missionary organization. Also, during those first years in Japan, I found myself writing a bit again; and some of my stories, such as "The Fear," "Dilemma," and "To Be a Missionary" found their way into *The Youth's Christian Companion*.

Perhaps most important in relation to the future was the request for me to offer English classes for adults at the church and also to do some teaching at one of the local high schools. In my classes with these students, I discovered two truths that would shape much of the rest of my professional life: (a) I liked teaching English as a language; and (b) there was much that I did not know about teaching English as a foreign language.

Subsequently, after we returned to the U.S. and moved to Cambridge, Massachusettes, in 1964 for Bob's graduate study, I was delighted to find, study, and teach under a professor at Boston University who knew a great deal about linguistics and English teaching to non-native speakers of English.

New Truths in a Once Familiar Country

However, after having lived in Japan for five years, I found life in the U.S. difficult. The cars drove on the wrong side of the streets—except on one-way streets—the relationship between yen and dollars was confusing, everything seemed surprisingly expensive in the stores, and I no longer had a young woman in the home to help with the housework and child care. Also, I no longer had any role outside the home. What was happening to me we can now identify as re-entry culture shock, but no one seemed to know anything about that diagnosis then.

Eventually one doctor made the suggestion that turned me around.

"I think you should go back to teaching," he said, and so I did, at Boston University's Metropolitan College and also Northeastern University's large part-time college. Fortunately, Bob could arrange his PhD course schedule, and I could plan my studying and teaching schedule so that one of us was always at home with the children.

My advice now to people who have lived abroad for a period of time is to have some kind of activity to return to that will engage their attention and enable them to feel productive in a meaningful way.

Bob's and my twenty-two years in the U.S. from 1964 to 1986 were filled with the delight of watching our children move through pre-school, primary school, high school, driver's education, and college to adulthood, and also of developing our own academic careers.

Everywhere we moved I found a university position teaching English composition and grammar and often literature to both American and non-native students until finally I was clearly viewed as a specialist in teaching English as a second or foreign language.

However, during our year in Princeton when Bob completed his dissertation, I stepped into another kind of occupation: that of the church secretary at Princeton's All Saints' Church.

When I telephoned to inquire about the position advertised in the newspaper as that of executive assistant to the rector of the church, the woman who answered the phone said, "Yes, Father Swartzentruber can talk to you now. That's S-w-a-r-t-z-e-n-t-r-u-b-e- r." I had known, of course, how to spell this common Mennonite name, but it did not occur to me that the rector of an Episcopalian church would be remotely related to anyone in my church.

When he answered, I inquired with some embarrassment, not sure how to begin, "I guess my first question is whether a Mennonite can work for an Episcopalian."

He laughed—a reassuring sound. "*I* was a Mennonite," he said, "and yes, a Mennonite can work for an Episcopalian."

This rector, as Bob now guessed, was the Orley Swartzentruber he had known in Europe after World War II had ended, the Orley Swartzentruber who had once planned with other young men like Dick Burkholder and John Litwiller to found a seminary in Argentina. Orley later explained that when the Mission Board said no, he had found himself at a loss about what to do next until John Howard Yoder helped him enter Princeton University, where he eventually earned his doctorate in Old Testament. At some point in those years his earlier difficulties with completely adopting Anabaptism and his developing convictions led him, he said, back to "the true church."

At first another woman was hired because the church wanted someone who would be in Princeton more than a year. However, when she quit her first day, Orley called me and offered me the job. It was a job that increased my confidence in dealing with people in the business world since I had to do all the ordering of office supplies. It was also a job that introduced me to the beauty of the Episcopal service and the ways it involved the whole congregation. I was accepted into the choir there; and in that church Orley baptized two of our children, Suelyn and Bobby, on their confession of faith. No, they are not Episcopalians today. Suelyn became a Mennonite, in which church she remained until she met and married the tall tenor in the choir at Luther Memorial Church in Madison, Wisconsin. Bobby and his wife, Elaine, are members of the Friends' Meeting in South Bend. Living and working in research in the Boston area, Steven has become an example for us in his ethical choices and his loyalty to his community and friends. After the year in Princeton, I happily resumed teaching, this time where Bob had accepted a position—at the University of Tennessee in Knoxville. There I also took several graduate English courses and was admitted into a doctoral program; but, asked to choose between that and a tenure track teaching position, I chose the latter. None of the possible majors really interested me; besides, I loved both helping American literature students discover that they liked poetry after all and also teaching in the English Department program for the international students, where I soon became fully involved.

Two Hurdles in My Timeline

During those Tennessee years, two painful things happened in relation to the church. One had to do with the Summer Bible School material the Mennonite Publishing House commissioned me to write for high school students and their teachers: an introduction to the New Testament. Bob was my best editor because he both helped me find relevant resources and also critiqued each chapter in helpful ways. Balancing this project with my teaching and homemaking was more difficult than I had anticipated, but I enjoyed the research and the challenge to provide interesting teaching methods. In the end, I often worked into the morning every other night.

The final books were in certain important ways a disappointment. Although I appreciated many of the changes made by the MPH editors, particularly in breaking up fairly long sections and giving them captions, I was unpleasantly surprised—as was Bob—upon discovering changes in content that had been made without my knowledge or agreement. One was, to my astonishment, the addition of a statement directly contradicting a fairly long quotation from John Howard Yoder's *The Politics of Jesus* and thus the whole point of that section. Another was the substitution of out-of-sync lines for some of my favorite lines in the dramatic reading I had written based on the book of Romans to bring it to life for my teenaged readers. Still another was the deletion from my material of the clear contrast between "then" and "now" that is basic in the structure of the book of Hebrews. Also, the cover design was a shock. Familiar with the covers of many high school textbooks, I knew that this design would strike teenagers as being childish. Moreover, one of the sketches in the book was an insult to people of other races.

Sometime later, when Willard Swartley, then on the Publication Board, met with the editors and questioned the changes, he found that the two men could often give no reasons for making them. Still, I hope that the students and the teachers who used the books made new discoveries in their New Testaments and learned to enjoy serious Bible study.

The second painful thing that happened in Knoxville occurred in the little Mennonite church there. We had been welcomed warmly, and Bob was invited to preach sometimes and I to lead the singing. Also, the church had voted for Bob to guide the planning involved in relocating the congregation to another section of the city, and he had organized task forces involving everyone interested. This whole truly energized situation came to a halt a year after we had arrived when we gave our church letters to the minister to move our membership there.

The problem was not an issue that I would have chosen. Briefly put, I found that, after years of not wearing the covering, I could not put it on again. In Japan I had come to see that it had no meaning there. In Boston no Mennonite woman in our congregation wore it. Now in Knoxville, when I thought about the other women attending this city church who were also interested in becoming members but who had not taken that step because they did not believe in wearing the covering, the missionary in me would not let me put the covering on again. How, in the late 1970s, could a city church grow if it continued to insist on a symbol that, contrary to the spirit of 1 Corinthians 11, continued to put women in an inferior position?

Bob supported my perspective—and with better Scriptural explication than I could give—and one of the Virginia bishops offered us enormous help and understanding in the painful months that followed: Harold Eshleman. He even proposed accepting Bob's and my membership letters in a Harrisonburg church, an invitation, however, that we all saw would bypass the fact that we were not then living in Harrisonburg.

In contrast, I discovered one day how completely the bishop involved in the district overseeing the Knoxville church misunderstood my motives, when he admonished me, "Nancy, you need to die to self." In the end, however, he followed my suggestion as a way out: he would accept our letters but add that he did not agree with me.

The atmosphere that particular Sunday morning was electric and joyful as, immediately after the bishop's words of acceptance of Bob and me, one after another person, including our daughter, stood up and said that he or she, also, wanted to become a member of this congregation. Having more than once almost disbanded over the refusal to allow Bob and me to move our letters there, this congregation now saw itself as a church where the members were free to be honest with one another about their convictions. And many of these new members were the ones who held that congregation together after we moved to Texas and when it had no pastor. Before we left Knoxville, however, Bob was able to help the congregation work together again and relocate the church. The Virginia Mennonite Mission Board helped with a loan, which the church members triumphantly repaid some years later.

New in My Timeline: China and Again Japan

After a brief return to Boston, we moved to Texas in 1980, where Bob held a chair at Southwestern University and I commuted to Austin and taught in the Intensive English Language Program of the University of

Texas. One of my special joys occurred there when I was asked to have UT graduate student interns help me and learn to teach. It was a beautiful experience to see them become confident, skilled English instructors of international students.

It was also during this time that in 1981 I first went to China—with a group of teachers and student assistants organized and sent by Goshen College—to what would become "my" university and where I would teach a total of 12 times—five semesters in different years and seven summers. It happened that in 1981 our daughter, Suelyn, also went to China with the second group of Goshen SST students sent to Chengdu. In fact, she landed in Beijing the day I left Shanghai.

It was during that summer that one Saturday morning, after listening to Wilbur Birky's lecture on Robert Frost's "The Road Not Taken," my students—professors, engineers, and a few graduate students—turned the topic of our conversation into what I thought was forbidden territory, the area of faith. Our conversation ranged through the basics of Christian belief and social response, including nonresistance; and as we talked, we all moved physically close together.

Finally, a man in the back stood up with a shining face. "Choice is a right!" he exclaimed. "Choice is a right."

Thus it happened that in this land with no choices at that time, for this small group of people there were now paths in the woods of faith that diverged for everyone.

On my way back to Texas at the end of our program and after a magical trip to major cities in China, I took time to visit friends and former students at Doshisha Women's College in Kyoto. Newly aware of how much Japan meant to me, I wrote the following short poem.

Kyoto Notes

In the West, water lilies jewel the reflection of a gold pavilion.
In the eastern hills,
    green spears beaded with rice
    bend near tall pines
    and palace gardens.
Among the ranks of silent Kannon

> with eleven faces and one thousand arms
> a thin, determined hermit speaks.

> I take off my shoes
>> and whisper in a white space.
> And I take off my shoes
>> for the little gray fish—upright on the small plate—
>> and friends.

> Then my small cup overflows
>> with the rain dripping from the temple roof
>> outside my window
>> and songs from another summer.

Before my other trips to China, we would move to Houston, where I taught at the University of Houston and was then asked to be the coordinator of the large program in the English Department for non-native speakers of English. While I enjoyed the organizational aspects of this administrative position, I was also happy for every opportunity to teach.

It was in Houston in 1986 that MBM's Ron Yoder (now the CEO at VMRC) asked Bob and me to go again to Asia. This time he gave each of us a different assignment: Bob was to do research in Japan, and I was to be a consultant and English teacher in China under China Educational Exchange since it was felt that China needed English teachers more than Japan did. As it happened, in 1989 I also taught in Japan at the same Japanese university where Bob was then teaching and then later for five summers in the Intensive English Language Program at Temple University Japan, a branch of Philadelphia's Temple University and the oldest U.S. university campus in Japan. In addition, Bob taught in China with me a couple semesters and part of a third. Thus, we were not away from each other as much as our assignments indicated we would be.

Too much happened during these years for all of it to be recorded here. However, I want to mention how good it was to share joys and concerns with Ruth and Charles Shenk, who were then based in Tokyo.

Also, I was active both as an invited speaker and later as a member of the planning committee in the annual interdenominational Women's Conference. In this group I met many wonderful women and learned to know better the problems and joys of living as an expatriate Christian woman in Japan.

Also, during one of these conferences, I saw something of the destructiveness of present American policy. It was the year our conference was held in Okinawa, the only part of Japan to witness combat on land in World War II. Here we not only saw the visible effects of this fighting and heard stories from people who had lived there at that time. We also witnessed the continued presence of the American military, which, in its exercises, was then in one area using live ammunition, threatening many homes—against the protests of the people living there. Indeed, after the failure of their appeals to their government to influence the American military to stop this dangerous practice, the people had gone out and lain down in the crucial street to stop the transporting of American equipment. The American military's solution? Simply to fly over these people in helicopters!

In addition, we learned something about the lives of the women in the brothel district, and we met the missionaries trying to help them.

World War II with its Hiroshima and Nagasaki was in the past, but neither there nor here was the past at an end.

Disillusioned, I, as an American, wrote this little poem.

Again

I walk barefoot on the hot white sands of Okinawa,
    looking for shells.
White winged gulls slant through the gentian sky,
    crying like violins
        in the uncertain hands of students.
Red hibiscuses lean over the shores,
    hiding the caves—
    bomb shelters.
A broken shell cuts the bottom of one foot.
Behind me as I walk,
    blood seeps again into the white sands
    of Okinawa.

Although I have been very grateful to have lived and taught in Japan, Maribel Kraybill, who was a member of our China Educational Exchange team the summer of 1997, made a very perceptive comment. It was the first time I had been back at "my" university in Shenyang since the fall semester of 1994. Our mornings were taken up with teaching and our afternoons with preparation for the next day, as well as with coping with the extremely hot July weather. Noticing the stream of visitors to my room, one of our CEE teachers commented about them, apparently concerned that I needed more rest.

Maribel replied, "Oh, this is her ministry."

Yes.

Don Snow, in his book *English Teaching as Christian Mission*, has explained well the ways in which Christian teachers can serve in China legally and with integrity both in terms of their academic profession and their faith, and the CEE orientation material is also helpful. Actually, in that totalitarian country I have found far more opportunities to be of service and to share my faith or some aspect of it than I have had in my own nation. They simply come to one, often in unexpected places and at surprising times; and I have learned to wait and listen and trust the Lord of the church there, as well as here, to guide me.

One of these opportunities I have already described. Another happened one autumn after I had been invited to be the sponsor of the English club, the largest, most popular club on the campus. In this capacity I helped select the English movie shown every other week on campus and led a discussion afterwards. Sometimes, to my dismay, a different movie would be substituted for the one on the schedule. That is how one night I found myself watching a fierce Rambo film in which Rambo, against orders, rescues American prisoners of war in a jungle. What was I going to do with *that*?

After it ended, I took the students through the story and then asked how Rambo solved his problem. No question: with a great deal of violence. Were there other ways to find solutions to problems? I wondered. And then I told the students packed into that room that I was a person of peace and that I hoped the world would look for nonviolent, positive ways to find solutions. Weren't there such ways? Several students nodded yes. Suddenly a student got to his feet and proceeded to say that they knew that I was a person of peace and that they appreciated the fact that I had left my country to come and live here simply and teach them. In a later year, that student identified himself to me in one of my classes of graduate science students. Did I remember that night and him? he asked.

A very special opportunity came when several of my former graduate English majors came to me for advice about the Master's thesis each was planning to write. As I met with them individually over a period of weeks, our friendship deepened and our conversations ranged over many topics, including sometimes Christianity. Then two wintry days they took me with them to the English department at Liaoning University, where, seated with the professors, I listened to them calmly make their defenses in fluent English. All of them passed, and I was intensely proud of them.

As part of my service in China, I tried to leave teaching material that would contribute to the ongoing English education of Chinese students and teachers. At the invitation of the leaders of the graduate English program for the science students, I wrote an English composition book and a detailed teacher's guide for the first semester, called *Developing English Writing Skills*. In my material, I related the content to Chinese culture and devised task-based discovery exercises instead of giving a great deal of advice. These volumes, along with a third one for the second semester (when I was no longer there) by another teacher, Janina P. Traxler (from Manchester College, Indiana), were published by the University Press in 1994 and later reprinted with a new cover. The books continue to be used by the undergraduate English majors and by the science and technology PhD students. Some of the CEE teachers in other universities have used them, and they have been purchased by other schools, also.

More recently, one of my former graduate English majors who is now my colleague and a professor at the university, invited me to be the advisor of what turned out to be a very time-consuming project: the development of four volumes and four CD-ROMs called *All Purpose College English,* published by the Higher Education Press in Beijing and later republished in Taiwan under the name *Smart Reading*. I became essentially the English editor and even author of many of the exercises in this material, and I welcomed the help of Jim Bomberger with the last volume. It felt good to be able to provide material that the Chinese students could trust to be accurate, not only in its exercises, but also in its readings. In more than one of the selected readings sent to me, I was able to correct information, even information directly related to Christianity. One particular essay had Christianity coming to an end before the Reformation!

Later I had the privilege of teaching some of the first volume and CD in the fall of 2001 with my Chinese colleague in the Distance Learning College. It was a new experience to teach in front of TV cameras with a live audience of not only the hundred students in the media classroom with us but those in other classrooms on other campuses. And it was this group I was scheduled to teach on the evening of the day the rest of the world woke up to the news of the destruction of the World Trade Towers. In the face of such an enormous tragedy, I felt very aware that I was inescapably an American as well as inescapably a Christian person of peace. I realized that before I and my colleague could conduct the class as usual, I would need to address the event.

With my colleague translating, I began that evening by saying that I understood that white was the color of grief and mourning in China. In my country it was black. Perhaps they had seen a video of Jackie Kennedy when President Kennedy was shot. (Heads nodded.) Well, I did not have a black dress here, but I was wearing the darkest dress I had to symbolize my sadness about the many people who had died.

Then I reviewed the facts as I had learned them via AOL.

Next I talked about how I felt. I was grateful for the messages of sympathy from around the world, such as the one sent by China's President Jiang Zimin. I was also very sad, indeed in shock, and the event did not seem real. I said I was worried about two of my former Northeastern University students who were now studying and living in New York. I had not yet heard from them.

And while I was terribly sad that terrorist attacks still happened in our world, I was also grateful for the people who were working for peace—and I mentioned my university with its peace center, to which people came from around the world to study ways to solve problems peacefully. I said that I was hopeful that in the future ways would be found to solve problems without violence. I named the recent Universiad in Beijing and China's Olympics 2008 as major ways of strengthening friendship around the world.

I ended, "When you reach out to me and I reach out to you, we know that we belong together in one human family."

I never felt in danger in Shenyang although the Director of the Foreign Affairs Department warned the three of us foreign teachers to be careful, pointing out that many Middle Easterners lived in Shenyang.

It is a continuing pleasure now to respond to the requests of CEE Director, Myrrl Byler, and to be in touch with and of help to Chinese friends both here and in China. Also, it is good to be in the classroom again at EMU's IEP (Intensive English Program).

Finally, I want to say that it has been a truly precious opportunity to attend church services in Shenyang and to see the churches there grow through the years. The largest one now has over 30,000 members, and the other one that I also attend, whose lead pastor is He Hong, a woman who attended seminary here at EMS, has over 10,000. As I think about these Christians, I realize that my witness and the difficult experiences in my life pale in comparison to theirs. In tribute to them, I would like to end with the following poem.

Sunday Mornings in China, 1993

The church I go to
>   in this country of stone walls, brick walls,
>   concrete-coated walls, adobe walls, and—
>   in the South–bamboo fences

has many doors—
>   simple wooden doors weathered into a quiet green,
>   doors whose locks hang loose
>   in this land of crisply snapped shut locks,
>   doors never locked even when darkness fills the alleys
>   outside.

This church I go to has many windows—
>   small-paned double windows set in green wood
>   along the south and north sides of the sanctuary,
>   anachronisms polished clean

in this flat dusty town dotted with smoke stacks
that is home to six million people.

The eastern sun pours in through the high door windows,
    reflecting off the white-washed arches
    and high ceiling
    and filling the room with such clear light
    that all two thousand heads of the people—
    gathered here for this second of three morning services—
    shine as though tipped with white fire!

In this church I go to
the people sing an hour before the service begins
and stay for the long sermon even though
the cushions on the hard wooden slats of the benches
are thin.

In this church I go to here
the people smile
now.

                                          February 2005

APPENDIX

An Unfinished Story: The History of the Anabaptist Center for Religion and Society

Calvin W. Redekop

It can be safely said that "higher learning" has been suspect among the descendants of Menno. There was danger in knowing too much. It was assumed that too much learning would lead to "worldliness" or secularism. In my German Mennonite heritage I grew up with a community, which repeated endlessly the aphorism, *"Je gelehrter, je verkerhter"* ["the more learned, the more perverted"]. Hence Mennonites were late in establishing "centers of higher learning" beyond parochial and Bible Schools.

But beginning in Russia, and then spreading to North America, Mennonites began establishing "higher learning" institutions. The first "higher" educational school in North America was Wadsworth Mennonite School begun in 1867; Bethel College was next, established in 1893. One of the main concerns the sponsoring Mennonite churches in all subsequent institutions of higher learning had was making sure that the "liberalizing" and hence "secularizing" aspects of the higher learning were restrained, and that the "learning" was consistent with, and supportive of, the Anabaptist/Mennonite faith.

One of the many unintended consequences of the establishment of Mennonite centers of higher learning is that they have become magnets for immigrants from the Mennonite "hinterlands." Untold graduates remained in the college communities after graduation for a variety of reasons, not the least being the "free air" of an academic community. Another was employment opportunities. Further, the rich cultural fare offered on the campuses, including performances in music, athletics, art activities, conferences, visiting speakers and the like were very attractive.

Another unanticipated consequence for college and universities in general was attracting retiree populations, and Mennonite centers were no exception. It is well known, that one of the reasons why Mennonite college towns prospered was the increasing number of retirees, including academics, that are flocking to these "cultural centers." This has been corroborated by comparative research, including a research project by a student at Hesston under my direction, who proved rather conclusively that the struggling town would not have survived the 1930s if it had not been for Hesston College.

Pro forma in this context, Eastern Mennonite College, now University, began attracting increasing numbers of retirees, including retired Mennonite professors. During the Joseph Lapp administration, retired college teachers from other institutions were given retired faculty status, which in my case, was a most welcome gesture: it did more to make me feel part of the university community than anything else I could imagine. (It may have given me more "ownership" than I deserved and created resentment among the "native professors," but I have not researched to check this out, probably mainly because I did not want to know that it was true). Many of us were given opportunity to teach a course or occasionally lecture in classes.

Another corollary of this "gathering" of retired academics was the realization that these people possessed a wide range of knowledge, expertise and experiences that might enhance the college community. One of the first specific intimations of this fact was an article that President Shirley Hershey Showalter wrote in the August 10, 1994, *Chronicle of Higher Education*, entitled "Senior Professors Can Open the Doors for Young PhDs." She argued that the venerated old professors should vacate their tenured positions so that the newly minted young and hungry PhDs could get jobs. As a consolation (or compensation) to these voluntarily abdicating tenured professors, they would become members of an "Institute of Senior Fellows" who could continue in their role as silver-haired oracles [my term] on college campuses, being paid with honor rather than paychecks. She proposed that the fellows of these "institutes" could do research on problems important to the community, hold symposia for community leaders and college faculties, be research consultants for faculty and students, help institutional evaluations, write proposals for grants, guide faulty graduate study, as well as student projects.

This article was circulated by Ray Gingerich to a number of retirees with an accompanying memorandum, entitled "An EMU Senior Fellows Institute for the Advancement of Higher Learning and Living" (October 7, 1994). His memorandum began: "Recently such widely respected church-persons (sic) like C. Norman Kraus and Cal Redekop have decided to live their senior years in the Harrisonburg-EMU community. We can anticipate _____ joining us within another year or two (this person did not arrive). How might these resources be used for the University, for the community and for the church?"

Other ideas pertaining to the using of senior retirees were circulating among local retirees and EMU faculty. This included the idea of publishing a journal sponsored by EMU and using senior retired faculty (see letter to Dean Hawk of January 29, 1999, by Cal Redekop). In the meantime the idea of an institute for advanced studies made up of senior faculty—modeled after the famous Institute of Advanced Studies at Princeton—was proposed by Robert Lee, who had been a visiting member at that Institute. He began discussing it among some of us who had been thinking about such a possibility. On March 30, 1999, Lee sent a proposal for an "Institute for Advanced Studies at EMU" to Vern Jantzi, Ray Gingerich, Al Keim and Cal Redekop. His orientation was rather specific and designed after the Institute of Advanced Studies, namely, "The purpose of an institute of advanced studies at EMU is to add academic excellence by establishing a formal faculty for advanced studies in the University."

An informal group composed of Ray Gingerich, Ted Grimsrud, Al Keim, Robert Lee, Vernon Jantzi and Cal Redekop discussed the idea. In the spring of 1999, Robert Lee, Vernon Janzti (who was designated as our official contact with EMU), and Cal Redekop met with Joe Lapp and

Beryl Brubaker about the idea of establishing some type of Advanced Study Institute to be sponsored by the EMU, though the exact purpose and structure of the institute was not yet fully defined.

On April 21, 2000, Vernon Jantzi wrote a memo to Calvin Redekop stating, "I met with Joe just before I left for New Zealand and that (the proposed institute) was one of the items that I raised with him, now that the Graduate Council has given its approval and encouragement for such an entity." Jantzi also stated that President Lapp was very concerned about the costs "because of a very tight upcoming budget." Vernon asked, "What next? If you and Robert would be willing to take the original proposal and specifically address the economic issue in such a way that you could demonstrate that the Center will not be an economic 'burden' for EMU, there is a good chance that it could move ahead next year. Do you think that there might be $5000 out there that could be captured for this purpose. If there is, I think that it is likely that we can move forward. If not, Joe doesn't feel that he can encourage our moving forward."

On April 28, 2000, Redekop responded to the concerns President Lapp raised by stating, "I am assuming that the IAS should be self-financing, meaning of course that there might be some planned subsidy from EMU, but by no means a majority of the cost. I am thinking that the charter members might be willing to each chip in some start-up contributions, and then think of a fee structure." President Lapp asked for more specifics on the proposed organization including structure, budget, space usage and anticipated programs and activities (letter, August 4, 2000).

After informal discussion by the "core group" a memorandum written by Calvin Redekop was sent to President Lapp on August 11, which included a paragraph on organizational structure—three local resident scholars, two persons from EMU recommended by the EMU-VP, all subject to approval by the president. This board would determine the goals and program of CAS (Center for Advanced Studies). A budget of $2,055 for the first years was proposed. The objectives included: (1) mutual enjoyment of retiree scholars, (2) mutual stimulation and encouragement of retirees' projects, (3) provide resources to EMU academic enterprise, such as (a) serving as consultants and guides for undergraduate and graduate students, (b) serving the same way for EMU faculty and staff,

(c) offering assistance in staging seminars and conference on various topics in which the retirees have expertise, and (d) team-taught courses on special topics. It was proposed that this type of entity on the EMU campus would "enhance the ability of EMU to call attention to its academic resources which are available."

There was continuing discussion including various oral and written proposals. For example one written proposal by Norman Kraus included an extended list of issues that this group could study including, "Is justice a valid moral end for those who understand the Christian ideal as agape and nonviolence? What is the relation of justice and love? Should Christians be responsible for social justice?" (September 24, 2001).

Many of us became convinced that the organization would not get off the ground unless some person was made available to spearhead and implement activities. Fortunately, Ray Gingerich was contemplating retirement and seemed to be the logical choice. On July 31, 2001, President Lapp sent an memorandum to Cal Redekop, stating "As mentioned to you the other day we are granting six-hours time to Ray Gingrich as service to the (whatever the name will be) for next year. I hope this (organization) can be a resource for intellectual stimulation and promotion of the mission of EMU." The "core group" was pleased by the very positive and supportive position taken by President Joe Lapp and Provost Beryl Brubaker, which they conveyed to the faculty and staff. Things were now beginning to move forward rapidly.

The issues of name of the organization, detailing the exact goals and structure of the organization and membership continued to percolate. Prospective names of members were circulated and on July 23, 2001, a roster of 24 men and 12 women who would be potential members and supporters was circulated. The first formal meeting of the Center for Integrative Studies (CIS) was held on August 7, 2001, and dealt with purpose of the center, membership, expectations, structure, and immediate tasks.

By mid-2001, a steering committee was established consisting of Myron Augsburger, Al Keim, Norman Kraus, Ed Stolzfus, and Cal Redekop. Vernon Jantzi was the liaison with EMU, while Beryl Brubaker was designated by President Lapp to be the University representative. Still called the Center for Integrative Studies, the goals, structure, and activities of the organization were debated and slowly hammered out.

On September 21, 2001, Ray Gingrich presented a report to the core group, entitled "Synthesis of Vision and Conceptualization: Based on Interview with Core Group and EMU Administration." The two page, single-spaced report included the following sections: (1) Purpose and Vision for the Center, (2) Membership, (3) CIS Expectations from EMU, (4) Organizational Structure, and (5) Projects. The "Purpose and Goals" section suggested the direction of the organization, which has pretty much predicted the course of what later became known as ACRS (Anabaptist Center for Religion and Society). The specific goals consisted of research and writing, mentor/consultant/advisor, sponsoring regular forums, sponsoring annual or bi-annual conference on particular topics, probing an institutional identity for colleagues after leaving EMU, promoting visiting scholars to be present on campus, and publication of significant works.

One of the major issues that continued to bother us was the basic identity of the organization. At the Wednesday, October 3, 2001, meeting, Ray Gingrich stated several issues in the Agenda. "At quite a few points I think there seems to be an emerging consensus. I've identified at least two points that I think need further process: (1) Are we agreed to have 'Anabaptist' as one of the key identifiers? If so, how broadly do we want to define Anabaptist? (2) How solidly academic should CIS be?" These and other issues were slowly processed and are too detailed to be described here.

It was felt that the quickest way for CIS to gain some credibility was to stage a conference sponsored by CIS. At the Friday, October 10th CIS meeting Ray stated, "The idea of a conference as related to the structuring of the 'Center for Integrative Studies' is that rather than attempt to conceptualize an organization in the abstract, we should focus on a compelling and engaging task together and allow the structure of CIS to emerge more organically." At the October 31st CIS meeting the topic selected was "Re-Imaging Our World." There were numerous "chaotic" meetings attempting to refine CIS identity and the nature of the first meeting on "Re-imaging Our World." (Parenthetically, this topic/slogan became something of a confusing focus for our identity and it remains unresolved.) The November 15th meeting minutes state, The name "Center for Integrative Studies" was reconsidered. Is what we are creating best-called a "center" or an "institute." Or is there some other term that better captures both essence and substance of what we are about? At the November 29th meeting a number of names were suggested, including "Center for Theological and Cultural Studies." Finally, at the January 17, 2002, meeting, the name "Anabaptist Center for Religion and Society" (ACRS) was adopted. The reasoning attending this decision are highly instructive and entertaining but cannot be enumerated here.

The ACRS "Steering Committee" continued to meet bi-weekly in lively and energizing discussions. As part of these meetings, the various members were invited to report on research and or publications they produced in recent months. On March 30, 2002, the Steering Committee produced a "Membership Guidelines and Statement of Purpose." This was refined, and in April of 2002 ACRS published its first brochure describing the organization. It was organized under the following sections: Purpose and Vision, Membership Guidelines, ACRS Steering Committee and Applications for Membership. Several revisions of the brochure have emerged subsequently and aside from several flyers of forums and seminars, provide the basic physical published evidence of our existence.

On April 11, 2002, the first forum was staged by ACRS and it featured Paul Peachey reviewing his book, *Leaving and Cleaving: The Human Significance of the Conjugal Union*.

On April 14, 2002 a forum was held featuring Basit Koshul, a Muslim scholar on the topic, "The Response of Traditional Islam to Modernity." On November 15, 2002, a forum was held on "Schleitheim and Iraq: A Reexamination of Our Sixteenth Century Heritage and Contemporary Mennonite Practices." These were the first of a variety of seminars and forums that followed.

Since the fall of 2002, an impressive variety of forums, seminars and colloquia have been conducted. One of the most notable and successful ACRS activities has been the monthly "Second Monday Morning Stories," in which ACRS members and others have told their stories of integrating faith and life and the world of thought. Mennonite community pastors and laypeople were invited to attend, and many community persons have participated. Thus far twenty-one seniors have told their stories, many of which were spellbinders. These personal stories/memoirs are to be published. You hold in your hands the first installment in this series.

ACRS continues to evolve. It is still searching for a firm identity. Finding a specific location/space for an office and meeting place continues to be a concern. A membership structure is still not established, and the relationship of "ACRS participants" to the larger campus and community is still not clear. But it could just be that the presence of "hoary heads" in an academic community holds, as Shirley Showalter maintained, potential promise for everyone—if the right understandings are reached. Could it be that there is a function for "elders?" Or was Solomon rationalizing his own position when he said, "Miss not the discourse of the elders"? (Ecclesiasticus 8:9)

April 20, 2006

NOTES ON CONTRIBUTORS

Esther (Kniss) Augsburger (DFA, Grove City College, PA) is an artist, teacher and speaker. Sculpture is her area of expertise. Having lived the first twelve years of her life in a jungle village in India with missionary parents, she creates art that reflects a combination of both the Western and East Indian traditions. After her and Myron's three children were in school, she earned her BA from Eastern Mennonite College and then crafted the art program at Eastern Mennonite High School, where she taught for almost eight years, interrupting one year to complete an MA degree from James Madison University. She has further studied in Europe and Washington, DC. She has used her gifts in developing an art program for inner-city children, in organizing art conferences for professional artists in Asia and Eastern Europe, and in speaking and teaching on art and faith in educational institutions and churches. Her sculptures, known for expressing peace, appear in collections in the U.S. and eight other countries. Best known is the large sculpture commissioned by the Metropolitan Police Department that she with her son Michael created, titled "Guns Into Plowshares." It contains three thousand actual guns from off the streets and now sits in Judiciary Square in Washington, DC.

Myron S. Augsburger (ThD, Union Theological Seminary, VA), President Emeritus of Eastern Mennonite University, has been involved for nearly 60 years in the service of Christ and the church: 15 years in pastoring and evangelistic ecumenical ministries; 15 years in education and theology as the president of Eastern Mennonite College (now University); 15 years in church planting in Washington, DC, and as the president of the Coalition of Christian Colleges; and since 1995 nearly 15 of his retirement years in Harrisonburg in a variety of activities, serving as an overseer in the Virginia Mennonite Conference, teaching in seminaries overseas, being active in ministries under the auspices of InterChurch, Inc., and accepting interim pastoral roles. He has written twenty-plus books and continues to write. In their retirement years he and his wife, Esther, enjoy their family of three children and two granddaughters.

Titus W. Bender (PhD, Tulane University) is Professor Emeritus of Eastern Mennonite University. He and his wife, Ann, have three children: Anita, Maria and Michael. In Mississippi he was pastor of Fellowship Mennonite Church in Meridian, a member of a statewide organization (Committee of Concern) that was involved in re-building places of worship destroyed in KKK-related activities, and Peace Representative in the South for the MCC Peace Section in the last half of the 1960s. After completing a doctorate in Social Work at Tulane University, he taught four years at the University of Oklahoma and then at Eastern Mennonite College/University for 22 years. Since 1981 he has been active alongside other community members in the initiation and development of *Gemeinschaft Home,* a Harrisonburg, Virginia-based program for the re-entry of addicted people from prison into the community. He and Ann are members of Lindale Mennonite Church.

James R. Bomberger (EdD, Columbia University) is Professor Emeritus of English at Eastern Mennonite University. Born in the depression, 1933, I survived a joyful childhood without any awareness of the plight of the unemployed. School was fun and reading was even better. Graduating from Mt. Joy High School, I went to EMU and signed up for an English major with an interest in education. What other job is there for English majors? In addition to teaching in high school and college, I found time to edit church publications. I also found teaching abroad stimulating: Liberia, China and Japan. I never wrote the great American novel. But work isn't everything. Church and family influenced me. As time goes by, I've learned more and more to appreciate the Mennonite church and its mission, especially its peace emphasis. My own nuclear family, Doris, Doug and Cathy, with the addition of spouses and grandchildren, has been the solid core of my life. Special friendships continue from the past. Now retired at Virginia Mennonite Retirement Community, I have time for reading, volunteering, fellowship groups, and sometimes work. I have a joyful retirement, but unlike in my childhood, I now have the awful awareness of world unrest.

Gerald R. Brunk (PhD, University of Virginia) is Professor Emeritus of History at Eastern Mennonite University. Born in Denbigh, Virginia, as the oldest of five children to George R. II and Margaret Suter Brunk, Gerald pursued a life of studying and teaching. At Eastern Mennonite University he earned a BA in Bible & Social Science, and at the University of Virginia he earned a Master's in Teaching, as well as a PhD in History. After teaching for 36 years at EMU, he retired in 2001. He married the late Janet High in 1960, and they had four sons. For several years he led the singing in the Brunk tent revivals. He also served with his family for two years as the first resident country representative in Egypt for the Mennonite Central Committee. He is the editor of *Menno Simons: A Reappraisal* and has given many impersonations of Menno, which he calls "My Road to Decision." In 1984 he married Shirley Nafziger, and they are enjoying their four grandchildren. He is a member of the Harrisonburg Mennonite Church, where he serves as an occasional Sunday-School teacher and song leader.

Ray Gingerich (PhD, Vanderbilt University) is Professor Emeritus of Theology and Ethics at Eastern Mennonite University and Director of the Anabaptist Center for Religion and Society (ACRS). He joined the EMU faculty in 1977, where his first major assignment came from Dean Al Keim: to establish an interdisciplinary peace and justice program. From this beginning of a minor, colleagues joined to carry the project further: an undergraduate major in Justice and Peace Studies, and the Summer Peacebuilding Institute which is now under the umbrella of EMU's multifaceted graduate program, the Center for Justice and Peacebuilding. Parallel to his teaching in church history and peace studies, Ray's focus has also been on the construction of a theology of nonviolence, including the nonviolent God. During the 60s, Ray and his wife, Wilma Beachy Gingerich, lived in Luxembourg (Europe), working with Eastern Mennonite Missions. To transcend the stereotype of a "foreigner" engaged in church work, Gingerich founded *Le Bon Livre*, a self-sustaining bookstore that specialized in Mennonite-Anabaptist books as well as a broad spectrum of religious literature and *belles lettres*. Ray and Wilma are members of Community Mennonite Church. They enjoy their family of four married sons, whom Ray now calls his mentors, and seven grandchildren.

Notes on Contributors

Samuel L. Horst (PhD, University of Virginia) is Professor Emeritus of History at Eastern Mennonite University. Born on July 18, 1919, in Lancaster, Pennsylvania, I was the third of eight surviving children. I was raised on a small farm along the borders of Berks and Lancaster Counties. The Great Depression emerged, and in 1933 at age fourteen I began five years of factory work in Reading. Drafted as a CO in 1940, I entered CPS in 1942, which broadened my outlook and gave me a clearer sense of direction. I married Elizabeth Good, and by 1961 we were the parents of six children. I received a BA from Goshen College, an MEd from the University of Virginia, an MA from American University, and a PhD from University of Virginia. In 1967 I was awarded a Fellowship by Johns Hopkins University and in 1969 a NEA Fellowship by Indiana University. Since my retirement in 1984 my faith and practice has been further enhanced by my ongoing involvement in historical study and writing.

Albert N. Keim (PhD, Ohio State University), Professor Emeritus of History, retired from Eastern Mennonite University in the year 2000 after thirty-five years of teaching. His field of study was recent American history; and he is the author of four books, among them his well received biography of Harold S. Bender, published in 1998. He also served as Vice President and Dean of the University for seven years in the 70's and 80's. Keim grew up Amish, was drafted in 1955 and worked as a conscientious objector in PAX Europe for two years. After the death of his first wife, Leanna, he married Kathy Fisher in 2000. They live near Harrisonburg and attend Park View Mennonite Church. He has a daughter and two grandsons

C. Norman Kraus (PhD, Duke University) is a retired college and seminary professor, author, and Mennonite minister and missionary to Asia. He served on the faculties of Goshen College and Associated Mennonite Biblical Seminary from 1951–1979. From 1980–87 he and his wife Ruth served the Mennonite churches in Japan, where he wrote the first of his two-volume theology, *Jesus Christ our Lord: Christology from a Disciple's Perspective*. Over the years he has served on various national and international boards and committees of the Mennonite Church and on various teaching, consulting, and reporting assignments for the Mennonite

Board of Missions and the Mennonite Central Committee in Asia, Africa and South America. Among his latest books are *To Continue the Dialogue: Biblical Interpretation and Homosexuality; An Intrusive Gospel?;* and *Using Scripture in a Global Age.* He and his wife, Rhoda, live in Harrisonburg, VA, where he continues writing and publishing articles for scholarly journals and anthologies.

Nancy V. (Burkholder) Lee (MA, Vanderbilt University), a Virginian married to an Oregonian, Robert Lee, views her life as a surprising series of relationships and opportunities. Mother, grandmother, high school and university English teacher (Rockway Collegiate in Ontario, Goshen College, various universities in the U.S., Japan, and China, and more recently EMU's Intensive English Program part time), the coordinator of the English program in the Department of English at the University of Houston for over a thousand non-native speakers of English, and writer (of curriculum material and other genre for Mennonite publications and of English education materials for university students and teachers in China and Japan), Nancy served in Japan and China under the Mennonite Mission Network and Mennonite Partners in China (MPC, formerly China Educational Exchange) for twenty-two years. Among the MPC teachers in China who have received honors, Nancy was named distinguished foreign professor by both her university and the city of Shenyang.

Harold D. Lehman (PhD, University of Virgina). Today I may be the oldest continuous resident of Park View. The defining events of my life, however, involved stepping out of the village. There was cross-town teaching at James Madison University and association with Semester in London programs. Traveling with my wife, Ruth, and TourMagination founders, Gleysteen and Cressman, brought on-site exposure to our Anabaptist heritage in Europe. With the Comparative Education Society I studied secondary and higher education on both sides of Europe's iron Curtain (1968) and later in Cuba. There were trips to visit family members in Bolivia and Kenya. With retirement came VS in England and residence in a Quaker community. Now at the Virginia Mennonite Retirement Community I am close to my first home and elementary school in Park Woods. Ruth and I are back in the village, now a Harrisonburg suburb, to stay.

John R. Martin (DMin, Lancaster Theological Seminary) is Professor Emeritus of Church Ministry at Eastern Mennonite Seminary. Earlier he served congregations in Walkerton, IN, Washington, DC, and Lancaster, PA. He also served as Executive Secretary of the National Service Board for Religious Objectors, Washington, DC, and Director of I-W Services, Elkhart, IN. In addition he served on several denominational boards and committees. He earned degrees from Eastern Mennonite College, Goshen Biblical Seminary, Eastern Baptist Theological Seminary and Lancaster Theological Seminary and is the author of four books: *Divorce and Remarriage: A Perspective for Counseling; Keys to Successful Bible Study; Ventures in Discipleship;* and *Calling the Called*. A native of Harrisonburg, VA, he was the sixth in a family of nine children growing up on a dairy farm on the edge of Harrisonburg. He is married to Marian Landis from Blooming Glen, PA. The Martins have three married children and seven grandchildren.

Paul Peachey (PhD, University of Zurich), beginning soon after WW II, served five years under the Mennonite Central Committee in Europe in post-war relief and rehabilitation programs, along with occasionally studying part-time in graduate programs at European universities. He then completed his studies in sociology and history, along with a doctoral dissertation, at the University of Zurich (Switzerland). This dissertation, written and published in German, was a sociological study of Swiss Anabaptist origins, 1525–1540. All this resulted in varied Mennonite and ecumenical assignments for himself and his wife, Ellen, in the USA, Europe, and Asia. For the second half of his career, he served as a sociology professor at the Catholic University of America in Washington, DC. During that period, he also participated actively until the Cold War ended with Christians Associated for Relations with Eastern Europe and the parallel Academies of Science related Institute for Peace and Understanding.

Calvin W. Redekop (PhD, University of Chicago) was born on September 19, 1925, at Lustre, Montana. After receiving a BA at Goshen College in 1949, he worked in Europe under MCC from the fall of 1949 to December 1952, where he helped with the development of PAX and European Mennonite

Volunteer Service. He earned an MA at the University of Minnesota in 1955 and a PhD in anthropology/sociology/religion at the University of Chicago in 1959. He has taught at a number of colleges: Hesston College, Earlham College and School of Religion, Goshen College, Tabor College, and Conrad Grebel College. His research and writings have focused on the sociology of religion, Mennonite identity, economics, and environment. After retiring in 1990, he continued to be involved in business entrepreneurship, the environment, and volunteering. He and his wife, Freda, are members of Park View Mennonite Church, and have three married sons.

Calvin E. Shenk (PhD, New York University) is Professor Emeritus of Religion at Eastern Mennonite University, where he taught in the fields of religion and mission from 1976 to 2002. Concurrent with his teaching at EMU, he and his wife, Marie, spent the spring semester for eight years (1994–2001) in Jerusalem as Mennonite Church representatives in inter-religious dialogue. Prior to moving to EMU, he served in Ethiopia from 1961–75, teaching at the Nazareth Bible Academy, Haile Selassie I University, and Mekane Yesus (a Lutheran) Seminary. Calvin has written two books: *When Kingdoms Clash: The Christian and Ideologies* (1988); and *Who Do You Say that I Am? Christians Encounter Other Religions* (1997). Beginning July 1, 2007, Eastern Mennonite Seminary has contracted with Calvin and Marie to explore the possibility of offering graduate courses at Meserete Kristos College in Ethiopia with the long-range possibility of developing an EMS extension there.

Edward B. Stolzfus (ThM, Princeton Theological Seminary) is Professor Emeritus of Theology at Eastern Mennonite Seminary, Harrisonburg, VA. He was pastor of Bethel Mennonite Church, West Liberty, OH (1950s), worked at Goshen College and Goshen Biblical Seminary, IN (1960s) and was pastor of First Mennonite Church, Iowa City, IA (1970s). He is a graduate of Goshen College, Goshen Biblical Seminary and Princeton Theological Seminary. He served on numerous Mennonite Church boards and committees. He and his wife Mildred (Graber) have four children and eight grandchildren.

INDEX OF NAMES AND PLACES

A
Addis Ababa, 278–9
Augsburger, Myron, 13, 31, 198, 209, 227

B
Barth, Karl, 32, 77, 78, 120, 245
Bender, H.S., 2, 26, 28–35, 47, 75, 95–6, 121–28, 135, 138, 145, 196, 247, 324
Berrigan brothers—Phil and Daniel, 77, 252
Bethel College, KS, 195, 313
Blanke, Fritz, 53, 244, 247
Bluffton College, *also* Bluffton University, 111, 195
Brackbill, M.T., 193
Brackbill, Ruth, 84, 221, 292
Bridgewater College, 194
George R. Brunk I (Bishop), 26, 173
George R. Brunk II, 31, 43, 95
Brunner, Emil, 32, 248
Burkholder, J. Lawrence, 30–32, 47, 98

C
Calcutta, 34, 260, 289
Catholic University of America, 252–4
Charles, Howard, 47, 85, 135
China, Peoples Republic of, 37, 222–28, 290–310
Christian Peace Assembly, 252–3
Civil War in U.S., 173, 182, 184–6, 213
Conrad Grebel College, 327
Cullmann, Oscar, 257
Cumberland Valley, 173, 187

D
Detweiler, Richard, 212, 228

Denbigh, 26–7, 29, 93, 173, 109–10
Dhamtari, 257

E
Eastern Mennonite College, EMC, 9–14, 65–8, 72, 84, 92–111, 118, 132, 136, 140-50, 157, 167, 178ff., 197–201, 209, 211, 221–2, 227–9, 248–51, 264–8, 270, 277, 291–295 314, 321–22
Eastern Mennonite High School, 116, 197ff., 263
Eastern Mennonite School, 27–9, 193–6, 238ff., 264
Eastern Mennonite Seminary, 128, 270, 327
Eastern Mennonite University, EMU, 2, 3, 13, 22, 28, 37, 67, 74, 83, 111, 163–4, 166,192, 207–29, 271–3, 292, 297, 310, 315–19
Egypt, 209–10, 282, 287
Espelkamp, 47, 246
Ethiopia, 35, 273–87
Evangelical Mennonite Brethren, 45

F
Fast, Henry A., 47, 196
Franklin County, Pa., 173, 187
Friedman, Robert, 196

G
Gehman, G. Ernest, 192–3
Gingerich, Melvin, 47, 249
Goshen College, 27–55, 67, 97, 118, 127, 136–38, 181, 185, 194ff., 293ff.
Graber, J.D., 98, 145, 259–60, 297–98
Griffin, John Howard, 185

H
Haley, Alex, 185
Hammer, Howard, 66, 96
Hartzler, Sadie, 193
Hershberger, Guy F., 31, 47–8, 55, 98, 107, 135
Hesston College, 48, 103,199,135, 312
Hokkaido, 35, 37, 297–99
Horst, Amos, 84
Horst, Irvin B., 31, 48, 84, 107, 199, 223, 277
Hostetter, C.N., 47, 196
Hostetter, D. Ralph, 193, 221

I
India, 34–37, 111, 257–73
Israel, State of, 133, 210, 282

J
James Madison University (JMU), 167, 198, 222, 267–8. *See also* Madison College.
Japan, 222–8, 248-55, 273, 283, 296–307, 322–5
Jordon, Clarence, 148–9

K
Kauffman, Ed, 196
Keim, Albert N., 315, 317, 323
Kemrer, 193
King, Martin Luther, 77, 164, 289
Kniss, Paul and Esther, 263
Kniss, Mark, 236–7, 257
Koinonia Farm, Americus, 148
Kraybill, Paul N., 85n8
Kuhn, Thomas S., 19, 70

L
Lapp, John A., 102–03, 183, 209, 258
Lapp, Joseph, 314–17
Laurelville Mennonite Church Center, 84, 199, 225
Lehman, Chester K., 27, 67, 107, 178, 192–3, 196, 239
Lehman, Daniel W., 191
Lind, Millard, 85n10

M
Madison College, 194, 198
Martin (Gehman), Margaret, 196, 264
Miller. Ira E., 10, 99, 101, 103, 197, 224, 227
Miller, John W., 31, 48
Miller, Marlin, 84
Miller, Orie O., 26, 32, 47, 145, 249
Mumaw, John R., 96–7, 104,181, 192–3, 197, 209, 227, 242, 265, 294

N
Nazareth Bible Academy, 278

P
Palestine. *Also* West Bank, 17, 282
Pannabecker, S.F., 196
Peachey, Paul, 31, 47–8, 107, 148
Pellman, Hubert, 84, 93, 103, 134, 221, 277, 294
Puidoux, 248, 251

R
Redekop, Calvin W., 135, 137, 294, 313, 315–17
Roosevelt, Franklin Delano, 25, 195, 206, 217

S
Schwerner, Michael (Mickey), 155–8, 160
Shank, David, 31, 48, 84n4, 85n9
Smith, J.B., 192
Snow, Don, 307
Soviet Union, 187, 207
Stauffer, J.L., 117, 136, 193
Stauffer, J. Mark and Eva, 96, 117, 133, 207, 265
Stauffer, Ruth S., 193
Stringfellow, Bill (William), 77

T
Tabor College, 195, 327
Tantur Ecumenical Institute, 282–3
Tel Hai Mennonite Camp, 199
Tokyo, 250, 297, 306

U
University of Virginia, 12, 184, 197, 207–8, 224

W
Waltner, Leroy, 84n4
Washington County, Md., 187
Wenger, A.D., 193
Wenger, A. Grace, 264, 292
Wenger, J.C., 47, 84, 98, 102, 135, 145
Wink, Walter, 87n25

Y
Yoder, Jacob Eschbach, 186
Yoder, John Howard, 48, 73, 77, 85–7, 98, 102, 107–8, 297, 299, 300, 301–2

Z
Zimmerman, Ada, 180, 291, 293

INDEX OF SUBJECTS

A
Amish
    Amish Mennonite, 63, 236
    attire and practices, 8, 9, 13, 94
    Beachy Amish, 9, 21, 63, 248
    community, 7, 20, 235
    Old Order Amish, 12, 236
    position on salvation, 8
    self-identity, 8, 64
African American, 66, 86, 151–163, 183, 184
Again. *See* Poems.
Associated Mennonite Biblical Seminary, *also* Goshen Biblical Seminary, 28, 29, 31, 66, 69–77, 85, 118, 127, 135, 140
    Eastern bias against, 97
Anabaptist, Anabaptism
    and Catholicism, 122
    commitment to, 2
    discipleship, following Jesus, 33, 53–4, 69, 85n10, 121, 142–45
    and education, 101, 107
    fellowship, 124,
    heritage, tradition, 45–6, 53
    mission, 36ff.
    movement, 75–6, 122, 142
    peasants' movement, 76
    peoplehood, 123, 127
    theology, 36, 78, 100, 110, 112, 127, 284
    vision, 2, 35, 124, 126, 128
Anthropology of religion, 59n1, 79–80, 87
Art
    relationship to Christian faith, 109, 269–73
    teaching art in non-Christian culture, 271–73
Attire, Mennonite, 46, 106, 116, 294–5, 302–3. *See also* Amish attire.
Authoritarianism, 18, 54, 74

B
Baptism, 43, 213, 237, 259, 291
Bible, 29, 32, 35. *See also* Scriptures.
    and community, 22, 32, 198, 207
    and culture, 30, 35, 78
    and hermeneutics, 11–13, 27, 30, 67, 70, 73, 78, 83, 120, 285
    as holy book, 11, 291
    infallible, 27, 86
    inspired by Holy Spirit, 35, 66, 69, 86
    reading the Bible, study of, 11, 68, 142–3, 291
Birmingham boycott, 147–8

C
Capitalism, challenges of, 49, 55, 87n23
Catholic Church, 3, 34, 86, 251–2
Catholicism, 120, 122–3
Cattle boat, 133–4
Certainty, certitude, 66, 69, 82
    of salvation, 51, 65, 77, 98
China Educational Exchange (Mennonite Partners in China), 226, 305–8, 310
Church
    as body of Christ, 77, 123
    as community, 2, 33, 123–4
    leaders, 25, 43, 194, 284
    mission of, 75, 100

Index of Subjects

as moral regulator, 9, 17
planting, 108–11, 164–5
as political arm, 86n15
theology of, 30, 158
Church Peace Mission, 249, 251–2
Civil rights
  movement, 32
  groups, activists, 155–8
Civil War, U.S., 173, 184, 213
  Southern Claiming Commission, 182
  Virginia Mennonites in, 182
Civilian Public Service (CPS) Camps
  Blue Ridge Parkway, 178, 195
  Greystone Park Hospital, 178, 180, 195
  National Forest Service Camp, 179
  Soil Conservation Camp, 179
  Vineland Training School, 195–6
Coalition of Christian Colleges and Universities, 111, 321
College
  academic freedom, 12
  integrity in academia, 51
  leaving for, 10
Concern group, papers, 11, 31, 48, 248ff.
Conscientious objection, objectors (COs), 2, 9, 48, 137, 178, 196, 239, 247
Conversion(s), 8, 43. 73, 76, 101, 117, 236, 259
  nature of, 45, 76, 117, 148–50
  as paradigm shift in truth/reality, 73
  second and multiple conversion, 51, 73
Cosmology, 72. *See also* Worldview.
Creation
  role of creation in theology, 49
  preservation of, 54
Culture(s), cultural 3, 11, 52, 66, 81, 84, 115, 228, 263, 278, 289
  accommodation, 65, 250

adaptations, 15, 71,
and church leadership, 33
comparative, 66
constructed by humans, 15, 124
pre-modern, 72
religion and, 287
shock, 27, 299
Mennonite c, 26
of selfishness, 155
shame vs. guilt, 36

D
Discipleship
  Anabaptist meaning of, 145
  interpretation of, 33
  heritage of, 69
  and incarnation, 122
  as nonviolent socio-political stance, 86
  seminars on, 121
Dispensationalism, 27, 30, 32
Doctrine, doctrinal
  gospel as doctrine, 76
  as human constructs, 74, 80, 120
  Mennonite d, 102
  orthodoxy, 27, 64, 124
  purity of, 67
  of scriptural inerrancy, 31
Dress restrictions, 8, 13, 200, 294–5. *See also* Attire, Mennonite.
Dutch-Russian heritage, 44ff.

E
East Africa Revival, 72
Eastern Mennonite Missions (*also* EMBMC), 70, 84, 272, 283
Economics
  and Anabaptism, 55, 85n12
  and organizations, 55
  involvements in, 56
Environment—crisis of, 56
Epistemology, 68-9, 78, 85n10, 87n26
Ethics, ethical life
  as discipleship, 127
  as basis of knowing Jesus, 78

in contrast to metaphysics, 78
religion substitutes for, 80
supercedes doctrine, 64
European Common Market, 70
European Peace Section, MCC, 84
Evangelism, 95, 96, 98
    Congress on Evangelism, 100
    methods of , 31
    personal evangelism, 133
    and justice, 284
    theology and, 101

F
Farming, 46, 67, 237
    in tension with other ministries, 134
    from farming to missions, 135
    not an option, 46
Forgive, forgiveness, 102, 155
    unique to Christianity, 228
Fundamentalism
    Anabaptism as paradigmatic option to f., 33
    epistemological precariousness of, 78
    shares Liberalism's epistemology, 78
    in conflict with Anabaptism, 25–36
    a heresy, 67
    child of Modernism, 86n19
    and revivalism, 33, 50

G
Gay, lesbian. *See* Homosexuality.

H
Hermeneutics, scriptural interpretation
    guidelines for OT, 74
    hermeneutic community, 11–13, 83, 85
    hermeneutic tools, 75
    and homosexuality, 325
    metaphors, symbols and interpretation, 119ff.
    premillennialism, 27
    sola scriptura, 35
Holy Spirit
    as "discussion stopper"
    empowered by, 92
    infilling of, 92
    inspired scripture and interprets, 35
    revealer of truth, 140
Homosexuality, 75, 77, 166, 325
Humility, humble, 64, 67, 105
    communal humility, 64
    self-effacing, 2
    and honored, 205
    humble spirit, 229

I
Idolatry
    of Bible, 86
    and human nature, 79
    of first-century worldview, 80
    as worshiping theological constructs, 80–1
Individualism
    within Amish context, 20
    and collectivism, 57
    and interdependence on others, 168
Inspiration, 74
    verbal inspiration, 86

J
Jewish-Christian dialogue, 283–84
Justice
    and Anabaptism, 54
    development and, 283
    economic justice, 54, 75, 164
    evangelism and, 284
    freedom and, 156,
    peace and, 149, 323
    social justice, 54, 78
    struggle for, 159, 163

K
Kingdom of God
    not bound by worldview, 81

symbolization of, 120–1
Koinonia groups, 31, 33
Korean War, 1, 47, 63
Kyoto Notes. See Poems.

L
Liberalism
    epistemological precariousness of, 67
    of the Midwest, 67
Lot for choosing minister. *See* Ordination.

M
Martyrs Mirror, 258
Mennonite Disaster Service (MDS), 110, 150
    in Mississippi in the 1960s, 158–162
Meserete Kristos Church
    growth of, 284
    persecution of, 279–80
Messianic Judaism, 283
Ministry—preaching
    call to, 28, 93, 132, 140, 225
    women in, 77
Missions, mission
    "city mission," 177
    mission-minded, mission-oriented, 64, 65
    theology for understanding, 81
    Welch Mountains, 225
Music
    love of, 223, 226ff.
    use of instruments, 105ff., 119, 299
    teaching, 294

N
Nonconformity
    social n. of Jesus, 76
Nonviolence
    among sixteenth-century Anabaptists, 76
    new foundation for nonviolence, 82

O
Ordination
    to ministry by lot, 125, 144, 177, 199, 237

P
Pacifism
    Christian, 246
    Civil War pacifism, 182
    quieter pacifism, 78
    versus Just War, 254
Pacifist
    pacifist God, 11, 20,
    nuclear pacifist, 100
    prophetic pacifist minorities, 76
    communicating pacifist convictions, 100–111, 246–254
Paradigm, paradigm shift
    Anabaptism as theological paradigm, 33
    paradigm shift as conversion, 73
    intellectual paradigm shift, 85
Peace church, historic peace churches (HPC), 185, 248
Pietism, pietist
    p. awakening, renewal, 45
    dualism shared with protestants and Catholics, 70
    American Mennonite missionaries as p., 72
Poems
    by Nancy Lee
        Again, 306–07
        Kyoto Notes, 304–5
        Sunday Mornings in China, 310–11
        Timelines, 289ff.
    by Robert Frost
        references to *The Road Not Taken*, 221, 293, 304
Puidoux theological exchanges, 248–51

R
Race relations, 155

Revelation
  biblical, 74
  direct revelation, 211, 229
  and knowledge, 120
  truth or revelation, 52
Revelation, Book of
  interpretation of, 67
Revival meetings
  expected attendance, 45, 51d
  experience at EMC, 93
  point of commitment to Christ, 93, 132
  Brunk Revivals, 207
Road Not Taken, The. See Poems.

S
Salvation
  Amish understanding, 8
  assurance of, 8, 51, 98
  individual, 64
  now or in afterlife, 77
Scriptural interpretation. See Hermeneutics.
Scriptures. *See also* Bible.
  as ahistorical Word of God, 78
  harmonizing, 66
  nature of, 86n21
Sociology of knowledge
  companion to anthropology, 80ff., 87n22
  reveals limitations of our knowing, 79-80, 87n22
  as tool for Anabaptist theology, 91ff.
  threatening to faith, 78
Sociology of religion, 48, 51, 78, 80

T
Tent evangelism, 31, 95, 97, 139, 207, 323
Theology
  American evangelical, 64
  of church leaders, 25–27
  communal, 64
  of salvation—assurance of, 98
Timelines. See Poems.

V
Vietnam War, 13, 33, 106, 159
Voluntary service, 3, 47, 134, 138, 199–201
  in Mississippi in the 1960s, 134–155

W
Witness, 117, 123, 127
  to government, 109, 135-7
  to Islam, 282
  of presence, 228
  to other religions, 286
World Council of Churches (WCC), 248, 251
Worldview(s), 7–23. *See also* Cosmology.
  basis of, criteria for worldview, 19 ff.
  and Concern Group, 48
  and cultural plurality, 19
  of East Africans, 61
  of first century CE, 72, 80ff.
  idolatry of, 80
  foisted upon us, 81
  Greco-Hebrew worldview, 81
  limitations of scientific w., 49
  provides meaning, 22
Mennonite worldview, 118, 119
  postmodern, 22
World War I, 25–6, 32, 228, 235, 238, 306
  impact on Denbigh, 206
  memories of, 238ff.
  wartime voyage, 260ff.
World War II, 1, 32, 46, 131, 145, 178,
  drafted for, 178

www.ingramcontent.com/pod-product-compliance
Lightning Source LLC
Chambersburg PA
CBHW070735170426
43200CB00007B/527